1008316851

Social Media and Mental Health

Social Media and Mental Health

Edited by
Allan House
University of Leeds

Cathy Brennan
University of Leeds

CAMBRIDGE
UNIVERSITY PRESS

Shaftesbury Road, Cambridge CB2 8EA, United Kingdom

One Liberty Plaza, 20th Floor, New York, NY 10006, USA

477 Williamstown Road, Port Melbourne, VIC 3207, Australia

314–321, 3rd Floor, Plot 3, Splendor Forum, Jasola District Centre,
New Delhi – 110025, India

103 Penang Road, #05-06/07, Visioncrest Commercial, Singapore 238467

Cambridge University Press is part of Cambridge University Press & Assessment,
a department of the University of Cambridge.

We share the University's mission to contribute to society through the pursuit of
education, learning and research at the highest international levels of excellence.

www.cambridge.org
Information on this title: www.cambridge.org/9781009010863

DOI: 10.1017/9781009024945

© The Royal College of Psychiatrists 2023

This publication is in copyright. Subject to statutory exception and to the provisions
of relevant collective licensing agreements, no reproduction of any part may take
place without the written permission of Cambridge University Press & Assessment.

First published 2023

A catalogue record for this publication is available from the British Library.

Library of Congress Cataloging-in-Publication Data
Names: House, Allan, editor. | Brennan, Cathy, 1968- editor. | Royal College of
    Psychiatrists.
Title: Social media and mental health / edited by Allan House, Cathy Brennan.
Description: Cambridge : New York, NY : Cambridge University Press, 2023. |
    Includes bibliographical references and index.
Identifiers: LCCN 2023017687 (print) | LCCN 2023017688 (ebook) |
    ISBN 9781009010863 (paperback) | ISBN 9781009024945 (epub)
Subjects: MESH: Social Media | Body Image–psychology | Self-Injurious
    Behavior–psychology | Mental Health | Adolescent
Classification: LCC HM742 (print) | LCC HM742 (ebook) | NLM HM 742 |
    DDC 302.23/1019–dc23/eng/20230706
LC record available at https://lccn.loc.gov/2023017687
LC ebook record available at https://lccn.loc.gov/2023017688

ISBN 978-1-009-01086-3 Paperback

Cambridge University Press & Assessment has no responsibility for the persistence
or accuracy of URLs for external or third-party internet websites referred to in this
publication and does not guarantee that any content on such websites is, or will
remain, accurate or appropriate.

....

Every effort has been made in preparing this book to provide accurate and up-to-
date information that is in accord with accepted standards and practice at the time
of publication. Although case histories are drawn from actual cases, every effort has
been made to disguise the identities of the individuals involved. Nevertheless, the
authors, editors, and publishers can make no warranties that the information
contained herein is totally free from error, not least because clinical standards are
constantly changing through research and regulation. The authors, editors, and
publishers therefore disclaim all liability for direct or consequential damages
resulting from the use of material contained in this book. Readers are strongly
advised to pay careful attention to information provided by the manufacturer of
any drugs or equipment that they plan to use.

Contents

List of Contributors vii
Foreword ix
Lizzie Mitchell
Preface xi
Acknowledgements xii

Section 1 Understanding Social Media

1 **Introducing Social Media** 3
Ysabel Gerrard

2 **The Legal and Ethical Status of Social Media** 12
Jon Fistein

3 **Social Media: An Everyday Reality** 23
David A. Ellis

4 **How Social Media Can Influence Group and Individual Behaviour: Practice Implications** 33
Jeff French and Melissa Blair

5 **Researching Social Media: Qualitative and Mixed-Methods Research Approaches** 45
Cathy Brennan, David A. Ellis, and Kim Heyes

6 **Researching Social Media: Quantitative Approaches** 53
Allan House

Section 2 Social Media and Mental Health

7 **The Harms and Benefits of Social Media** 67
Maša Popovac, Philip A. Fine, and Sally-Ann Hicken

8 **Social Media and Disorders of Mood** 81
Allan House

9 **Social Media Use, Body Image, and Eating Disorders** 90
Rachel Rodgers and Katherine Laveway

10 **Social Media and Gambling** 98
Thomas B. Swanton, Sascha Callaghan, Nicola C. Newton, Vladan Starcevic, and Sally M. Gainsbury

11 **Social Media, Self-Harm, and Suicide** 109
Cathy Brennan and Allan House

Section 3 Social Media as a Resource

12 **Safely Navigating the Terrain: Keeping Young People Safe Online** 121
Jo Robinson, Louise La Sala, and Rikki Battersby-Coulter

13 **Technological Interventions for Adolescent Mental Health** 131
Arjuna Ugarte, Renee Garett, and Sean D. Young

14 **Online Outreach and Support Provision: An Empirically Informed Approach and Case Illustration** 139
Stephen P. Lewis

Afterword 150
References 152
Index 168

Contributors

Rikki Battersby-Coulter
Research Assistant, Orygen, Centre for Youth Mental Health, University of Melbourne, Australia

Melissa Blair
Lecturer, Faculty of Health Sciences, Brock University, Canada

Cathy Brennan
Associate Professor of Psychological and Social Medicine, University of Leeds, UK

Sascha Callaghan
Senior Lecturer, Sydney Law School, University of Sydney, Australia

David A. Ellis
Associate Professor of Information Systems, University of Bath, UK

Philip A. Fine
Senior Lecturer in Psychology, University of Buckingham, UK

Jon Fistein
Visiting Associate Professor, School of Medicine, University of Leeds, UK

Jeff French
Visiting Professor, Brighton University, UK; CEO of Strategic Social Marketing, UK

Sally M. Gainsbury
Professor, Gambling Treatment & Research Clinic, Brain & Mind Centre, School of Psychology, Faculty of Science, University of Sydney, Australia

Renee Garett
CEO and Founder, ElevateU, USA

Ysabel Gerrard
Senior Lecturer in Digital Communication, Department of Sociological Studies, University of Sheffield, UK

Kim Heyes
Senior Lecturer in Health and Social Justice, Department of Nursing, Manchester Metropolitan University, UK

Sally-Ann Hicken
PhD student, University of Buckingham, UK

Allan House
Emeritus Professor of Liaison Psychiatry, School of Medicine, University of Leeds, UK

Louise La Sala
Research Fellow, Orygen, Centre for Youth Mental Health, University of Melbourne, Australia

Katherine Laveway
Graduate student, APPEAR, Northeastern University, USA

Stephen P. Lewis
Professor, Department of Psychology, University of Guelph, Canada

Nicola C. Newton
Professor, The Matilda Centre for Research in Mental Health & Substance Use, Faculty of Medicine & Health, University of Sydney, Australia

Maša Popovac
Senior Advisor for Digital Literacy and Online Safety, Alannah & Madeline

Foundation, Australia; Honorary Research Fellow, University of Buckingham, UK

Jo Robinson
Associate Professor, Orygen, Centre for Youth Mental Health, University of Melbourne, Australia

Rachel Rodgers
Director, APPEAR, Northeastern University, USA

Vladan Starcevic
Professor, Nepean Clinical School, Sydney Medical School, Faculty of Medicine and Health, University of Sydney, Australia; Department of Psychiatry, Nepean Hospital, Australia

Thomas B. Swanton
PhD candidate, School of Psychology, Faculty of Science, University of Sydney, Australia

Arjuna Ugarte
Research Associate, Department of Emergency Medicine, University of California, Irvine, USA

Sean D. Young
Professor, Departments of Emergency Medicine and Informatics, University of California, Irvine, USA

Foreword

Lizzie Mitchell Psychology graduate with personal experience

Social media in itself is a very contentious topic – people either love it or hate it. Add the impact on mental health to the social media conversation and suddenly things become even more divided. And as a young person with experience of poor mental health, including self-harm, I can see why.

When accessing certain content, social media could be a place of comfort, connection, safety, and recovery inspiration, giving me a sense of belonging, connection, and support I didn't have offline. But it was easy to get sucked in, and 10 minutes of mindless browsing quickly turned into hours of obsessive scrolling. The addictive aesthetics of Instagram, TikTok, and Snapchat pictures invited me to succumb to a pressure of living up to this 'perfect' online life I was seeing, and meeting expectations of peers, influencers, and celebrities who dominate social media. This led to social media being a risky place full of competition, envy, judgement, and self-loathing. It affected my brain in a way that I didn't understand – even if I didn't want to self-harm, somehow social media could tempt me in a way nothing else could.

Young people are often told to 'use social media appropriately', but I didn't know what that meant. The knowledge and research in this book helped me to understand what that could mean and taught me the relationship between social media and mental health, particularly self-harm, is individual and complicated, and taps into a variety of psychological, social, and technological constructs that most young people would be unaware of. Comprehensive, accessible, and useful for researchers, clinicians, young people, and parents alike, this book helped me question and reflect on my own use of social media and how to better navigate a complex, ever-evolving, and potentially triggering online space.

With each new social media platform that pops up, there will inevitably be new problems, potential triggers, and casualties, but as the research in this book shows, the onus isn't all on young people. We need a collective effort from society, including technology professionals, researchers, clinicians, educators, and young people, to come together to create generations of social media-savvy young people, who can access the realm of benefits social media can bring and use it to empower, not destroy, themselves. I believe this book acts as a vital educational resource to assist this change.

Preface

It is estimated that half the global population – more than four billion people – uses social media. There are marked age differences, with more than 80% of people aged under 50 years old saying they are users compared to fewer than 50% of those over 65 years old. In light of such figures, it is particularly striking, and concerning, to read so many reports suggesting that social media use is harmful – and especially so for the mental health of young people.

As researchers we have been struck by how strongly worded such criticisms can be – to the point at times of seeming one-sided and melodramatic. Our own research suggests a more complicated picture than is represented by the idea of social media as a toxic exposure from which vulnerable young people need to be protected. The effects of the same content can vary from person to person and even for the same person at different times, so that what is harmful for one can be helpful for another, or harmful and helpful to the same person on different occasions. To take one example, we have found that looking at and responding to images of self-harm can cause distress for some people while leading others to feel less isolated with their own self-harm and more able to appraise their own circumstances.

It isn't possible to ask simply of social media, are they a resource for good or are they harmful? Instead, we have to ask, paraphrasing our Leeds colleague Ray Pawson,[1] what works (for good or ill), for whom, and under what circumstances? To answer a question like this we need more than a single study supplemented by the personal interest stories so favoured by the popular media. We need a wide-ranging and unbiased review of the evidence with all its contradictions and uncertainties – and interpretation of that evidence by experts who are familiar with the strengths and limitations of any research in this tricky and rapidly evolving area.

Our main aim in preparing this book is to provide a resource for the interested non-specialist who wants to understand the terrain and make informed judgements about the unfolding debate regarding the impact of social media on mental health. We wanted a balanced account of social media that discusses their potential benefits as well as harms and one that acknowledges where there are uncertainties. With that in mind we have invited academics with recognized relevant expertise to summarize what they see as the key issues in their own area. A print book cannot possibly stay up to date with every advance nor provide, in an accessible format for a general readership, an exhaustive survey of such a far-reaching phenomenon. It can however lay out and illustrate the basic facts and principles that are likely to remain salient for a foreseeable future, and it is that aim that we have asked our authors to help us achieve with this volume. We hope you agree that they and we have succeeded in doing so.

---

[1] Ray Pawson, Professor of Social Research Methodology in the School of Sociology and Social Policy at the University of Leeds, has been a leading figure in realist evaluation. See, for example, his seminal book *Realistic Evaluation* (co-authored with Nick Tilley; Sage Publications, 1997).

Acknowledgements

We would like to thank Faye Ambler for helping in the preparation of this book, especially the hours of work checking, creating, and inserting the references for each chapter.

Section 1
Understanding Social Media

We want to start this book about social media and mental health by stepping back and surveying the landscape. Before we get to mental health, we ask some questions about social media more generally:

What is social about social media? Perhaps we all have a mental picture of young people hunched over a smartphone and swiping at the screen, but what do we really know about who uses social media, how, and why?

How can we understand the potential advantages and disadvantages of social media use and how social media might exert their influence – directly through the form and content of online material, or indirectly by time taken away from other activities, sleep disruption or whatever?

Social media represent something new – not just in the technology used in delivery but in their characteristic as user-generated and yet hosted on a platform provided by others. This raises legal and ethical questions such as who owns any material produced, who is responsible for content, and who can be held accountable for its consequences?

Research into the effects of social media is needed if we are to move beyond the public debate being dominated by individual opinion. To some degree the way in which we undertake such research is just the same as the way in which we undertake much research – we do not need to be blinded by the novel aspects of the subject of our studies. On the other hand, there are particular problems posed by research in this area. How should we undertake, and read, research into the association between mental health and social media use? What methods are available to us and what are their strengths and limitations?

The chapters in this section provide some answers to these scene-setting questions.

Chapter 1

Introducing Social Media

Ysabel Gerrard

I write this chapter at what feels like a turning point in the short yet rich history of social media.

Instagram – a photo- and video-sharing app founded in 2010, which has since attracted near-global popularity – has been accused of being 'toxic' to teenagers' mental health, especially girls' [1]. Whistle-blower Frances Haugen leaked several internal documents sourced during her tenure at Meta (the company that currently owns Instagram) to the *Wall Street Journal*, which included findings from an internally conducted survey of a sample of Instagram's teenage users. In slides from a presentation posted to the company's staff message board in March 2020, the survey findings revealed that Instagram 'make[s] body image issues worse for one in three teen girls' [1].

This is one of many high-profile reports about the link between social media and mental health, and it sits within a broader social climate where people are asking pressing questions about the extent to which social media can 'affect' or 'impact' individuals. It is natural to fear new and fast-growing technologies [2] but regressing to the media 'effects' models that have for so long been discredited (remember the hypodermic needle model, anyone?) may not be helpful, or indeed accurate. One of the aims of this chapter is therefore to argue that social media are not one *thing* and to introduce instead several aspects of the phenomenon to readers, briefly tracing standout phases in their evolution, the characteristics that differentiate them from older media technologies, their (increasingly controversial) business and governance models, and finally their use and non-use among particular social groups.[1]

The Evolution of Social Media

The phrase 'social media' was first used in the English-speaking language around 1994 [3], but it wasn't until the mid-2000s that it gained widespread currency. At that time, US tech companies were recovering from the 2001 dot-com bubble crash, with many embracing the opportunity to start afresh and create what they imagined to be a *different* Web [4]. This new wave of internet history was known as Web 2.0, a term coined by O'Reilly Media's Dale Dougherty and Tim O'Reilly at a Web industry conference to represent a turning point in the internet's (albeit short) history [4]. However, as Jamieson explains, it's notoriously difficult to pin down exactly what Web 2.0 *is*: a business model, a technical development, a social change, or perhaps all the above [4]? Many of the features packaged as Web 2.0 – such as user participation and user-generated

---

[1] I commit to the phrase 'social media *are*' throughout this chapter for precisely this reason.

content – were present in Web 1.0 applications such as wikis, online journals, and blogs, which means Web 2.0 might best be thought of as a *discourse* as opposed to a set of unique technologies.

Nonetheless, the term caught on in the West, evoking excitement for a new phase of Web history. This sentiment was famously captured when *TIME* magazine named 'You' its Person of the Year in 2006, hailing the potentialities of 'the new Web' for enabling ordinary people to create and share media, the supposed actualization of 'the many wresting power from the few' [5]. Around the same time, within academic circles, the term *participatory culture* was coined to denote the seemingly new opportunities afforded by a move away from the one-to-many communicative style of television shows, magazines, some older websites, and more. The move to a participatory Web, it was said, increased opportunities for average internet users to share user-generated content such as text, images, videos, emoji, and GIFs. The term *participation* contrasted with older notions of passive media audiences/receivers, hence the rise of hybrid terms like *prosumer* (*producer* plus *consumer*) in the mid-2000s [6] (though decades of media and communication research teach us that audiences are, of course, never wholly passive).

The history of social media is often told from a Western, US-centric perspective, but this evolution looks very different around the world, and changes according to local infrastructure, politics, economics, and culture. There is therefore no singular rise of social media, and this history depends on how you tell it.

For example, similar technological and societal developments took place in Japan long before Web 2.0 emerged as a discourse in the USA. While Japan was seen as being late to the internet age, partly due to the complexities of displaying non-Western language characters on digital keyboards, the country was a front runner in the development and uptake of 'person-to-person communication' [7]. These technologies emerged in Japan in the late 1980s and were known as 'personal computer communications' (or *pasokon tsūshin*), which were 'basically bulletin board systems that enabled users to seek out information from various news feeds as well as participate in online discussions and send email to other users' [7]. While these early systems were not taken up by the Japanese population en masse, they found their place in certain communities such as feminist women, those living with chronic illnesses, and among trans people and gay men [7].

Although bulletin board systems might not count as 'social network sites' according to boyd and Ellison's (2007) definition [8], which I discuss in the next section, these developments should remind us that the rise of social media as we know them today was not strictly driven by Silicon Valley. Long before 'participatory cultures' were celebrated by Western academics, Japanese writers spoke of the potentialities of 'revolutionary' new 'networks' (*nettowāku*) [7]. But what makes social media different from their technological predecessors?

The Characteristics of Social Media

In what has become a go-to source for those seeking a definition of *social network sites*, boyd and Ellison [8] explain that they are

> web-based services that allow individuals to (1) construct a public or semi-public profile within a bounded system, (2) articulate a list of other users with whom they share a connection, and (3)

view and traverse their list of connections and those made by others within the system. The nature and nomenclature of these connections may vary from site to site.

Readers might notice that this is a definition of 'social network sites' as opposed to 'social media', a term on which this book is based and which we now more commonly use in the English language. This shift in terminology is tough to trace, and it is difficult (and certainly controversial) to decide what counts as the world's first example of 'social media'. Instant messaging and bulletin board services evidently count as *social* forms of media technologies, but if the creation of a profile and the ability to share lists of connections was central to boyd and Ellison's definition of a 'social network site', then one of the earliest examples was SixDegrees.

Founded in 1997, SixDegrees 'allowed users to create profiles, list their Friends and, beginning in 1998, surf the Friends lists' [8]. While these features existed on other sites, SixDegrees was the first to combine them [8]. Although boyd and Ellison's 2007 definition continues to be heavily cited, what we now know as *social media* platforms have more complex characteristics than their predecessors, and these changes invite us to question the endurance of the profile and friends list to more contemporary definitions of what counts as 'social media'.

Let's take Myspace (launched in 2003) as another example. Myspace users were invited to create their own profile, which displayed a profile picture along with their name, age, and location – their ASL, or age/sex/location, as we used to call it (see Figure 1.1). Users could also choose their Top 8 friends and browse each other's social connections, leave comments on people's profiles, send messages, and display biographical information. Crucial to Myspace's success, however, was the editability of the profile: 'Myspace users needed to learn basic HTML and CSS to creatively customize their profiles'; affordances that are, unfortunately, 'mostly absent from contemporary social media platforms' [9].

Figure 1.1 A static clone of Tom's iconic 2006 Myspace profile page
(image sourced from https://github.com/wittenbrock/toms-myspace-page)

It's easy to see why, in 2007, boyd and Ellison centred the profile and friends list as key defining features of social network sites. However, the functionalities and characteristics of *social media*, as we now know them, have advanced considerably since the days of SixDegrees and Myspace. Current social media users can record and edit videos on TikTok and Douyin (a Chinese equivalent of TikTok), send ephemeral pictures through Snapchat, livestream a video on Facebook, or buy clothes for their dog on Instagram.

What distinguishes 'social media' from 'social network sites' might therefore be the shift from the profile – and the showcasing of friends and networks – to the creation and sharing of media *content*. This change is reflected in Burgess et al.'s [10] more recent definition of 'social media technologies', which they define as 'those digital platforms, services and apps built around the convergence of content sharing, public communication, and interpersonal connection' [10]. While social media are still, of course, used to communicate with people, this definition also rightly includes content creation and public communication, core elements of their business models that I now discuss in greater depth.

The Business Model(s) of Social Media

MARK ZUCKERBERG: The Facebook is cool and if we start installing pop-ups for Mountain Dew it's not going to be cool.

EDUARDO SAVERIN: Well, I wasn't thinking Mountain Dew, but at some point – and I'm talking as the business end of the company – the site...

MARK ZUCKERBERG: We don't even know what it is yet. We don't know what it is. We don't know what it can be. But we know that it is cool. That is a priceless asset I'm not giving up.

It might be surprising to readers that social media companies don't always generate profit straight away. In the quote above, taken from *The Social Network* – a 2010 biographical film chronicling the invention of Facebook – the company's founder (Mark Zuckerberg) and chief financial officer (Eduardo Saverin) debate the point at which they should start monetizing their then-new site.

Facebook – and plenty of other social media companies – make most of their money by displaying advertisements for external products and services. They make some money by charging sign-up fees, but the big players in today's social media game tend to offer their sites for free [2].[2] Currently popular platforms find increasingly sophisticated ways to show people ads. On Instagram, for example, users might see ads as they scroll down their Feed, or as they browse through people's Stories. For those unfamiliar with Instagram, this means paid-for posts are interspersed with content from a person's social network. Businesses can also pay to advertise their products in more creative ways, such as Snapchat filters, as shown in Figures 1.2 and 1.3.

To decide which advertisements to show to a particular user, social media companies will analyse that person's data: their clicks, shares, likes, follows, and even their activities on other sites hosting 'like' buttons for social media sites [11] – a process called *social*

---

[2] It is beyond the scope of this chapter to engage in an extensive discussion about the other 'costs' of free social media use, and whether this counts as a form of labour.

Figure 1.2 Photo of a sponsored Disney PhotoPass Lenses Snapchat filter, taken by Dr Phoenix Andrews

media data mining. This information is of great value to people paying social media companies for advertising space, as they know their ads will be seen by the people most likely to engage with their products or services. Less discussed academically, however, are instances when social media platforms become incredibly popular but make no money at all. Let's take the failed app Fling as an example.

Founded in 2014, Fling invited users to send – to *Fling* – photos and videos to complete strangers around the world. The app was an instant hit, but it was soon overrun with pornographic images and sexual harassment, leading to its removal from Apple's App Store. Anonymous app Sarahah met a similar fate. Part of the 'honesty app' trend, Sarahah, 'which means "frankness" or "honesty" in Arabic' [12], allowed users to ask a question for anyone with a link to answer anonymously. Sarahah quickly rose to the top of app stores in several countries, becoming 'particularly popular in Arab-speaking regions and also among English-speaking teenagers' [12]. However, the app's founder – who had originally designed it for corporate settings, as a tool for workers to give feedback to their employers – hadn't imagined the site would become so popular with teens. Predictably, Sarahah was removed from app stores and its founder never made a penny.

Apps like Fling and Sarahah are what I call *popular by surprise* [13], and apps that fit into this category typically make little if any profit as their popularity is too fleeting for

Figure 1.3 Photo of a sponsored Ben and Jerry's Sundae Snapchat filter, taken by Ysabel Gerrard

founders to meaningfully monetize them. In essence, they failed because they were *too* popular, leaving their founders unprepared to govern them safely.

The Governance of Social Media

Fortunately (or unfortunately, for some), we can't just say what we want on social media. Every space facilitating user-generated participation – not just social media but, for example, comments sections of online newspapers, or buyer reviews on shopping websites – is governed by a set of rules dictating what people can and cannot say. But it's not just about what people *say* via text; it's also about what they post – videos, images, emoji, and so on. Let me give you an example.

Emoji – 'small digital images used in online communication' [14] – might seem like harmless, playful forms of digital communication. Emoji are immensely popular, with over five billion used every day on Facebook Messenger alone [14]. But their harmless facade can be used to 'cloak everyday microaggressions in humour and play' [14], as online abusers weaponize smiley emoticons to mitigate their abuse. Emoji are also sometimes used to display opposition to certain religions or to incite hatred to those of certain ethnicities.

As Matamoros-Fernández [14] explains, emoji pose unique challenges for content moderation: they cannot be switched on and off (unlike, say, switching off the comments underneath a post), and platforms can't filter out keywords or previously banned images/videos, like they can with other kinds of social media content. It is also extremely difficult for human content moderators – known within the tech industry as commercial content moderators [15] – to decipher the context of their use. While academic and public discussions focus mainly on the moderation of text, images, and videos, significantly less attention is paid to the moderation of emoji.

This example is one of many to highlight the failures of currently popular social media giants to effectively regulate their content. As Gillespie [16] explains, the relatively recent popularization of the term 'platforms' by tech giants signals a shift in social media's history, particularly in terms of their reputation. In stark contrast to the excitement surrounding Web 2.0 technologies, social media companies face growing distrust and backlash from their users, for everything from their failures to act on online harms to their opaque data collection processes. Rather than helping the average, everyday media user to wrest 'power from the few' [5], social media have instead given new, indeed quite frightening, forms of power to a small handful of tech giants. McChesney puts it best by saying: '[I]t is supremely ironic that the Internet, the much-ballyhooed champion of increased consumer power and cutthroat competition, has become one of the greatest generators of monopoly in economic history' [17].

The emergence of the term social media *platform* therefore does not mark a technical shift in the way Web 2.0 perhaps did but is instead a discourse popularized by online content providers in their efforts to make 'strategic claims for what they do and do not do, and how their place in the information landscape should be understood' [16]. By describing themselves as 'platforms' in press releases and other public-facing communications, Gillespie argues that this carefully chosen term does the discursive work of helping tech giants to elide responsibility for the often-problematic content they host. The term *platform* implies 'a kind of neutrality towards use – "platforms" are typically flat, featureless and open to all' [16], but social media are, of course, anything but. Interestingly, in recent years we have seen a growth in nostalgia for Myspace and similar social sites like Bebo, BlackPlanet, and Neopets; a nostalgia that is, in part, connected to a discontent with failures in current social media governance, and with their inflexible features for representing the self [9].

The Self on Social Media

Social media platforms often share similar features, many of which I have already described. But each platform fosters its own *culture*, partly due to the identities people are and are not allowed to maintain. As Gibbs et al. [18] note, each social media platform has its own 'vernacular': its unique combination of style, grammar, and logic which distinguish user experiences from platform to platform. This is perhaps best represented by comparing two platforms with contrasting approaches to identity.

In response to evidence that users may have several different accounts, and that use of pseudonyms is common, some platforms, like Facebook, want you to use your 'real' name and to tie you to a form of government-issued ID if necessary. But others, like Reddit and 4chan, actively discourage the use of legal names. The founders of Facebook and 4chan famously went head-to-head with their differing views on social media identities, with Facebook's Mark Zuckerberg claiming 'the default is now social', with users required to bring their 'real' identity [19], and 4chan's Chris Poole arguing 'anonymity *is* authenticity' (emphasis added) [20].

Zuckerberg's argument resonates to some extent with recent academic theories proclaiming the 'embeddedness' of 'online' and 'offline' lives, spaces, and selves [21]. While these theories hold true in many contexts – particularly around the near-global uptick in smartphone and smart-device users – the distinction between online and offline identities is enduringly meaningful to people who want to use social media to be a different version of themselves, and this is precisely Poole's point. One example comes from my own research, led by Anthony McCosker, which found that people often run pseudonymized meme accounts on Instagram as a way of talking about their experiences of depression [22]. This form of dark humour and identity concealment could only be made possible on platforms that allow users to maintain pseudonymous identities, separating themselves from legal names and documentation. For these individuals, the online/offline distinction is complex. Further, pseudonymity can offer safety to particularly marginalized or outlawed identities, such as LGBTQ people in unsafe environments. Pseudonymity is therefore not just a tool for privacy and identity play; it has real, bodily stakes for many people around the world.

A platform's vernacular is *crucial* to user experience, and Goffman's work on performativity can help us to make sense of this. Goffman broadly explains that people present different versions of themselves according to their audience; a theory that has been used to inspire more modern research about how difficult it is to know who your online audience is, and therefore how to 'perform' [23]. On a given social media platform, especially one with large cross-demographic uptake (such as Facebook), different social groups – family members, co-workers, neighbours, acquaintances, ex-partners, friends of friends, people from hobby/interest groups, past and present students, etc. – are now collapsed into one: the friends list. This phenomenon is known as 'context collapse' [24]. Because of this, Hogan argues that people define the *lowest common denominator* of what is appropriate to post on a certain social media platform (or, in other words, the least controversial thing to say) [25]. These complexities mean people present different facets of their identity according to the vernacular of a given platform; something van der Nagel calls the 'compartmentalisation' of the self [26].

Expanding on Goffman's theories, Ditchfield proposes the 'rehearsal stage' as a phenomenon unique to social media through which a person prepares their communication and carefully tends to their imagined audiences (thereby putting to bed any grand claims that the quality of communication has declined because of social media) [27]. What's particularly interesting about this theory is that it allows for people to choose *not* to be social. Put differently, using social media is not necessarily about being social, or even about disclosing any aspects of the self to a public audience. Sometimes people want to be present on social media but not say or do very much, and this is called *lurking*.

The participants in Ditchfield's research often agonized over how much (or little) to say in a Facebook Messenger chat, or whether to abstain from replying altogether. Some people go further than this by avoiding social media altogether; downloading apps to restrict their use of certain platforms, deleting their accounts, or keeping their accounts but avoiding them. In short, there are myriad ways of *avoiding* social media; a concept that has received significantly less academic attention than social media 'use'. While it might seem odd to include points about avoidance in a section on the self, I would argue that in certain pockets of society – where smartphone uptake is high and using social media commonplace – a decision to not use social media still means you have a relationship to them, however distant, or troubled.

Writing about Social Media: A Final Thought

While this chapter has outlined several key aspects of social media – their evolution, core characteristics, underpinning business models and governance structures, and capacity to enable explorations of the self – it should perhaps end by acknowledging that social media platforms are not 'everywhere', as some might dramatically claim.

Not everyone has access to the Internet or internet-enabled devices, and not everyone chooses to use them. Some social media platforms become globally popular (Facebook), and others are regionally popular (VK); some attempt to appeal to all (YouTube) where others focus on particular demographics (BlackPlanet); and some are not available to everyone who wants to use them. Famously, China's 'Great Firewall' screens out many social media platforms popular in the West, such as TikTok and YouTube. This means social media are not experienced or understood universally, and there are still many, many people who are yet to use them. Some individual platforms, like Instagram, have so many features and nuances – Posts, Reels, Stories, Direct Messages, Comments – that it's inaccurate to even describe Instagram as one 'thing' anymore.

In short, and as the writers included in this book will tell you: social media are very, very complicated.

Further Reading

Baym, N., *Personal Connections in the Digital Age*. 2nd ed. 2015, Cambridge, UK; Malden, MA: Polity Press.

Gillespie, T., *Custodians of the Internet*. 2018, New Haven, CT: Yale University Press.

Chapter 2

The Legal and Ethical Status of Social Media

Jon Fistein

This chapter considers some of the legal and professional implications of social media use. These are discussed from two perspectives: firstly, how the law is changing to help ensure harmful and false information is not distributed, and secondly how professionals should use social media responsibly. To illustrate each of these, the chapter focuses on proposed reforms to the UK law and the UK General Medical Council's (GMC) guidance for doctors. The principles discussed will apply to other jurisdictions and professional groups, but individual professionals should ensure they are familiar with the frameworks within which they practise.

As will be seen, although social media are relatively new, many of the legal and professional issues they present are not. Social media present new opportunities for the more effective dissemination of health information, offer new ways to communicate with individual patients and the public about health matters, and can provide valuable support networks for vulnerable individuals who might otherwise be isolated. However, they also offer more opportunities for people to be misled by information that is wrong or posted deliberately to cause harm, and they make it easier inadvertently or deliberately to spread information relating to particular individuals. This is not new: misinformation has always been in the public domain, and it has always been possible for recipients of such misinformation to be misled or harmed. Confidentiality and privacy have been safeguarded by laws and professional rules that have been in place for many years. The GMC (and other professional bodies) has guidance in place advising doctors and other professionals to be considered in their communications, to ensure they and their professions remain trusted.

The questions we address here are: do existing laws offer sufficient protection given the ease and scale of misinformation seen on social media, and how should existing professional principles be applied to social media?

The Case for Law Reform

> Amy is diagnosed with an eating disorder. She goes online, looking for information about the condition and support from others going through similar experiences. She finds several helpful blogs in which people have documented their own recoveries. She also finds a closed social media group in which people encourage and support each other to maintain dangerously low body weight. Amy is distressed by what she reads and finds it harder to cope with her own eating disorder, losing significant weight as a result. Have the members of the social media group done anything unlawful?

The pace of legal change often lags the pace of technological change. In the UK, new law is either passed by government or developed in the courts. This process can take several years and is often reactive. When new technology emerges, the courts apply the existing rules to the new technology, developing the law where possible to ensure their rulings are consistent with existing law, but also fair in the case in question. However, existing law may not be applicable where there has been a radical change, and periodically there may be the need for central law reform from the UK Parliament to revise and consolidate existing laws to ensure they are fit for purpose. This process is currently under way for social media. We will describe these proposed reforms, focusing particularly on how they aim to prevent social media causing physical and mental harm.

In 2014, the House of Lords considered whether the current laws needed revision given the uptake of social media. Jean-Baptiste Alphonse Karr might have said of its position 'plus ça change, plus c'est la même chose'. It argued that the then existing laws applied to social media, and 'there are aspects of the current statute law which might appropriately be adjusted and certain gaps which might be filled [to cover social media]'. It was 'not persuaded that it [was] necessary to create a new set of offences specifically for acts committed using the social media and other information technology' [1]. One example, discussed further later on in this chapter, is the offence of encouraging suicide – which is illegal under the 1961 Suicide Act [2] regardless of the medium used for the encouragement.

Its argument was that, at their core, social media share some fundamental similarities with traditional media. In both cases there are content creators, publishing channels, a publishing process, and recipients of the published information. One should therefore expect the legal and professional considerations surrounding social media to be very similar to those surrounding more traditional publication channels. There are existing laws that create civil liabilities and criminal offences for harassment, defamation, threatening communications, and for communications that are grossly offensive, indecent, obscene, or false, which would also apply to social media.

However, all has not 'remained the same'.

In traditional media there is more control over the publishing process than there is in social medial publication, and this can place safeguards on material that appears in the public domain. For example, in traditional media, authors are commissioned based on their knowledge or expertise in a particular topic, and the content they create undergoes a review process to ensure its accuracy and veracity. Publishing houses place their reputation on the quality of the information they produce and hold themselves to ethical standards that entail not misleading their audiences. Reputable publishers additionally make explicit any editorial or advocacy position they take, enabling reasonably informed readers to be able to distinguish fact from opinion.

The traditional model has its downsides, too: routes to publication can be slow, expensive, and restrictive as only certain 'approved' authors may be able to air their views. The net result may be that content is filtered, such that only content deemed worthy of publication may see the light of day. In extreme cases this can lead to oppressive control by publishing oligarchies, limiting individuals' freedom of expression. Individuals' access to information may also be restricted, as readers may, for example, be required to pay to enable publishers to recoup their production costs.

Social media have countered these negatives by providing platforms that enable content creators to release material with minimal editorial filtering. This enables readers to access (and interact with) unfiltered content, during which process they become creators themselves. Access to information is not only more open (and potentially cheaper) than in traditional media, but also is less passive. Readers don't merely seek the information they may need, but information can be tailored to their needs and be 'pushed' to them in real time. Virtual communities can self-organize to offer mutual support and information-sharing. This may seem like a utopian position, where information is free and provided to users when and where they need it, but it can have negative consequences where inaccurate information is presented as fact to readers who may be harmed when they rely on information that is designed to manipulate or mislead them.[1]

In the UK, the Law Commission (the statutory body that keeps the law under review and recommends reform where it is needed) recognized 'the difference', observing that:

> The revolution in online communications has offered extraordinary new opportunities [for people] to communicate with one another and on an unprecedented scale. However, those opportunities also present increased scope for harm: the physical boundaries of a home now afford no haven to the bullied; the domestic-abuser can exert ever greater control over the life of the abused; many thousands of people can now abuse a single person at once and from anywhere in the world. The examples are many [3].

It published its recommendations in July 2021 [4] concluding, contrary to the earlier House of Lords Committee, that 'the current criminal offences are ill-suited to addressing these harms'. It argued that the expansion of social media, the ease of access to it (as a publisher or a reader), and the ease with which misleading or harmful information can be distributed represented a 'fundamental change' in the way people communicate, which has greatly increased the 'scale and varieties of harms' that may flow from online communications. It argued that existing laws both under-criminalize some behaviours (leaving damaging communications without criminal sanction) and over-criminalize others (permitting prosecutions that may constitute an unjustifiable interference in freedom of expression).

The Law Commission, following an extensive consultation, therefore proposed reform in four areas of law, three of which are the more relevant here:

1. The creation of a 'harms-based' communications offence, to make it illegal to send communications that could cause harm to others.
2. Offences of sending knowingly false, persistent, or threatening communications, making such communications illegal.
3. An offence of encouraging or assisting serious self-harm, similar to the existing offence of encouraging or assisting suicide.[2]

---

[1] There has been much public debate about the role of platform providers who host harmful material. Some hosts cast themselves as impartial conduits who are therefore not responsible for any harmful content they host, notwithstanding the fact that they have control over what is posted on their sites. A fuller discussion of the role of platform hosts is outside the scope of this chapter; however, it should be noted that in the UK, the proposed Online Safety Bill, discussed in this chapter, will place a duty of care on organizations hosting user-generated content not to host potentially harmful material, which should provide extra safeguards against the appearance of potentially harmful material online.

[2] On 4 February 2022 the UK Government Department for Digital, Culture, Media and Sport agreed to accept the Law Commission's recommendations on creating a harms-based

We will explore each of these in turn, considering the aspects of the proposals that are particularly relevant to mental health.

The Creation of a 'Harms-Based' Communications Offence

> **Recommendation 1**
>
> 'We recommend that section 127(1) of the Communications Act 2003 and the Malicious Communications Act 1988 be replaced with a new offence with the following elements:
> (1) the defendant sent or posted a communication that was likely to cause harm to a likely audience;
> (2) in sending or posting the communication, the defendant intended to cause harm to a likely audience; and
> (3) the defendant sent or posted the communication without reasonable excuse.
> (4) For the purposes of this offence:
>   (a) a communication is a letter, article, or electronic communication;
>   (b) a likely audience is someone who, at the point at which the communication was sent or posted by the defendant, was likely to see, hear, or otherwise encounter it; and
>   (c) harm is psychological harm, amounting to at least serious distress.
> (5) When deciding whether the communication was likely to cause harm to a likely audience, the court must have regard to the context in which the communication was sent or posted, including the characteristics of a likely audience.
> (6) When deciding whether the defendant had a reasonable excuse for sending or posting the communication, the court must have regard to whether the communication was, or was meant as, a contribution to a matter of public interest.
>
> We recommend that "likely" be defined as "a real or substantial risk".'

The Law Commission set out several elements that would need to be proven for an offence to have been committed under the proposed new law. These include:
- defining harm: establishing thresholds for harm and the likelihood of harm;
- the likely audience of any communication;
- the intention behind the communication;
- whether there is a reasonable excuse for the communication; and
- whether there should be a distinction between communications that are 'sent' versus those that are 'posted' on social media platforms.

The practical implications of these regarding harms to mental health are considered later in the chapter.

The Law Commission recommends that 'harm' should be defined as 'at least serious distress', to exclude other, more minor harms to individuals. Although the line between minor and more serious harm may seem nebulous, the concept of 'serious distress' has already been established in English Law, as distress that has 'substantial effect' on the victim's usual day-to-day activities. The Law Commission noted that 'serious distress' would include 'recognised medical conditions' and 'substantial adverse effects' on the

---

communication offence, a false communications offence, and a threatening communications offence. It is considering whether to adopt the offence for encouraging or assisting self-harm.

victim but should go beyond these as the bar for defining harm in the context of social media should be lower.

The Law Commission recognizes that 'distress is often more difficult to prove than physical harm' and that its broad definitions, if taken in isolation, might incite trivial or vexatious legal actions. To counter this, it argues that the proof of harm would be only one of the several elements required for a successful conviction, all of which would need to be proven, and which only taken together would lead to a conviction. It also recommends that there should be guidance to accompany any law to provide indicative, non-exhaustive examples of the kinds of distress that courts should (and should not) interpret as being within the definition. It notes that harm could follow a single communication, as distinct from the series of communications that would need to have occurred to establish harassment.

It is important to note that for a communication to be an offence under the proposed law, there is no requirement to prove that actual harm resulted but there is the requirement to prove that the communication is 'likely to cause harm' (of the serious nature already described). This is, again, not a new principle, and is seen in other offences such as assault and battery, for which there is also no requirement for actual harm.

This provision is important for two reasons. Firstly, it makes sense to make it unlawful to communicate material that could foreseeably cause harm, as a preventative measure to avert actual harm to potential victims. Secondly, this limits the scope of the offence to exclude cases where it is unlikely that harm would be caused by the communication, even if unexpected harm did occur, thereby limiting the risk of 'vexatious complaint'.

In considering the likeliness of potential harms, the nature of the potential victim needs also to be taken into account. The Law Commission resisted adopting a 'reasonable person' test, which was proposed by some respondents to its consultation who wanted to ensure that causing 'harm' to individuals who are uncommonly and unreasonably sensitive (and likely to be caused distress) was excluded. Instead, it argued that is better to focus on the likelihood of harm resulting from the communication and the potential victim – 'if the sender knows the likely audience is unusually susceptible to a particular type of harm and exploits that to their serious disadvantage, the sender should not be able to argue their innocence by appeals to a reasonable person'. It also argued that this is important to protect potential defendants, who should be able to 'predict at the point of sending whether they are about to commit a criminal offence', that is, whether they are likely to cause 'serious harm' to a likely audience, who may be in a vulnerable group.

As material can be posted on social media without any specific recipient in mind, the Law Commission also recommended that consideration should be given to whether the communication was likely to be 'seen, heard or otherwise encountered' by potential victims. This is to protect potential victims even if they are not specifically targeted, by making it an offence to post harmful material if there is a likelihood that it will be seen by those potential victims (presumably including where they may be 'targeted' by algorithms pushing content to them). The Law Commission recognizes that there needs to be a balance, though, between the need to prevent the posting of information with the intent of causing harm (which would be illegal under the proposals) and the requirements not to disproportionately restrict rights of freedom of expression (as outlined in the Human Rights Act), for example by criminalizing legitimate discussion of contentious or emotive topics, which may lead to harm, even though that is not the intent.

The proposed law therefore considers the intent of the sender as well as the content of the message, proposing that an offence should only be deemed to have been committed if the sender intended to bring about the harm. This excludes recklessness (cases where the sender may be aware of the potential risk of harm but does not intend to cause harm). The Law Commission additionally proposes that for communications to be unlawful, they must be made without 'reasonable excuse': the prosecution would have to establish the lack of such reasonable excuse for the communication for the prosecution to succeed. This should further ensure that there is 'no interference by the criminal law in reasonable communications or legitimate freedom of expression ... even when someone has sent a likely harmful communication intending to cause harm'. Although this may sound like a high burden and standard of proof, the Law Commission also notes that other legislation is in progress (such as the Online Safety Bill [5]) that will protect potential victims.

Offences of Sending Knowingly False, Persistent, or Threatening Communications

> **Recommendation 3**
>
> 'We recommend that the existing offences in sections 127(2)(a) and (b) of the Communications Act 2003 be replaced with a new summary offence targeting knowingly false harmful communications with the following elements:
> (1) the defendant sent or posted a communication that he or she knew to be false;
> (2) in sending the communication, the defendant intended to cause non-trivial psychological or physical harm to a likely audience; and
> (3) the defendant sent the communication without reasonable excuse.
> (4) For the purpose of this offence:
>
>   (a) a communication is a letter, electronic communication or article (of any description); and
>   (b) a likely audience is someone who, at the point at which the communication was sent by the defendant, was likely to see, hear, or otherwise encounter it.
>
> We recommend the offence should have a limitation period of three years from the day the offence was committed and six months from the day the prosecution becomes aware of sufficient information to justify proceedings.'

As well as the harms-based offence, the Law Commission made several recommendations relating to the posting of false and threatening information. The most relevant of these here is Recommendation 3, shown here, relating to the posting of false information.

The Law Commission was careful to point out that for a communication to be unlawful under this offence, the information must be false and the sender must know it to be false. This would mean that a communication that was false, but which the sender sincerely believed to be true, would not be unlawful. This position was adopted to recognize that the criminal law should only play a role in cases where false communications are made with 'malign purpose': the aim is to ensure the offence targets 'culpable false communications and has robust protections for freedom of expression' [4].

The false communications offence is proposed as a complement to the more general harms-based communication offence already described. It mirrors the harms-based offence in several ways. For example, a key element of the proposed offence is that the instigator of the communication must have 'intended to cause non-trivial psychological or physical harm to a likely audience ... without reasonable excuse'. The relevant legal principles are covered in the previous section.

An Offence of Encouraging or Assisting Serious Self-Harm

> **Recommendation 14**
> 'We recommend that encouraging or assisting serious self-harm should be an indictable offence with the following elements:
> (1) A person (A) intentionally encouraged or assisted another person (B) to cause himself or herself serious physical harm.
> (2) B need not be a specific person (or class of persons) known to, or identified by, A.
> (3) A may commit this offence whether or not serious physical harm, or an attempt at causing serious physical harm, occurs.
> (4) Physical harm is serious if it would amount to grievous bodily harm under the Offences against the Person Act 1861.'

'While encouraging or assisting suicide is [already] a specific offence, criminalised under the Suicide Act 1961, encouraging or assisting self-harm is not' [4]. The Law Commission proposes a specific new offence to complement both the Suicide Act and its proposed harms-based communication offence, to criminalize the encouragement or assistance of non-suicidal self-injury such as self-cutting, disordered eating, and self-bruising. It draws many parallels to S.2 of the Suicide Act 1961, which sets out the conditions for the offence of the encouragement of suicide and draws on definitions from the harms-based communications offence.

The proposed offence is an 'inchoate' one – that is, an offence would still be committed regardless of whether anyone actually self-harmed as a result of the encouragement. Such inchoate offences normally relate to the encouragement of other crimes, but it is noteworthy that the self-harm is not in itself a criminal offence (nor is there an intention to make it one). This is similar to the offence of encouragement of suicide, which remains an offence in its own right, notwithstanding the decriminalization of suicide in the Suicide Act 1961.

The proposed offence targets those encouraging self-harm in others. However, the intent of the communication is important here as well. The sender must have intention of causing harm for the offence to have been committed. This is to ensure the offence does not have a disproportionate effect on vulnerable people by ensuring they are not criminalized or stigmatized if they share information about their experiences with self-harm on social media as part of a support community or when seeking help. 'Those expressing their own experiences with self-harm without any intention to encourage others to self-harm' would not be committing an offence.

Similarly to the harms-based communications law, the proposed law on self-harm is limited to cover 'serious physical harm'. Many of the arguments about the seriousness threshold covered in the section on the harms-based offence apply here too, but there is an additional consideration. There are cases where someone can inflict harm on another, but this is not illegal if the person who is harmed gives their consent. The Law Commission does not desire to criminalize 'the encouragement of an act that, when actually committed against another, would be legal'. The aim of the proposal is to protect against 'at least serious harm ... [which is] more than transient or trifling harm', which could lawfully be 'committed by A against [a] willing [i.e. consenting] B'. Although this approach may seem over-cautious, for example, excluding many cases where the self-harm is 'disordered eating', the Law Commission was satisfied that this should be excluded from this proposed offence as it 'may well be captured by' the other offences it proposes, as we have already set out. As with those other offences, the Law Commission stresses the need for guidance to accompany any proposed new criminal law, in particular to ensure that 'acts of vulnerable people are not inadvertently criminalised' [4].

> It is unlikely that the blogs looked at by Amy are unlawful. Even though they are discussing harm, the intent is to promote recovery, not to encourage harm.
> Considering the postings of the social media group supporting and encouraging low body weight, under the proposed harms-based law, this may be unlawful. The communication is likely to cause serious distress and/or harm to likely recipients and is likely to reach those recipients as it is posted to a group for people with eating disorders. Whether this is unlawful would most likely hinge on the intent of the posters: if they intended to cause distress or harm (for example, by trying to reinforce a vulnerable person's already distorted body image by commenting on a picture of them, saying they are fat and giving them strategies to lose more weight) it is likely that this would be found to be unlawful due to their intention to cause the recipient to be harmed (by intending to bring about weight loss that would be harmful, even if they thought they were helping) and it is unlikely that there is a 'reasonable excuse' in these circumstances.

Professional Conduct on Social Media

> Dr S, a GP, discovers that Dr T is posting information on a social media platform espousing the discredited theory that the MMR vaccination causes autism. She is worried that this misinformation might lead to her patients and the public becoming vaccine hesitant, making their children vulnerable to measles, with potentially serious consequences in terms of their morbidity and mortality. What should she do?

The first section considered what protections should be in place to prevent harmful material being posted on social media. This section looks at social media from the perspective of professionals who may use social media themselves, and who may have to counter misinformation online in discussion with service users. We will take the professional standards expected of doctors, set out by the GMC as our exemplar, but similar guidance exists for other professions such as teachers [6]. It should be noted that professional regulators often expect, for those registered with them, higher standards than the legal standards that apply to the general public.

The GMC has issued specific guidance on the use of social media by doctors [7]. The GMC recognizes many of the benefits of social media, such as enabling public health and policy discussions, establishing professional networks, and facilitating patients' access to information about health and services. However, it reminds doctors that the 'standards expected of [them] do not change because they are communicating through social media rather than face to face or through other traditional media, but new challenges can arise'.

We will consider two of these challenges here: how doctors should respond to information that is inaccurate or misleading, and doctors' own conduct on social media.

Responding to Inaccurate or Misleading Information

Doctors may encounter material they believe may cause harm to either to their patients or to the public in general. Doctors have a duty of care to their patients, and part of this is to provide information to them that allows them to make informed decisions about their care. Doctors should therefore be careful to provide reliable sources of information to patients, and to direct them away from sources that are misleading. They have a duty to work with their patients to help them be discriminating about the quality and reliability of the information they rely on, for example by explaining how they can check their sources, consider any potential hidden agendas, and be reassured that the information is not false or likely to cause them harm.

Doctors may have a wider duty to correct misinformation [8]. Where doctors encounter information that they feel is misleading and which is aimed at a more general public audience, they should consider their response carefully. The GMC's *Good Medical Practice* requires doctors to treat colleagues 'fairly and with respect' and requires doctors to ensure their 'conduct justifies [their] patients' trust in [them] and the public's trust in the profession' [9]. Doctors must also maintain appropriate boundaries and should not mix their personal and professional relationships. The GMC reminds doctors that they should not 'bully, harass or make gratuitous, unsubstantiated or unsustainable comments about individuals online' and that the laws relating to defamation (making unjustifiable statements about individuals or organizations that harm their reputation) also apply.

In the face of misleading information doctors should therefore, in most cases, resist the temptation to get directly involved with the poster. Rather, they should assess the impact of the information on their patients, and on the trust of the profession and should work to correct the information with their patients. If the information is posted by another doctor, they should be careful not to get dragged into spats on social media. Concerns could be raised with the GMC, and in the future could potentially come under the proposed 'harms-based' or 'false information' laws we have described.

Professional Conduct on Social Media

Doctors may also use social media themselves. Where doctors post material on social media, the GMC reminds them to consider the implications of what they post: that such information is likely to be taken on trust and may potentially be taken to represent the views of the profession more generally [7]. The British Medical Association has also emphasized that a doctor using social media 'is still a doctor' and that the 'ethical and legal standards expected [of them] by the GMC and the broader, less well-defined professional expectations of their peers can still apply online as in any other part of everyday life' [10].

Doctors should also consider the implications of their social media use in relation to laws on privacy and confidentiality [11]. Both of these laws apply to social media, and the ease by which information can be transmitted, copied, disseminated, etc. can increase the chance and extent of potential breaches.

Privacy is the (qualified) right for individuals to conduct various aspects of their private and family life without unwarranted interference [12]. Doctors should consider their own privacy and also that of their patients. As online information can potentially be accessed by others, doctors should be careful to consider whether information they post might lead to breaches of privacy for themselves or others. They should particularly be aware that there might be additional risks to privacy due to the nature of the medium, such as the disclosure of location information in metadata that is associated with posted images and should use appropriate safeguards to protect against these.

Confidentiality is an important professional and legal duty for doctors, and its principles apply when using social media in other settings. It is obvious that doctors should take care to ensure that they do not use publicly accessible social media to discuss individual patients' care, even with those patients themselves, due to the potential risk that the conversation might be intercepted or otherwise compromised. Doctors should also be aware of the risks of 'jigsaw' identification [13], where 'individual pieces of information [that] do not breach confidentiality on their own' are shared but, when taken with other information published online, could be enough to identify a patient or someone close to them.

In summary, social media provide potentially useful ways for doctors, patients, and the public to communicate with each other, and existing professional guidance recognizes this. However, doctors and other professionals must take appropriate care to ensure they are aware of the potential risks and that appropriate safeguards are in place.

Dr S should:
- talk to her patients, to explain the evidence for the safety of the MMR vaccine and its efficacy in preventing serious illness;
- report the misleading information to the social media provider;
- report Dr T's post to the GMC; and
- consider posting accurate information to counter the misinformation.

Dr S should not:
- post anything that personally attacks, disrespects, or defames Dr T.

Conclusion

- Misinformation has always been out there. It is more easily spread now through social media as it is unfiltered and can appear to target vulnerable individuals.
- Many of the existing UK laws provide some protections against the posting of harmful and misleading information.
- However, it has been recognized that these leave some loopholes, so there are proposals for UK law reform to:
    o place responsibilities on social media platform providers to not allow the posting of harmful or misleading information; and
    o introduce new offences of:
        - encouraging harms;
        - false communications; and
        - encouraging self-harm – potentially.

- When faced with misinformation online, these may provide routes for professionals to report crime to the police, and further action may be taken by them to investigate and then recommend prosecution.
- Professionals should take care when considering whether to intervene directly if they discover misinformation. They should consider:
    - their professional obligations relating to their behaviour and the reputation of the profession;
    - the impact of the misleading information on their patients, and how they can work with their patients directly to counter any misinformation; and
    - the impact of any action they take on their patients' trust in them and the public's trust in their profession.
- Professionals should also consider their own behaviour on social media, considering, for example:
    - privacy and confidentiality, particularly when information is being stored on remote systems over which they do not have control; and
    - their professional obligations relating to their behaviour and the reputation of the profession.

Further Reading

British Medical Association, *Social media, ethics and professionalism*, www.bma.org.uk/media/1851/bma-ethics-guidance-on-social-media-2018.pdf

Law Commission, *Modernising Communications Offences* (Law Com No. 399, 2021).

Chapter 3

Social Media: An Everyday Reality

David A. Ellis

In the space of a single generation, social media have transformed how billions of people make friends, build communities, and share knowledge. However, approaches that suggest harm occurs based solely on time spent using social media disguise this everyday reality. In response, this chapter points towards the importance of understanding who uses social media in daily life, why and how. While we have more data than ever to help us explore the impacts of new technologies, including social media, everyday experiences require description *alongside* careful theorizing about the mechanisms that might cause benefits or harms. This collectively shifts research priorities towards applied applications that can mitigate problems, injustices, and inequalities that social media and other digital cultures can foster.

Technological Innovation and Social Media: As with many innovations, social media have evolved from technologies that previously existed in other forms. Computer-mediated communication in the 1980s took place on forums or bulletin boards, and these online messaging services were often referred to as virtual communities. Here, small numbers of users could exchange messages with groups that shared common interests. Graphical web browsers in the mid-1990s, alongside the proliferation of internet connections and 'multimedia' computing, followed. Increased internet speeds and Web 2.0 technologies allowed even more people to create and share online material in the following decade. Smartphones in the early part of the twenty-first century simultaneously drove a further wave of connectivity that allowed for location awareness where social media can be associated with an individual's location. Collectively, social media services today encapsulate a variety of Web-based technologies that can support online and offline relationships. Of course, as with the offline world, social media provide an outlet for potential harm including digital exclusion, misinformation, and harassment.

Large numbers of people have been building digital communities and communicating online for over four decades. Staying connected via social media has become an unavoidable part of everyday life for much of the world's population as it facilitates social and occupational activities. Software developers at any level can also quickly become fundamental figures in the socio-technical systems that characterize modern

---

Funding Statement: David A. Ellis was supported in part by REPHRAIN: The National Research Centre on Privacy, Harm Reduction and Adversarial Influence Online, under UKRI grant: EP/V011189/1.

Acknowledgements: I would like to thank Heather Shaw who provided helpful comments on an earlier version of this manuscript.

society. These technological movements have continued during the worldwide pandemic, as some services (such as Microsoft Teams) have become integrated with the world of work.

The Social Sciences and Social Media: Seemingly rapid changes to society rightly raise many questions, especially in terms of how technologies might impact well-being. Stakeholders are often looking for guidance – for example, whether time with technology should be reduced remains the most pressing concern. Researchers have recently demonstrated that bold claims about the impact of social media hold little value because of how social media activities are measured and subsequently analysed [1]. Studies typically require participants to estimate the total time spent using digital services, which is then correlated with measures of well-being. Almost all such research comes to a similar conclusion: the relationship between time spent in social media use and well-being is close to zero, and below a threshold for harm that would require intervention (e.g. Orben and Przybylski [2]). Very little of this has reached the public, yet the notion of small to non-existent effects should not be wholly surprising. Alongside the enormity of confounding variables, the psychological processes and the technology that underpins any positive or negative impact will not be universal.

When theoretical frameworks are referenced, they tend to fixate on a linear dose–response relationship derived from medicine. A pathologized approach towards social media goes further and compares overuse to a 'drug, demon or doughnut' [3]. Such concepts have their origins in 'usage scales' that are built around constructs, plucked from thin air, with little to no clinical input [4]. This preoccupation with time spent online as harmful serves to repeat problems associated with research that focused on the negative impacts of many other screen-based technologies, systematically moving from television and video games to the Internet and smartphones. Beyond drawing attention away from harmful *content* – including misinformation and online abuse – social media research has often ignored the fact that for the vast majority, social media use remains a core function of everyday life. This neglects human agency and an individual's capability to shape the consequences of digital connectivity [5].

Many researchers are rightly interested in how social media are changing people and society, but this also needs to be reflected in how we conduct research in the digital age. Therefore, the remainder of this chapter describes *why* people use social media, *who* uses social media, and *how*. While not mutually exclusive, the answers provide a basis from which to understand how social media interacts with everyday life.

Why People Use Social Media

We have an intimate desire to connect with others. Sociability and the subsequent generation of interpersonal relationships are inherently linked to emotional well-being [6]. Conversely, the breakdown of relationships is often considered one of life's more traumatic experiences. Long-term social separation also has a negative impact on general health and well-being. So, in the first instance, social media can support such a desire to affiliate, which drives people to form positive and lasting personal relationships. A second major motivation for social media use concerns self-presentation, which in many cases leads to further affiliation [6]. Examples include Facebook activities that accomplish self-presentational goals, including posting photographs, profile information, and wall content.

These two answers concerning *why* are, as with our understanding of social media impacts, rather general, given the variability of affordances[1] provided by different platforms. For example, some people report using social media to curate memories via photographs or videos, but this feature is not available on all platforms – for example Snapchat deliberately deletes content. Similarly, while Facebook profiles generally represent accurate self-presentation, the *why* may change when content is posted anonymously as for example on Reddit.

Given this variation, social media has become more segmented despite increased levels of hyperconnectivity and collective ownership of popular services. There are likely to be nuanced reasons *why* users engage with specific social media platforms based on the types of relationships they wish to form, the online identity they wish to present, and whether any content is cross-posted to other platforms. One can hypothesize that Facebook is the location for family and friends to keep in touch, LinkedIn is the place to build professional networks, and Twitter becomes the site of choice for news or topic-based arguments with strangers. The rapid adoption of smartphones has also led to the second wave of dating services including Tinder and Grindr. Using data from How Couples Meet and Stay Together (HCMST) surveys, Rosenfeld, Thomas, and Hausen [7] demonstrated that meeting partners online has now displaced all other ways of meeting. Other mobile services (such as Snapchat) are used to build relationships with people who are often already known offline. These more focused motives still align with the general drivers of affiliation and self-presentation.

Variability between individuals who regularly engage with multiple platforms adds a further layer of complexity. Motivations can be aligned with the *uses and gratifications theory* (see Chapter 9), which aims to understand *why* and how people actively seek out specific media to satisfy specific needs. For example, after asking participants to generate words or phrases to describe motives for Facebook use, Joinson [8] identified several unique uses and gratifications: social connection, shared identities, photographs, content, social investigation, social network surfing, and status updating. Of course, a variety of other demographic and changing individual circumstances will cause motivations to evolve. Relationship status has been shown to impact the use of Facebook, and a variety of micro-variations in motivations will apply when it comes to dating platforms depending on the type of relationship desired.

Various personality factors have also been associated with different motivations. For example, extraversion has been associated with people who want to create new connections with those higher in neuroticism being more likely to use social media as a form of escapism [9]. Seidman [10] explored associations between personality and the key motivators belonging and self-presentation. Belonging was best predicted by high agreeableness and high neuroticism. Self-presentation was best predicted by low conscientiousness and high neuroticism. Personality differences appear to be more consistently linked with core motivations rather than platform selection or usage [9]. However, this remains somewhat an open question as correlates between personality and social media rarely involve objective measurements of use [4].

---

[1] Affordances are the opportunities offered to a user of a particular platform – they are therefore not fixed properties of the platform but emerge out of interaction between the platform and the user.

Who Uses Social Media?

More than 3.5 billion people are online out of a world population estimated to be around 8 billion. Over three billion of these online people use Meta platforms, which includes Facebook, Instagram, and WhatsApp. Many other platforms, including YouTube, also have more than one billion users. A conservative estimate would suggest that social media platforms are used by one in three people in the world and more than two-thirds of all internet users. In rich countries, where access to the Internet is nearly universal, almost all young adults use social media. Gender differences exist for some platforms. The share of women who use Pinterest is more than twice as high as the share of men who use this platform. For Reddit, it is the other way around – the share of men is almost twice as high.

A Life-Course Approach?

As with *why*, *who* uses social media is dynamic and likely changes across an individual's lifespan. While new services continue to appear and grow at pace (e.g., Tik Tok), many other platforms that were once popular have almost disappeared (e.g., MySpace). Beyond technological changes, which are often difficult to predict, the most popular social media platforms have historically been adopted by adolescents and then expanded out to other age groups. For example, earlier studies on Facebook suggested that females, younger people, and those not currently in a committed relationship were the most active Facebook users, but these differences are less pronounced today. However, aggregate numbers can mask a great deal of heterogeneity across other platforms with popularity dropping much faster with age in some instances. For example, the age gradient for Snapchat and Instagram is especially steep. Since these platforms are relatively new, it is hard to know how much of this age gradient is the result of a cohort effect. In other words, it is unclear whether today's young people will continue using Snapchat as they become older. If they do, the age gradient would narrow as it has with Facebook.

Assuming today's young adults continue using some form of social media throughout their lives, then social media will become even more universal, especially as internet adoption expands throughout lower-income countries.[2] An increasing number of careers also require the use of social media to accomplish tasks and share information with other colleagues within their company on a location-independent basis, which has been further amplified by the COVID-19 pandemic.

On the other hand, changes to *who* are unlikely to be consistent across platforms at an individual, group, or country level – there is considerable variation in *who* appears across different services. People already engage with a sophisticated management of their online identity [11]. The choices people make regarding where they appear are therefore not random. This has implications for research that depends on data from particular social media platforms. It also offers helpful lessons on how to reach different population segments when trying to communicate to diverse audiences.

Even towards the end of life, or in death, *who* is on social media continues to evolve. Some research has focused on how individuals manage their presence towards the end of life and how people who know they are dying document and process those events. According to some forecasts, Facebook may become the largest cemetery in human

---

[2] https://ourworldindata.org/grapher/share-of-individuals-using-the-internet

history, a digital graveyard that will contain archives, biographies and testimonies, obituaries and eulogies, and traces of social bonds. Such changes may help or hinder the grieving process [12]. The long-term impacts of this remain unclear as visiting the deceased's profile or having unexpected 'encounters' with the deceased through pop-up reminders or personal mourning posts may lead people to move to other platforms or leave social media altogether.

Who Is Missing: Short Term?

Irrespective of the life stage, a constant level of connectivity has fuelled theoretical and empirical research on how individuals and organizations might best manage everyday experiences. Digital detox apps (that force reduced usage) may have obvious benefits while undertaking work that would otherwise be dangerous such as driving. Recent research has observed higher levels of well-being for those who use such apps, although it is difficult to interpret when researchers combine those who use detox apps with those who use screen monitoring apps (that simply advise about usage).

Beyond an occasional detox, one could leave all forms of social media. Some studies have found that complete withdrawal from social media can have adverse consequences such as lower satisfaction, boredom, feelings of social pressure, and fear [4]. This supports the notion that a sudden lack of social media use may be an early warning sign of social withdrawal. While giving up a digital existence for a short time may let people reconnect with other aspects of their lives, this is often a temporary state that is impossible to maintain. Most people will simply return to prior habits that have become an essential part of everyday life. The notion of digital management is more realistic than total disconnection for most people. Such decisions determine *who* can be driven by *why* or where.

Disconnection can mean different things for different people or groups [13]. This might include intrinsic psychological concerns, technological factors, social influence, and privacy and security concerns. However, we know comparatively little about how the removal of one form of social media is supplanted by another form of online or offline communication. Some social media services may no longer serve their original purpose. For example, if someone is now in a happy relationship or no longer wants to find a partner via a dating platform, then it will no longer be required. Alternatively, avoiding a technology may be deliberate and may have specific underlying reasons tied to an individual or location where reduced usage is preferable.

Who Is Missing: Long Term?

Barriers or a lack of access are not always obvious when billions of people use a specific technology. Digital inequality can be broadly considered as the systematic differences between individuals of different socio-economic backgrounds concerning their access to, skills in, uses of, and outcomes derived from engagement with digital media [14]. In terms of who is online, one would conclude that those from developing countries, those who are in low socio-economic areas, and those over the age of 65 are poorly represented.[3] However, a lack of access to specific services can be problematic at any point in

---

[3] www.ons.gov.uk/peoplepopulationandcommunity/householdcharacteristics/homeinternetandsocialmediausage/articles/exploringtheuksdigitaldivide/2019-03-04#how-does-digital-exclusion-vary-with-age

life. For example, for adolescents who are digitally excluded (lacking the computer or internet access needed to successfully participate in online-only education), educational disruptions will be greater.[4]

Worldwide, access to the Internet varies considerably and some states such as China block access to specific social media platforms. However, the latter can often be navigated with the use of virtual private networks. In the UK, almost 20% of people are not online. This presents a dilemma for governments that want to reach and support people as more public services move online. Identifying barriers to the adoption of specific services should remain of equal importance when placed alongside research that aims to improve our understanding of *who* can benefit or become excluded from new technology, including social media. Similarly, scholarship that interrogates the link between social media use and well-being must also account for the role of social stratification in this relationship [14]. For example, large numbers hide large disparities between different services, with less than a quarter of Americans visiting Twitter or Reddit [15]. British Twitter users have also been reported to be younger, wealthier, and better educated than those in the sample who were offline, which also has implications for research where representativeness is important.

How People Use Social Media

How people seek information (or misinformation), manage profiles, and communicate dominates most social media activity. This frequently overlaps with offline activities. For example, searches or exposure to information can play an important role in shaping users' decisions or actions pertaining to health. Many adults, including many people with chronic illnesses, turn to social media for health information. Others use social media to seek help during unpleasant life events, including relationship breakdowns.

Many systems also attempt to recommend content that can have unintended consequences. Specifically, algorithms that control content often lead people down wormholes that confirm biases and stereotypes that might be inaccurate [16]. This can also be driven by Facebook friends, who shared substantially less cross-cutting news from sources aligned with an opposing ideology. One might conclude that, at least within the domain of political news, selective exposure drives attention. Other findings, however, have suggested that social media *and* news portal browsing do not contribute to the avoidance of news or restrict diversity [17]. This suggests that confirmation bias may be driving many of the above effects rather than the availability of information alone. Like other online dangers, being exposed to misinformation or offensive material generates a risk, but the overall effects will not always be negative. For example, being exposed to anti-vax material may lead to a positive outcome by reminding individuals that they should get vaccinated.

The flexibility of information seeking also extends to *how* people develop social media profiles. Specifically, people can have behavioural signatures/profiles which are stable in situations that are perceived psychologically as being the same. This type of context-based behavioural change is both normal and expected by those around us. For example, Vasalou and Joinson [18] found that users were likely to create a more attractive avatar for a dating profile and a more 'intellectual looking' avatar for an online

---

[4] www.suttontrust.com/wp-content/uploads/2021/01/School-Shutdown-Covid-19.pdf

gaming profile. People appear to actively separate their professional (such as LinkedIn) and social (such as Facebook or Instagram) oriented platforms typically by self-censorship of posts rather than utilizing audience management tools [11]. However, while there was overlap between participants, their usage and reasoning behind *how* they chose to appear on different platforms were relatively unique.

The main *how* for most social media activities involves social interactions or responding to online content directly. Social media can allow for group cooperation on a larger scale, with virtual communities often founded on common interests or goals. Despite the efforts of some countries to control technology, collective group action, for example, has also become possible where this would have previously been dangerous in face-to-face contexts. As part of everyday life for the majority, however, almost all relationship development occurs following rapid switching between offline and computer-mediated interfaces, including social media. This is especially prominent when developing new relationships, as the flow of information about a potential friend or partner can, in turn, impact how a relationship develops over time. Specifically, people using dating platforms will chat online and then continue interactions offline. People can then use social media to maintain relationships or deliberately ignore those same people.

The three most common relational maintenance behaviours on social media are social contact, response seeking, and relational assurances [19]. Behaviours might include sharing photos, updating one's relationship status, or including a romantic partner in a profile picture. However, these are not always viewed as mutually beneficial. Taylor and Bazarova [20] found that frequent checking in with a partner across the interpersonal media ecosystem is associated with feeling the security of availability from a partner; however, others find that such availability can produce stress and relationship dissatisfaction [21, 22]. The experience of breaking up has also been transformed. While social media can create a rich digital record of life together, modifying or removing such content can be difficult to accomplish and cause additional stress. Irrespective of these choices, social media can also be used to engage with surveillance, stalking, or inadvertently discovering whether a former partner has moved on.

Summary and Implications

People use social media for a variety of reasons, which may or may not be due to the affordances of a specific service. At a macro level, *why* people engage with social media is psychologically similar to why they engage with any other form of social relationship. However, this likely remains a dynamic process at the micro level, although we know far less about how motivations change within and between platforms and what the impact of shared (or distinct) audiences might be longer-term.

Despite this, for many people social media use is driven by something more fundamental, that is, the necessity to engage and live in the twenty-first century. For example, online dating platforms are part of single life during emerging adulthood, especially where opportunities for offline interactions are limited. In adult life, linked streams of data and logins support a range of public sector (such as health) and private (such as banking) enterprises. Such systems were already core to social and occupational organization, which became even more apparent during the COVID-19 pandemic. Regardless, increased levels of connectivity before and after the pandemic have led people to directly question the *why*. Large surveys suggest that people of all ages report that the most frequently experienced *potential* harm is simply spending too much time online.[5] This is somewhat removed from what people feel is a *greater risk* of harm including matters pertaining to privacy and security. Collectively, individual, and societal, expectations mean that opting out of digital ecosystems becomes increasingly difficult and, in many cases, almost impossible.

As with *why*, *who* engages with specific platforms evolves over time. This can be a function of technology, but people can self-regulate where they appear [5]. Social media accounts have become paramount to the modern economy, and this makes understanding *who* is absent even more important. Many studies continue to focus on a single social media service such as Twitter or Facebook. Social media are now used to recruit participants at scale, but we need to ensure samples are not biased, which, in turn, limits the applied impacts of subsequent interventions that could instead create new inequalities. For example, the World Health Organization has flagged the importance of social media communication in crisis situations, yet it remains unclear which channels should be used to ensure effective population-wide communication [23]. Horvát and Hargittai also argue that a failure to understand *who* appears on different platforms can generate inefficiencies; for example, if two platforms have largely overlapped user bases, there is no reason to spend resources on both [23].

Ensuring that we engage with groups who are poorly represented can reduce inequality, but also support new technologies that might benefit those groups. For example, while many older adults are absent from social media, they bring rich and critical perspectives on the role of technology in society, that are grounded in extensive lived experiences across their life courses. Barros Pena and colleagues [24] conducted interviews with retirees over the age of 60. Experiences of technology across the lifespan significantly undermined the participants' sense of competency, independence, resilience, agency, and control. Dissonances between what participants valued and the perceived values of technology have led them to become critical adopters of technology and resist its intrusion into certain aspects of their lives.

In the same vein, failing to understand *how* people use such platforms every day has also led to enormous gaps in current understanding. Once social media has become integrated with everyday life, the *how* can become consistent for longer periods. Social affiliation models that focus on homeostasis help explain how people consistently use social media. Just as people regulate a variety of behaviours (like sleep), they also control the level of contact with others, keeping it both stable and close to the desired level. Of course, it is possible to further regulate habitual digital interactions by modifying apps, notifications, and modality switching. Research has recently begun to explore how such decisions relating to notifications might improve or hinder well-being. How feedback might encourage people to reflect on or change social media habits remains an open question [25]. However, there remain clear differences between individuals and groups. Variations in *how* have become increasingly valuable for prediction. A considerable volume of research has started to link *how* people use social media to mental health, personality, age, gender, sexuality, and political affiliations. Data from social media that

---

[5] www.ofcom.org.uk/__data/assets/pdf_file/0024/196413/concerns-and-experiences-online-harms-2020-chart-pack.pdf

include location can also be used to predict offline behaviours including attendance at events (e.g. Hinds et al. [26]).

While people develop interpersonal relationships and groups that can quickly move offline, we know less about the relational processes that underlie social media connections, disconnections, or offline actions that occur between contexts [27]. Research concerning online to offline transitions has typically relied on survey-based designs. Future research will therefore require more advanced methods to capture offline and computer-mediated communication over time. For example, these could start to test or extend integrative models that have attempted to explain distinct romantic relationship stages based around familiarity and attraction that occur in different contexts. It remains unclear, for example, *how* people interact with different platforms as relationships develop. We might predict, for example, that moving topics across different platforms (media multiplexity) and reducing communication interdependence is indicative of a stronger relationship [28], but how this interacts with offline interactions is less clear. Because relationships sit at the heart of why people use social media, this theoretical and methodological development might help answer other questions, including those concerning effects on well-being [27].

Conclusion

Rapid changes brought about by technology continue to generate lines of research that replicate the narrow priorities of the past [5]. Specifically, in the context of social media, many question whether these new communication technologies are having an impact on well-being. However, research that has often made grand claims rarely acknowledges the everyday reality of *why*, *who*, and *how* people engage with technology in the twenty-first century. Experiences are often reduced to a single duration estimate of general use or captured via a survey, yet when using these measures, research that adopts the highest methodological standards paints a much more complex and nuanced picture.

Recent work in support of an everyday perspective is largely descriptive yet remains systematic and highly revealing in terms of how social media might be impacting people across their lifespan and society more broadly [29]. These issues often relate to inequality or the exposure of people to content that risks genuine harm. Understanding the daily impacts of social media may collectively benefit from an even greater focus on description for many areas that are less theoretically developed [30]. However, the development or adoption of existing psychological theory also provides sensible starting points, especially with regards to habit formation, intra-individual consistency, self-esteem, and self-regulation. Other forms of theorizing that are 'digital specific' will likely require something truly interdisciplinary.

Over 20 years ago, Albert Bandura suggested that technological innovation alone does not lead to inevitable outcomes [5]. Social media, therefore, are not a unidirectional force. Acknowledging this complexity, even in passing, gets closer to understanding *how* specific affordances might influence *who*, and *why* impacts occur in offline and online environments [1]. For example, *why* a specific individual or group (*who*) is engaging in an activity (*how*) will be of far greater significance than any general measure of screen time. This includes what is arguably the biggest threat to most members of the public where social media can allow a small number of people (*who*) with extreme views (*why*) to connect with each other (*how*) and carry out acts of terrorism.

Why one person over another might be affected by social media also remains open to debate. For example, those who are depressed may have specific negative (cognitive) thinking styles or neural markers that mean their interpretations of social media content are in line with responses expected in other offline and online environments. Similarly, while the use of social media to facilitate social interaction might support someone who is introverted and motivated to develop new skills, it could also exacerbate a pre-existing mental health condition [4]. Considering responses between groups or individuals who are more susceptible to *specific* social media impacts should generate larger effect sizes, but the results may simply reveal an effect that is not technology-specific.

Further Reading

Bandura, A., Growing primacy of human agency in adaptation and change in the electronic era. *European Psychologist*, 2002. 7(1): p. 2–16.

Bayer, J. B., I. A. Anderson, and R. Tokunaga, Building and breaking social media habits. *Current Opinion in Psychology*, 2022. **45**: p. 101303.

How Social Media Can Influence Group and Individual Behaviour
Practice Implications

Jeff French and Melissa Blair

This chapter will cover some of the key theoretical and practice issues associated with how social media have an impact on group and individual behaviour. The chapter will also address practical issues of relevance to professionals considering using social media as part of their efforts to promote mental health. In the opening section of the chapter, we set out an introduction to relevant behavioural theory and its implications for social media practice and how it can be used to promote positive engagement with social media.

The chapter will also examine how social media can be harnessed to promote mental health and provide guidance about the design and use of social media in the field of mental health promotion. The chapter will provide practitioners with understanding about how social media can have negative influence on both personal and group behaviour and how this can be minimized. The chapter will conclude with practical examples about how to utilize social media in mental health promotion and guidance that can be given to clients about how best to use social media as part of their own mental health promotion. The chapter will be illustrated with case studies and examples from a variety of countries.

Theoretical Foundations of How Social Media Influence Behaviour

The potential and actual impact of social media on well-being is explored in depth in other chapters of this book. Despite the ubiquitous nature of social media globally we are in fact still at the early stages of our understanding about their influence, limitations, and potential as a force for good or ill. As recent research has shown, there is no strong evidence that associations between adolescents' digital technology engagement and mental health problems have increased in recent years [1]. We are however not starting from scratch as we have a great deal of theoretical understanding about how and why social media engender participation in their use and why so many people find them compelling and potentially addictive, helpful, and in some cases harmful [2]. In this first section of this chapter, we will briefly explore some key theoretical perspectives that can help us understand both the role of social media in society and the basis of their potential to influence.

There are obviously multiple theoretical perspectives that have relevance to an understanding of social media and their impact on mental health and the other chapters in this book explore such theories. We are concerned in this chapter with the application of social media in the promotion of mental health, so we will briefly consider three theories that are focused on the nature of social influence, the mechanisms of social influence, and how these manifest themselves as functional elements of social media. Namely, we will explore the theoretical influence of Habermas's theory of social spheres,

Horton, Wohl's parasocial interaction theory, Fogg's functional triad of computer persuasion and Dahl's 7s framework.

According to Jurgen Habermas, modern society depends on our ability to criticize and reason collectively about our own traditions. Technology, including social media, is one method of achieving this. Reason, according to Habermas [3], sits at the heart of everyday communication and is driven by interrogating people's actions through questions such as why did you do that? why do you think that? why did you say that? Habermas puts forward the view that reason is not about discovering truths but rather our need to justify ourselves to others. People undertake this reasoning in what Habermas calls the 'public sphere' which over time builds consensus, strengthens society, and ultimately brings about change. In this way society is developed through a process of active communication, sharing, and criticism. In term of the relevance to social media of Habermas's theory of the consequences of the 'public sphere', many social media channels offer opportunities for such dialogue between individuals and opportunities for millions to both observe and participate in social dialogue. However, if social media platforms, like more traditional media such as newspapers and TV, are controlled and/or regulated by powerful state or commercial interests such opportunities can be diminished or stopped altogether. Social dialogue is then, if we accept Habermas's view, essential to social development but it needs to be facilitated and exhibit critical reviews. This position obviously has implications for questions about monitoring, moderating, and restricting views or criticisms that are deemed by communities and social media providers to be inappropriate, offensive, and/or dangerous.

One of the key features of the social media communications sphere is that in theory everyone has an equal voice. In reality, however, some voices are louder and more pervasive than others. The impact of famous people's voices on issues and as a way to endorse products, services, or ideas has been shown to not only boost awareness of issues but also have a measurable impact on the sale of products and services and increase the acceptance of ideas. This influence can be measured using tracking systems such as the Adly Influence Index (www.adly.com). One of the key features of social media and its impact is the role played by people perceived to be significant by groups of social media users. Parasocial interaction theory has useful explanatory power when considering this feature of social media. Parasocial interaction theory [4] is focused on specific communication circumstances where communication is perceived by the recipient as immediate, personal, and also reciprocal but not by the sender.

People who follow a celebrity, for example on Twitter, develop a sense of a relationship and intimacy with them which can lead to even more influence. In reality, the relationship is one-sided with the celebrity having little or no personal awareness of the follower. It has been shown surprisingly however that social media-aided parasocial communication such as this can be perceived by followers as comparable with an actual social relationship and in that way can act as a powerful driver of both opinion and behaviour [5]. In a world of increased social media engagement, understanding the persuasive potential of parasocial communication should be a priority for those seeking to influence positive mental health. A good example of how influences can be used is that of the 2020 TikTok campaign as part of mental health awareness month in the USA. TikTok videos were developed featuring influencers including Jaci Butler, Parker James, Sav Palacio, Hailey Sani, Sara Schauer, Enoch True, and Madison Vanderveen, promoting aspects of mental health awareness and resilience [6].

The final theoretical perspective we will cover in this opening section of the chapter is focused on two conceptual models that can help us understand how social media can be used as a practical tool to encourage and persuade people to adopt and sustain positive mental and physical health. The two models are Fogg's (1999) [7] functional triad model and Dahl's 7s framework (2015) [2] which together give a set of principles that can guide the design and development of persuasive social media strategy and applications.

Fogg identifies three dimensions of how technology can influence people. The three functional elements are:

1. to provide an experience;
2. to increase an ability; and
3. to create social relationships.

Fogg's model has been used to design persuasion modes in a variety of contexts [8]. This tool is a helpful way for those interested in designing social media interventions to conceptualize what functions they will build into their social media applications and how they will position them as ways of increasing people's abilities, providing engaging experiences, or helping them to build what they perceive as being meaningful relationships or a combination of these valued benefits.

Dahl's 7S framework (2015) is a useful complementary set of features that can be perceived as sitting at the heart of Fogg's triad model. Dahl has identified seven principles that should be considered when building social media and other forms of technology-based persuasive applications and services. These seven principles can be applied across a range of applications. The seven principles are:

1. simplification including ease of use and interaction;
2. sign-posting including links to other resources and support;
3. self-relevance including the ability to customize and control;
4. self-supervision including feedback on progress towards personal goals;
5. support including feedback and encouragement;
6. suggestion including problem-solving solutions; and
7. socialization including support for sharing success, and connecting with and helping others.

These seven principles can be used to guide the development of social media applications and as a checklist to evaluate the robustness of existing applications.

In summary, there are many theoretical perspectives that can help us understand how social media can influence personal and community beliefs, attitudes, and behaviours. The application of the theories already set out and those that appear in other chapters of this book can help identify the best ways to both understand what social media interventions might be needed and how to design them to enhance mental health.

The Range of Social Media Platforms and How They Impact Mental Health

As outlined in Dahl's 7S framework (2015), the seven principles of social media applications have been applied in many well-established global social networking platforms including Facebook, Twitter, Snapchat, and Instagram, but also in newly formed and growing platforms including TikTok, Clubhouse, Parler, etc. Over time, the types of social media have not only diversified, but have increased the ease of access [9]. Outside of the typically considered social networking apps, there are many other platforms where people spend time online engaging in their interests and passions with like-minded communities. These include online gaming, online gambling, e-learning, and online coaching and counselling. These are massive networks all focused on enabling people to do something they enjoy and share their interests with others. These users are not just mindlessly browsing, they are constantly engaged, invested in what they're doing, and often contributing to the community.

The list of positive mental health impacts of these social networks is considerable. For individuals who use social media as part of everyday routine, including responding to content that others share, such use has been positively associated with three health outcomes: social well-being, positive mental health, and self-rated health [10]. Social media can also help individuals overcome barriers of distance and time and allow them to connect and reconnect with others to strengthen their in-person networks and interactions [10]. Additionally, social media may increase social interaction or social connectedness, or act as a mechanism for meeting potential people who share the same interest, thoughts, and feelings and in so doing promote belongingness [11]. For youth, social media may also help to develop their identities and culture perspective [12].

However, a growing body of research has demonstrated that there are also negative impacts associated with social media use including an increased risk of depression and anxiety symptoms and a variety of other serious mental health impacts, many of which are explored in other chapters of this book. The way people are using social media has been found to have a greater impact on mental health and well-being than the frequency and duration of their use. Examples include behaviours such as checking apps excessively out of fear of missing out, or feeling disconnected from friends when not logged into social media [13]. Excessive use of social media has also been found to be correlated with self-esteem, general and physical appearance anxiety, and body dissatisfaction [10].

Cancel culture is also a new and growing complex and multifaceted problem. Such problems are often called wicked problems and require complex responses [14] that have the potential to destroy people's reputations, damage mental health, and create a negative online environment. There is no one definition of cancel culture, but Sarah Hagi, magazine writer and victim of cancel culture, defines it in her *TIME* magazine article as '[t]he idea ... that if you do something that others deem problematic, you automatically lose all your currency. Your voice is silenced. You're done' [15]. Cancel culture has however also been described by some as a form of online activism with both negative and positive effects. For the positive side, cancel culture has worked to emphasize the representation and voice of women during the #MeToo movement against sexual harassment, especially at workplaces. On the other hand, cancel culture has a reputation for being 'activism-for-bad' when it seeks to silence the voice of people that contribute challenging ideas to public debate around disputed issues.

How Practitioners Can Use Social Media to Promote Positive Mental Health

Social media platforms have become a high-priority channel for organizations to disseminate behaviour change communications. Platforms such as Instagram, Twitter, and

YouTube are giving rise to a new phenomenon in which users treat their accounts like chat rooms for mental health, amassing tens of thousands of followers in the process. Influencers and brand owners alike have begun using their feeds to raise mental health awareness and even share their personal struggles.

Over the last few years, extensive growth in the e-counselling sector could be seen and has, despite various other ramifications, led to a need for information and guidelines for customers of such services. Due to these needs, in 1997 the International Society for Mental Health Online was founded, an international organization that aims to research the effectiveness of online mental health services and clarify licensing processes and therapy guidelines [16].

It is increasingly important for organizations to strategically decide on the right platforms suited to their target audience and behaviour change objectives. Similar to offline outreach tactics, it is not necessary to use every single platform. Including a variety of social media channels can increase participant involvement in a campaign, with the proviso that running a campaign well across the most appropriately suited social media channels makes more sense than trying to include networks that will not enable your target audience to take the action that your campaign is seeking. The box below outlines four key components necessary to consider before deciding to create a presence on a social media platform. It should be noted that these are necessary to review for each social media channel that is being considered.

> When developing a social media presence on a platform it is important to consider the following components.
> - **Character/persona** – Who does your brand sound like? If you picture your social brand as a person, who is that character? Are they inspiring, friendly, professional, authoritative?
> - **Tone** – What is the general vibe of your brand? Scientific, clinical, honest, personal?
> - **Language** – What kind of words do you use in your social media conversations? Fun, jargon-filled, insider?
> - **Purpose** – Why are you on this social media channel in the first place? What is your social currency?

For most social media marketers, the burning questions are how best to reach out to social media users and what types of messages and tactics cut through the online clutter and engage the target group? A key way to formulate answers to these questions is reflected in social marketing practice which advocates a shift away from a focus of offering single motivational exchanges to the creation of sustained value [17].

The majority of social media users subscribe to a channel with the intention to follow and connect with family, friends, or like-minded people from which they derive continuous value. With the increasing presence of organizations and brands on social media platforms, users can also make a conscious choice whether or not to follow that brand or organization if they perceive it also provides them with some form of value. In terms of mental health promotion in social media, individuals ultimately decide if they are willing to engage with the campaign and, in order for them to want to do that, it must also provide a similar sustained value to them. Value also comes from participation: successful social media campaigns help users to feel like members of a community and establish identity by allowing participants to express part of themselves to others [18].

> **Case Study Example 1:** The Holistic Psychologist – Using Instagram as a Movement for Mental Health #selfhealing
>
> The Instagram account, @the.holistic.psychologist, was developed by founder Dr Nicole LePera (see Figure 4.1) who is a registered psychologist previously practising out of Philadelphia, PA. A typical Holistic Psychologist post has a few key elements: a colorful graphic with a small illustration or chart, accompanied by a caption, usually a couple of hundred words long, that elaborates on the central topic. Dr LePera's posts ground her advice in her own experience as a mental health practitioner (see, e.g., Figure 4.2); however, her primary directive for her four million+ followers is learning to 'self-heal'.
>
> Dr LePera's teachings and the #selfhealers movement at large present an alternative for people who feel let down by traditional systems of mental health management. This could be due to inaccessibility or another alienating factors such as a lack of concrete results, sheer fatigue, or some combination of these obstacles. She also offers many other online free mental health management tools to use including an e-newsletter, and a YouTube channel where she posts a new video every Saturday.
>
>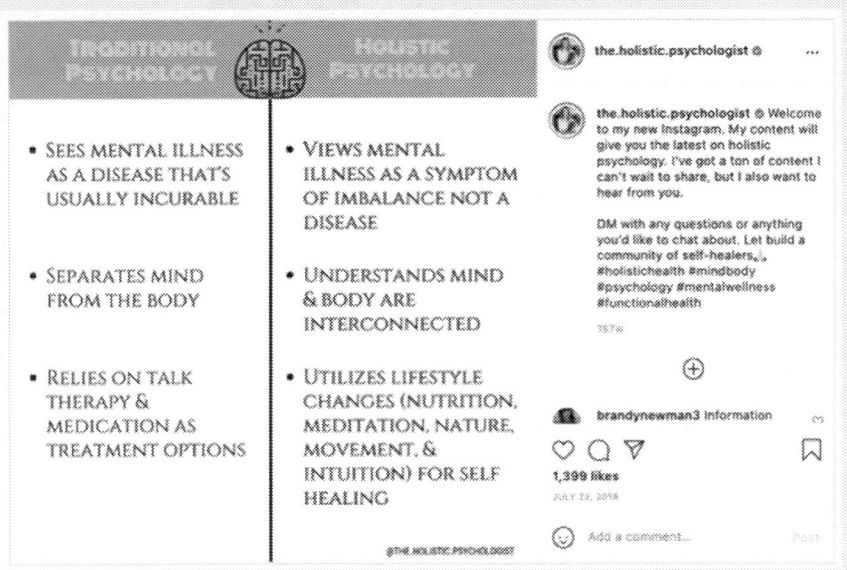
>
> **Figure 4.1** @the.holistic.psychologist's first Instagram post making her intentions on the platform explicit from its inception

Case Study Example 1: (cont.)

Figure 4.2 A post from @the.holistic.psychologist sharing the cycle of trauma responses, which received over 57,000 likes and 934 comments

As we have demonstrated in this chapter, social media is an umbrella term covering a varied field of applications and platforms. The social media ecosystem is also a dynamic field subject to constant change. Various forms of social media also appeal to different kinds of people at direct life stages. Some people use social media as a source of information and opinion formation, others use it as a source of news. Many others still use social media as a way of maintaining or expanding their social networks and building a wider circle of connection and influence. Others focus on using social media to share their life experience and interests. Some people are active content providers sharing personal news, opinions, and other news they feel is interesting and/or important.

Given this variety of usage when considering the use of social media in support of mental health promotion it is important that individual professionals, teams, organizations, and governments consider their objectives and how social media can be utilized to achieve them rather than starting from the default position that social media is important and should be used. Objectives come first; selecting social media as part of an execution mode should come second.

The following two sections set out how professionals and organizations can use social media as a part of their strategy for promoting mental health, and tips that can be given to clients and citizens about how to work with social media to protect and promote mental health.

Some Examples about How to Use Social Media to Promote Mental Health

- Positive preventive mental health awareness raising
    - for example, www.nhs.uk/every-mind-matters/mental-wellbeing-tips/your-mind-plan-quiz/
- Service promotions and help-seeking promotion
    - for example, using service GPS location to help someone find the nearest clinic, support service, or mental health services – Google Maps
- Building communities of interest/support
    - for example, The Truth campaign leveraged TikTok to build interest – www.thetruth.com/activity/tik-tok-challenge-werk-it
- Community building, facilitating ongoing connections with individuals and/or groups
    - for example, AdvocatesForYouth uses TikTok around social advocacy issues: www.tiktok.com/@advocatesforyouth/video/6802276039780355334?lang=en&is_copy_url=1&is_from_webapp=v1
- Providing online consultations, tele medicine, therapy, coaching, and counselling
    - for example, Talkspace: www.talkspace.com/online-therapy/
- Social and professional networking, and professional development
    - for example, Mentorloop: https://mentorloop.com/
- E-learning and team platforms (bite-sized education)
    - for example, Udemy: www.udemy.com
- Tracking population mental health concerns
    - for example, WHO real-time tracking of people's social media concerns: World Health Organization – EARS (Early AI-supported Response with Social Listening; Citibeats.com; Help Guide: Social Media and Mental Health: www.helpguide.org/articles/mental-health/social-media-and-mental-health.htm
- Positive social norms promotion
    - for example, Man Therapy in Australia: https://mantherapy.org/

Case Study Example 2: BetterHelp: The Pros and Cons of Using Online Influencers to Promote Mental Health Services

BetterHelp is an app which describes itself as 'making professional counseling accessible, affordable, and convenient' (see Figure 4.3). It provides customers direct access to behavioural health services online through the form of e-counselling. E-counselling, also known as e-therapy or online therapy, describes platforms that provide mental health services through the various means of online communication such as email, text messaging, video conferencing software, or online chats. BetterHelp was looking to build a strong online brand presence that would help it connect with its customers better. The company decided

Case Study Example 2: (cont.)

(a)

(b)

(c)

(d)

Figure 4.3 (a–d): BetterHelp's static online creative

> **Case Study Example 2:** (cont.)
> to create a series of online campaigns that would contribute to building BetterHelp's brand identity. The challenge was to build an online presence for a multichannel platform in a sensitive industry that communicated the value proposition without any distortion.
>
> A huge part of BetterHelp's advertising strategy has been the use of influencer marketing. Its campaigns expanded over several social media platforms such as YouTube or Instagram, and it used intermediary platforms such as Popular Pays to recruit large amounts of influencers interested in participating in the campaigns. BetterHelp offered brand partnerships to some of the biggest influencers on social media, including YouTubers Shane Dawson and Philip DeFranco. The strategy is to have these influencers post very 'personal videos' about their struggles with mental health and encouraging their followers to seek help. They then promote the BetterHelp services and affiliate links which reportedly earn them money for every subscription contracted by one of their fans. While this has been an extremely successful strategy for the widely advertised online counseling app, some users reported that they felt the app was less reliable than it was promoted as being. It also shed light on the role of influencers who used affiliate links to the BetterHelp app which could be seen as capitalizing on their followers' mental health as they earned a commission for every subscription to the therapy services.

Social Media Engagement and Measurement

Organizations that find the most success in their social media communities are those that can develop highly relevant content. Examples of high-value social media content are those that provide the following:

- tips and tricks (life hacks), for example top 10 ways to reduce anxiety;
- practical and easy applications to everyday life, for example 5-minute breathing exercises;
- myth-busting factual information, for example triggers versus emotions;
- inspiration, for example I can do that;
- aspiration, for example I want to do that/I want to be like that; or
- entertainment and evokes emotion.

Social Media Measurement

Using existing in-built social media tools, analytics and metrics can be easily captured to assess how successfully campaigns have engaged with participants and audiences. Typical social media analytics include the number of 'views', 'shares', 'comments', and 'likes' [19]. However, it takes very little effort to like a campaign on Facebook, and there may be no direct link between the number of likes and the likelihood of behaviour change [19]. Therefore, large numbers of followers or participants may actually mean very little in terms of how important or meaningful a campaign truly is [20].

Deeper engagement would be considered as people sharing content as a form of advocating with the organization with the capacity to influence others. However, for academics and practitioners it is essential to establish if there is a connection between engagement and behaviour change. Measuring actual participation offline as a result of some exposure to a social media campaign should be a measurement objective such as making an appointment for counselling [19]. Suggested methods for this include analysing the content of any online comments and interactions for evidence of behaviour change and conducting surveys and interviews with campaign participants to directly ask about their behaviour [19].

Tips for Clients on How They Can Manage Their Use of Social Media to Promote and Sustain Mental Health

1. Set Limits to When, Where, and How You Use Social Media[1]

Excessive and compulsive use of social media can negatively impact on real face-to-face communication with family and friends. A good way to manage overuse of social media is to set certain times each day when your social media notifications are off or your phone is in airplane mode. Another good tactic to avoid overuse is to decide not to have access to or not to check social media during mealtimes with family and friends and when playing with children or talking with a partner. Not taking a mobile phone into the bedroom or switching it off after a certain time in the evening is also a good tactic. Excessive use of social media at work can add to pressure and interfere with work efficiency and performance. So, again, set limits to social media interaction while at work.

2. Share Your Story

Use social media to let others know about how you are managing your mental health. Share tips that you have found have worked for you and seek advice and support. Also try to focus your online interactions with people you also know offline. Talking about mental health is very important. It helps us to not internalize and recognize when we might need help.

3. Maximize the Benefits of Your Online Time

A few short spurts of focused uses of social media interaction can be less tiring and less stressful than spending a long time scrolling randomly through multiple feeds. Setting limits for interacting with different platforms can also be a good tactic to avoid this random scrolling. It is also a good tactic to try to be as active as possible when using social media. People who actively contribute rather than passively consuming others' posts feel more positive and more in control.

4. Prune and Detox

Try to keep your social media life manageable. Over time, you have likely accumulated many online friends and contacts, as well as people and organizations you follow. Some content is still interesting to you, but a lot of it probably is not. Try to regularly prune your contacts, making your life more manageable. It's a good idea also to schedule regular multiday breaks from social media. Studies have shown that breaks from using Facebook can lead to lower stress and higher life satisfaction. It may be difficult at first to prune and disengage from social media so seek help from family and friends by publicly declaring you are on a break or that you have certain times when you are positively offline.

---

[1] These tips have been informed by: '6 Ways to Protect Your Mental Health from Social Media's Dangers' (theconversation.com).

5. Prioritize Your Real Life

Using social media to keep abreast of your cousin's life is fine, as long as you don't neglect to visit or talk in person. Tweeting with a colleague can be engaging and fun, but make sure those interactions don't become a substitute for talking face to face or via a live video platform. Social media are useful additions to our social lives, but only a flesh-and-blood person sitting across from you can fulfil the basic human need for connection and belonging.

6. Be Supportive and Positive

It is important to remember that your choices and use of social media affect others. Do not spend your time online being cruel to people. Rather, spend time supporting your contacts. It is not your job to judge others online. Criticisms and negativity can significantly impact on others' mental health. Use your social media profile wisely, be supportive and understanding – do not cyberbully.

Conclusion

This chapter has focused on some of the key theoretical and practice issues associated with how social media have an impact on group and individual behaviour. Social media platforms and campaigns have the potential to produce positive mental health benefits and well-being, but also have the potential to increase negative health outcomes.

For practitioners who are looking to implement mental health interventions and are considering using social media as part of their intervention mix, they first need to be very clear about who they are trying to help, what they know about them, and what their objectives are. To do this they will need to either undertake research or draw on previously published research and data before beginning any intervention design or implementation.

Subsequent to: strategic decisions about objectives; target group consideration of the right social media platforms to use; the development of content that can add value to people dealing with mental health issues or seeking to promote their mental health, an intervention can be developed and pilot tested.

Currently there is a lack of high-quality research and evaluation studies focused on the contribution of social media to the promotion and maintenance of mental health. There is then an imperative that practitioners and academics seek to capture the learning from interventions and make the learning and results available to others so that practice can be improved and mistakes avoided. A consideration of how social media fit with other aspects of mental health promotion and support services and interventions is also key as is the application of systematic social marketing planning procedures as they can assist substantially with this process [21].

Researching Social Media: Qualitative and Mixed-Methods Research Approaches

Cathy Brennan, David A. Ellis, and Kim Heyes

To understand the relationship between social media and mental health we need research that examines what people are doing and how this relates to other, measurable, variables such as their personal characteristics and the outcome of their social media use. We also need research that explores how and why people use social media and their experiences of doing so. The chapter on quantitative methods focuses on the former; in this chapter we will look at research that explores how and why people use social media and their experiences of doing so. This type of research is referred to as qualitative research.

Qualitative research is that which seeks to understand rather than measure social phenomena; it uses non-numerical data such as interviews, written text, images, and observations. Qualitative research can offer rich insights into the experience of people on social media; it can explore their motivations for being online, what they do when online, their reaction to content, and their interactions with others in particular online spaces.

In this chapter we will present an overview of qualitative approaches that focuses on methods of data collection and analysis. We will discuss the main approaches to data collection and offer some important pointers to bear in mind when evaluating the results of studies that use these methods. For those interested in a more in-depth exploration of qualitative methods there are some suggestions for further reading at the end of the chapter.

Qualitative Data Collection

To some extent, qualitative approaches can be divided into two types of data collection methods: those that ask people directly about their experiences through either one-to-one interviews or focus group discussion and those that observe what people are doing and make inferences about what has been observed, commonly called ethnography. Research studies can use more than one method of data collection within a project. For example, some studies can make observations about how people interact on social media and also interview participants to gain insights into the meanings they might ascribe to what they are doing.

Because of the personal detail uncovered by observational research there are key ethical issues with it. Social media can seem like a public space in which it is possible to make observations and collect data without the knowledge and consent of those being observed, and yet at the same time the content is personally contributed by individuals who will have their own views about what can be used for research by others. This is especially so when observing communities on social media where the interactions are asynchronous, often publicly accessible, and there is already a possible layer of anonymity afforded by the online space. In contrast to seeking informed consent to interview participants, much virtual ethnography is undertaken without the knowledge and explicit consent of the users who are posting and interacting with content.

Interviews and Focus Group Discussions

Interviews and focus group discussions (FGDs) are the mainstays of qualitative health research and are used to explore with participants their understanding or experience of a particular issue. Individual interviews can be very structured where the same question is asked of each participant but with open format responses. More often though interviews are either semi-structured, using a topic guide that maps out the areas to be explored but allows scope for the interview to pursue directions of interest within that map, or less structured (often called depth or narrative interviews) where participants are set off on an idea by an initial very open question and the interview follows where the narrative goes using probing and clarification questions to get more detail on particular areas of interest as they are raised by the interviewee.

This sort of interviewing has been called 'conversation with a purpose' and like any conversation it can be more or less fruitful. Some obvious ways to judge include how long the interview or discussion lasted and what topics were covered. An interview lasting about an hour and touching on three or four key themes is likely to be more productive than a single-issue interview lasting 15–20 minutes.

Example: Researchers in the UK were interested in suicide-related internet use in two groups of young people [1]. They interviewed 20 young people who had attended the emergency department following an episode of self-harm and who had reported using the Internet for suicide-related purposes during their assessment. They also interviewed 13 young people who were part of a different, population-based, study who had responded positively to questions as part of that study about suicide-related internet use. In-depth interviews explored their self-harm, internet use, and the impact of their internet use. In the results, the authors described different patterns of internet use according to the severity of suicidal feelings. The participants from the cohort study mostly described disorganized browsing without a clear purpose except to make sense of their feelings, they also reported accessing help content and sharing feelings online. The participants from the emergency department sample generally described more focused searches to research methods of self-harm; they rarely reported accessing help content.

This interview study demonstrates the value of talking to people about their experiences to gain insights into how people use social media. Insights can be gained from interviewing a relatively small sample as you are not seeking to make judgements about how likely different experiences are, only what types of experience there are or might be. In evaluating interview or focus group studies, the questions you ask about samples are different from those in quantitative studies. You want the people who have been interviewed to have something to say about the complexity of the research question under consideration – they should be 'information rich'.

A good sample for a qualitative study should therefore be chosen with purpose (a purposive sample). The researcher will identify the type of informants they need to talk to and actively recruit participants who meet this criterion.

In research where the key informants may be difficult to identify, a form of sampling called snowball sampling may be more appropriate: the researcher asks an initial participant to identify other possible participants. Snowball sampling is useful when the research wishes to access the experience of groups who may not be easy to identify and recruit. For example, in a study to develop online resources to support those with eating disorders, researchers used snowball sampling to identify and recruit a sample of men to interview as these are often underrepresented in research on eating disorders [2]. These participants were important to include as they reported a lack of gender-appropriate information and resources for men and suggested that this may lead to delayed help seeking.

Group discussion formats are useful when the aim is to gain insights into shared understandings of a particular issue, to explore different perspectives, or to establish areas of contention or disagreement. The emphasis is on the interaction of the group and therefore they are less useful for exploring individual nuances within a particular topic. Group dynamics are important in FGDs so it is vital that the participants are chosen in a way that will allow full participation by all group members. Real or perceived power imbalances between participants, for example because of age or status differences, may stifle contributions by some participants and lead to distorted discussions. The groups also need to be of a size that allows debate but isn't too unwieldly so that not everyone is able to contribute; groups of between 8 and 12 participants are usually seen as the ideal.

Example: Researchers in the UK were interested in how adolescents viewed social media and their potential impact on their mental health [3]. They held six separate focus group discussions with adolescents aged 11–18 years old, with 54 adolescents taking part in total. They were asked about their understanding of mental health, their use of social media, and the potential of social media to promote mental well-being. The authors reported that the adolescents overwhelmingly held negative views about the impact of social media on mental health. They identified three themes from the focus groups: 1) social media can cause stress, depression, low self-esteem, and suicidal ideation; 2) social media opens people up to bullying and trolling; and 3) social media are addictive.

Interestingly, although the consensus was that social media were bad for your mental health, few of the participants reported negative consequences personally. The authors concluded that the adolescents were identifying perceived risks rather than actual experiences, perhaps down to them buying into the dominant social discourse about the dangers of social media. It could be that a group forum was not conducive to explore more personal narratives in this situation. Whichever interpretation, studies of this nature are useful for exploring perceptions but are not able to answer questions about if and how much social media are detrimental to mental health.

Ethnography

Ethnography has its origins in anthropology and is useful when exploring the social, cultural, and relational aspects of a topic. It usually involves immersion of the researcher into the community being studied and observation of the values and practices of the community through exploring the interactions between group members. When these communities are online it is sometimes referred to as virtual ethnography. Observational data are often supplemented with interview data from key informants within a community. Traditional ethnographic methods use participant observation, where the researcher becomes part of the group under study and participates in community life. Some ethnographic research uses non-participant observation, where the researcher observes the interactions but without full immersion into the community. In virtual ethnography, data can also include the social media content created, shared, or commented on.

Example: UK-based researchers undertook an online ethnography to understand the ways in which self-harm is defined and discussed on social media [4]. They collected data from communities on Instagram, Twitter, and Reddit. These data included images and text-based content about self-harm as well as the conversations that formed around the content posted. All forms of expression were collected, including memes, gifs, and emojis. The ethnographic data were supplemented with interview data from 10 young people who had reported using social media to engage with self-harm content. The results suggested that young people were already engaging in self-harm prior to seeking content about self-harm on social media and that most online interactions were about giving and receiving peer support.

The researchers obtained informed consent from the interviewees but they collected the social media data without the consent or knowledge of those posting. They considered the ethics of this and only collected posts that they defined as public (visible without needing to sign in). To respect the privacy of the social media users, they did not give specific details of any of the content when reporting the results.

Qualitative Data Analysis

Analysis of qualitative data involves exploring the data for potential patterns or themes. Analysis can be inductive, where the analysis starts with the data collected to generate themes, or deductive, where the analyst will have some predetermined categories or framework and then explores the data to see how they fit into this. Whichever approach is taken, there is likely to be a degree of interpretation involved in presenting the results: sometimes a little, sometimes a great deal. It may involve, for example, efforts to understand the language somebody uses when talking about a particular topic, or what to make of apparently contradictory statements from the same person.

For this reason, in qualitative research the issue of subjectivity is important. That is, most qualitative researchers would accept that any interpretation of qualitative data is contingent on the researcher's own context and experience. There is never one definitive interpretation. Good qualitative studies would therefore generally include a reflexive statement that allows the reader to understand the position of those doing the interpretation and how that has shaped the research. An assessment of validity therefore is about how credible you feel the interpretation presented is – does it fit with the data that they have collected?

There are many different theoretical underpinnings that can inform this sort of interpretation in qualitative analysis and it is beyond the remit of this chapter to go into that level of detail. The suggested further reading will give more background to approaches such as grounded theory, discourse analysis, or interpretative phenomenological analysis. For this chapter we will give a brief overview of a common approach to analysing text-based data – thematic analysis – and then look at ways to analyse the content of social media posts.

Thematic Analysis

Most qualitative data analysis will report on themes or patterns that the researcher generates from the data. As such, a thematic analysis is the bedrock of much qualitative research. It is a way to look conceptually across multiple perspectives and participant responses to identify themes that have importance for the research question under investigation. Thematic analysis is a flexible analytic method that allows scope for the research to draw on different theoretical traditions [5]. A good analysis goes beyond simply describing or summarizing the data to give an interpretation of the whole corpus of data. A thematic analysis starts with the researcher becoming familiar with the data and then generating initial codes to categorize segments of the data. These codes are then grouped thematically, defined and refined, before being written up as final themes accompanied by excerpts of text (typically participant quotes) that exemplify the concept which the theme encapsulates. The stages are often iterative with multiple generating, defining, and refining of themes to establish the most applicable interpretation of the data. A good analysis should contain sufficient participant data that a reader can see from where the themes have been generated.

Example: A UK study interviewed 21 young people (aged 16–24 years), recruited via adverts on Facebook, to understand their perception and use of online images of self-harm [6]. A thematic analysis was presented in three sections: 1) the role of the Internet in young people's self-harm, 2) the influence of online imagery on young people's self-harm, and 3) the use of online media platforms for displaying self-harm imagery. The main conclusions from the study were that images rather than textual interactions were the primary cited reason for using the Internet and that viewing online images served an important role for many young people as part of a ritualistic practice of self-harm.

Example: A UK study recruited 25 participants via Facebook, Reddit, and a well-known mental health forum, to understand the supportive benefits of online communities for people with mental ill health [7]. Three key themes were identified: 1) Safety – this theme focused on how some participants felt safer talking about their health online than offline; 2) Support – many of the participants were happy to offer supportive comments to other users, which helped them to feel as though they were useful members of the community; and 3) Network Sociality – feeling accepted within an online community helped to reduce isolation, however, negative experiences increased these feelings. The main conclusions were that online communities are not for everyone, but many people who struggled to communicate about their mental health offline found that they were able to be open and honest online, and received the support they needed at that time.

Content Analysis

There are some types of studies that straddle the divide between qualitative and quantitative studies – they can sit in either camp and where to place them is a subjective decision in relation to the level of quantification that goes into the analysis. Content analysis is one such approach. Content analysis is important to cover in any chapter on research methods in social media because the nature of what people are interacting with is an important component of the social media experience. This is especially true for research on mental health as much discussion is about the role of particular types of content in contributing to poor mental health outcomes. Content analysis is used when you want to describe the content of a phenomena. In its most basic form it is a count of the number of times a certain form of content appears within the data, such as reporting the amount of likes or retweets certain types of content get.

Content analysis can also be a way of classifying the nature of content found online and will often involve some subjective classification of important variables. For example, there is much interest in the type of imagery that is shared on social media and some researchers have used content analysis to classify and quantify the type of images that are associated with self-harm-related hashtags. This can lead to quite divergent results depending on both the sampling choices and how the researchers have chosen to define key variables. A review of research on online self-harm and suicide content found that the amount of graphic imagery of cuts identified in studies ranged from none to 75%. This was largely attributed to the different ways in which the authors had defined graphic; for some this category included any images of scars, for others graphic was defined as images of deep wounds [8]. How a study chooses what content to analyse is also important to consider: one that samples a small selection of content from a hashtag search using only one or two terms is unlikely to give an accurate representation of the type and range of content that someone might encounter when browsing, or actively searching for content of that nature.

Example: A German study used content analysis to describe Instagram posts associated with a suicide-related hashtag [9]. The researchers searched on the hashtag #selbstmord at one time point and downloaded the 250 most recent posts. These had all been posted within one week. Each post was rated for the presence or absence of a number of predefined variables including reference to suicide and the demographics of the poster. They checked the reliability of the ratings by double rating 10% of the posts and comparing the results. They found that there was an explicit reference to suicide in 45% of the posts and 34% depicted at least one specific method. Although the double rating was undertaken by the same researcher, albeit at different time points, they reported poor agreement for some variables, especially the demographics with determining age and sex being reported as particularly problematic.

Given the small number of posts in the sample all coming from a single hashtag search at one time point, it is unlikely that the results can be taken as indicative of the range of content that might be found on Instagram. The lack of reliability in the ratings for certain variables also highlights a particular dilemma for research on content on social media – it is not possible to know with certainty anything about the person who has posted the content.

Visual Analysis

Much qualitative work focuses on the collection and analysis of narrative or textual data and many of the core research methods have been developed with this type of data in mind. There is a more established tradition in the analysis of non-textual qualitative data in art history, visual anthropology, and visual sociology. In recent years, visual methods have become more prominent in psychological and health research, although much of the focus has been on the use of visual prompts, such as photographs taken by participants, to stimulate discussion in interview or focus group situations. The analysis in many of these studies centres on the narrative data collected with the use of visual props rather than on the nature of images themselves.

Given the extent of visual content on social media – videos, photographs, drawings, gifs, memes to name just some – methods to explore and interpret visual data are important if we are to understand how content on social media, and an individual's interaction with it, may affect mental health. Content analysis can go some way to categorizing the type of content to be found across platforms. However, more interpretative methods are needed to explore potential meanings within image-based data and therefore how these may be experienced and interpreted by those interacting with content.

There are some frameworks for analysing visual data that offer a model to structure interpretative analysis. For example, the press photograph story analysis model [10] prompts the researcher to consider questions of denotation (what kind of information is in the image) and connotation (what kind of emotional response comes from the image) and consider these from the point of view of the creator of the image and the viewer. Often images on social media will be accompanied by some further contextual data such as hashtags, labels, and commentary posts. This can support an interpretation of the image from the position of the person posting it and, when there are responses from others in the comments, from the position of people viewing it.

Other frameworks suggest researchers consider the technological (how images have been produced), the compositional (the material qualities of the image), and the social (the range of economic, social, and political relations, institutions, and practices through which an image is produced and viewed) [11]. However, all frameworks acknowledge the importance of recognizing the polysemic nature of the visual – that any image can have multiple meanings. This then raises the question of subjectivity – how much might the interpretation offered by the researcher differ from that intended by the poster of the content or indeed someone else viewing that post?

Example: A study explored the nature of images tagged as self-harm on popular social media sites [12]. A total of 602 images were collected from Twitter, Instagram, and Tumbler and were analysed for literal visual content (using content analysis), and thematic content (using thematic analysis), both guided by a framework for analysing visual content. The content analysis noted that over half the images did not explicitly represent or refer to the act of self-harm. Where there was reference, self-injury was the predominant form of harm and 6% of the images portrayed self-injury that was rated as severe (showing bleeding or a wound that needed medical treatment). The thematic analysis identified four themes: communicating distress, addiction and recovery, the presentation of gender and the female body, and identity and belonging. The authors concluded that much of the imagery was being used to express difficult emotions, but there was also much positive imagery that celebrated recovery and offered support to others. They reflected that social media could be a powerful tool for peer support and communication.

Mixed-Methods Research

Social media are not one thing and the space is complicated. Research that seeks to explore the role of social media in mental health outcomes needs to engage with this complexity.

Mixed methods go beyond traditional divides between qualitative and quantitative research. The commonest sort of mixed-methods research uses each method to inform the other. For example, researchers wanting to conduct a large-scale online survey may choose some or all of the questions to ask by conducting preliminary interviews that are analysed qualitatively. The survey may then answer a question the qualitative study can't, which might be how common certain experiences or attitudes are in the general population. Alternatively, an interview study might seek possible explanations for the pattern of responses that have already been obtained via a quantitative study.

However, single estimates or general surveys of social media use (as in quantitative research) or one-off interviews with social media users (as in qualitative research) tell us comparatively little about *how* someone engages with people or content on a daily basis, which can be difficult to recall. Making distinctions between active use (such as writing a tweet) and passive use (such as browsing a Facebook feed) are instead best captured in the moment [13].

In response, ecological momentary assessment designs can deliver prompts (perhaps via a smartphone) to simultaneously request recent information about social media use and mood. Related probe-based methods can include 'walking' interviews, which involve interviewing participants as they engage with technology. These interviews can capture participants' thoughts and experiences in real time as they move around a particular digital environment [14].

Conclusion

Because of the personal and immediate nature of the findings of qualitative research, they can, for some, appear more convincing than the rather abstract-seeming results of statistical analysis of a quantitative study. We need nonetheless to read qualitative studies with a critical eye: how the participants were selected and with what purpose; whether data were collected in a systematic way; whether the analysis was conducted rigorously so that the results clearly came from the study uninfluenced by the researchers' biases and so on.

In considering the implications we need constantly to be reminded that any insights are, by nature, about subjective experiences and should not be taken as general principles to be applied across all populations and contexts. It is a common mistake to slip into talking about qualitative research findings as if they are in fact quantitative even though it is unlikely that a pattern of qualitative responses can be generalized to an entire population.

Regardless, with these basic principles in mind qualitative research can provide us with important insights into how and why people use social media, and their perceptions of how they make them feel.

Further Reading

Denzin, N.K. and Y.S. Lincoln, Editors, *The SAGE Handbook of Qualitative Research*, 5th ed. 2017, London: SAGE Publications Ltd.

Fielding, N., R.M. Lee, and G. Blank, Editors, *The SAGE Handbook of Online Research Methods*, 2nd ed. 2017, London: SAGE Publications Ltd.

Silverman, D., Editor, *Qualitative Research*, 5th ed. 2020, London: SAGE Publications Ltd.

Chapter 6

Researching Social Media:
Quantitative Approaches

Allan House

Summary

In this chapter I review the main quantitative research designs, indicating their strengths and limitations. Even the best-designed and conducted studies run the risk of being influenced by the ever-present threats of chance, bias, and confounding, terms that are explained and illustrated with examples, and of sampling and measurement error. The informed reader should therefore look beyond the results of a study to ask whether the study's design, sample, and measures are robust enough to allow the findings to be taken as likely to be accurate.

I will discuss three questions it is worth asking of a research study you might read – is the design strong enough to answer the question being posed, who is being studied (often described as the study sample), and how has the information about them been collected (the measures used)? The studies used as examples are chosen only to illustrate the topic of the chapter (study design) and should not be taken as having any significance other than that are typical of certain types of study. Many are about self-harm and suicide, simply because that is a particular interest of the author.

Research Design: The Basic Structure of the Study

In thinking about quantitative research it is useful to consider not just the topic being studied or the reported findings, but the specific method used – what is often called the *research design* [1]. Each design has its own strengths and weaknesses and this section outlines the common quantitative research designs used in social media research and their advantages and limitations. Its aim is to introduce an approach to reading research reports that has been described as *critical appraisal*; that is, thinking in a careful way about the degree to which a given study reduces our uncertainty about the topic under consideration. Reducing uncertainty may seem a rather downbeat way of describing the outputs of research that we'd like to think of as revealing the truth, but it's a more valuable approach in the long term than being led by the over-definite assertions of media reports or the pronouncements of 'experts' with a particular viewpoint to promote. In truth no research finding can be taken as 100% certain, however confidently some people talk about what the evidence shows us.

The main quantitative research designs can be grouped according to their purpose. *Descriptive studies* simply tell us what a particular phenomenon looks like: studies of single cases; case series or clusters; descriptions of the features of a larger group (often called a population, or a sample from a population). *Analytic studies* go further, providing a more nuanced picture by identifying what factors are associated with (linked to) our main phenomenon of interest. *Intervention studies* examine the effect of exposure to a deliberate action, which might typically be a medical treatment but which could also be a newly introduced public policy, a piece of legislation, or a change to an aspect of healthcare provision. We will look at each of these in turn.

Descriptive Studies

Single case reports are one of the most widely used devices in mainstream media. Typically, they are used to add 'human interest' to a story that otherwise seems too impersonal, so it is easy to miss that they are often in their own way a mini-research study. In fact until the modern era the single case study was one of the mainstays of medical research. In quantitative terms the case study can be thought of as measuring something in a sample of one. The approach that takes the case report beyond the anecdotal and into quantitative research involves making multiple standardized measurements over time.

Example: Researchers in Australia wanted to explore in detail the effect of various mental health apps on symptoms of depression or anxiety [2]. In their protocol they suggested taking multiple measures over time, with a baseline period followed by a period of use of the app and then a second period without the app. They illustrated how their results might demonstrate whether the apps led to sustained improvement or not (see Figure 6.1).

The strengths of the *single case design* are that it is (usually) easier to collect detailed information about one person than about many hundreds or thousands and the resulting account has an immediacy and understandability that is appealing – we can recognize and perhaps identify with what is being said. The limitations are that it is rarely possible, for obvious reasons, to know everything that might be relevant about a named individual, and it is difficult to generalize to a wider population because one person can never, in some senses, be typical.

Series of cases attract attention when the cases share unusual features – an example is the congenital abnormalities that led to identification of the importance of infection with the Zika virus during pregnancy. Case series also invite study when they occur in clusters, several cases presenting over a short period of time in the same place. Again to take an example from outside mental health, the possible clustering of cases of leukaemia and lymphoma around a nuclear power station raised the possibility that radiation exposure might be responsible. Study of clusters has had a place in research in mental health. For example, in thinking about what the common feature might be in suicide clusters a recent review [3] suggested that '[t]he internet and social media might have particularly important roles in spreading suicidal behaviour'.

The strength of case series or clusters is that they can reveal previously unidentified risks. An important limitation is that it can be difficult to define what constitutes a cluster – how close to a particular place does a case need to have arisen to be included, or how near in time do events have to be to count? Cases can appear to cluster together because we are looking for patterns when in fact what we are seeing is a chance occurrence – a bit like tossing a coin and getting the same answer six times in a row; these things sometimes just happen.

Example: A case series that attracted a great deal of attention in the UK was identified in Bridgend in South Wales [4], where there appeared to be a cluster of suicides in young

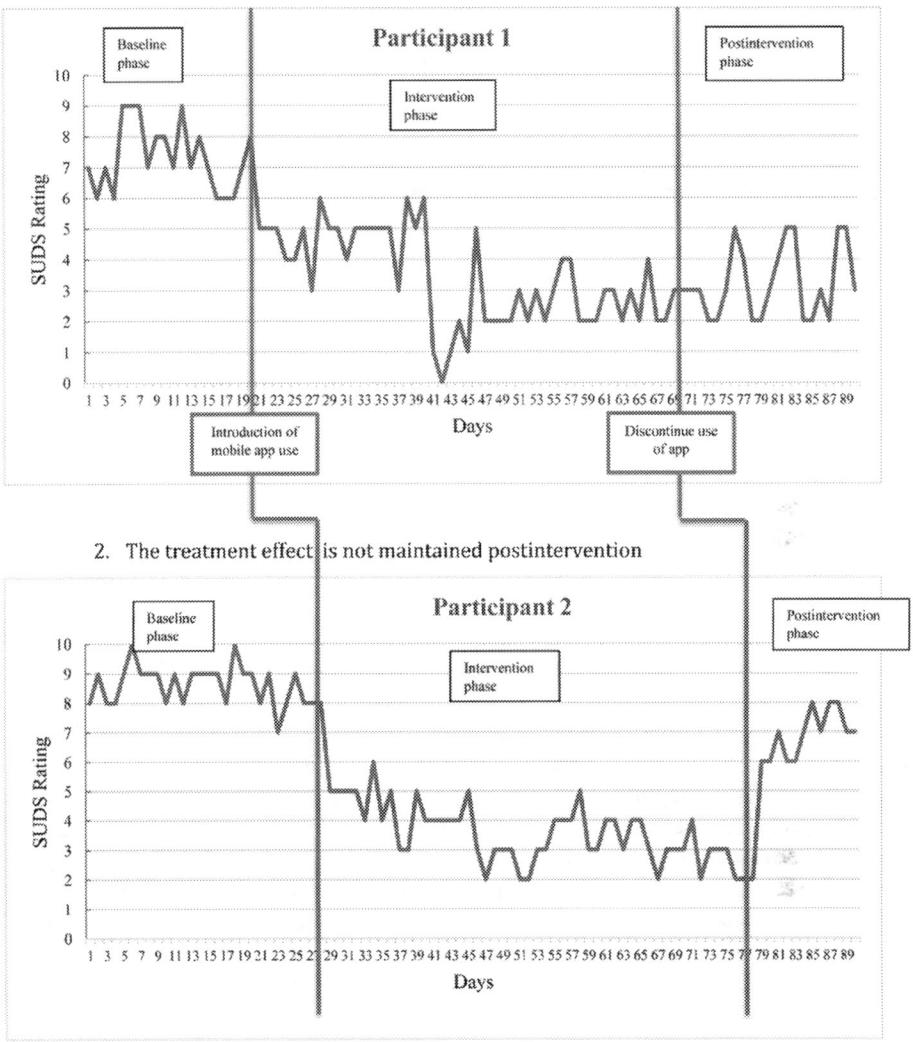

Figure 6.1 An illustration of repeated measures taken from two participants before, during, and after use of a mental health app

people. The media coverage of these events (which was widely criticized as sensational and insensitive) took it for granted that the deaths were related and floated ideas such as the presence of a suicide cult. Research analysis eventually concluded, in much less certain terms: 'There was a *possible* [emphasis added] suicide cluster in young people in Bridgend between December 2007 and February 2008. This cluster was smaller, shorter in duration, and predominantly later than the phenomenon that was reported in national and international print media.' No definite link between the people involved has ever been established.

Larger group studies such as population surveys will typically recruit more substantial samples – in the hundreds or even thousands – to describe features of interest with more precision.

Example: A study of young people in Bristol in the South of England [5] reported how many of them had seen online material about self-harm in the preceding months, and whether that was a result of searching for information, or for sites in which self-harm and suicide were actively discussed by participants. Studies like this have achieved wide coverage because they bring to attention just how common it is for people to access unsettling material online.

One particular type of large group study involves *social network analysis*, that is, how people interact with each other, who knows who, how often they interact and so on. In smaller studies, such networks can be analysed by interviewing the people involved, while larger studies of online social networks are made possible by the use of digital science to track interactions directly on line.

Example: Researchers [6] developed a social network map (see Figure 6.2) by studying the interactions between people participating in an online platform for patients with mental health problems. It suggests that some people are highly connected – in touch with lots of others on the platform and interacting often with them – while others make little or no contact with others. The researchers suggested that the place of individuals in the network is associated with their recovery.

A strength of larger studies is that the bigger numbers make it less likely that a finding is due to chance – if we get the same answer every time for 100 consecutive tosses of a coin we need to look closely at the coin, because such things just don't happen by chance. But what large samples don't do is remove the possibility that the participants are truly typical or representative of the whole population. Like the coin, the sample may be *biased*. Bias in research is a systematic error that distorts (biases) the results. The issue of sample bias is discussed later in this chapter.

Researchers try hard to avoid bias, but it isn't always possible. So what they may do instead is estimate how big an effect any bias might have on their results by undertaking various tests to see how different their sample is from the population they are interested in, or how possible it is that a different result could be obtained. A so-called sensitivity

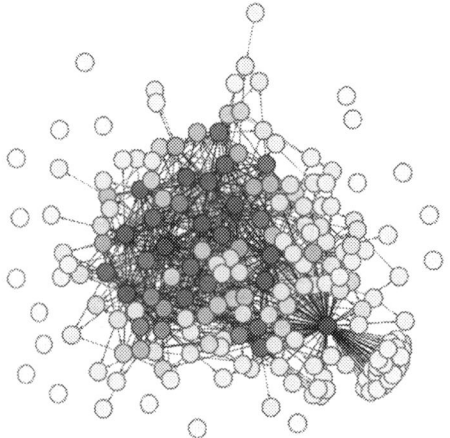

Figure 6.2 A map showing an online social network of 200 people using a platform for people with a mental health problem

analysis might ask, for example, suppose none of the people who didn't respond to our survey had looked at social media sites about self-harm, what would our figure be then? Or suppose all of them had, or 50% had? We then get a range of possible answers based upon more-or-less plausible scenarios.

Analytic Studies

Cross-sectional Between-Group Comparisons

The basic facts that can be obtained from single-group studies can be built upon by making comparisons between two groups. For example, in the study from Bristol already discussed, researchers found that young women were (slightly) more likely to have accessed suicide- or self-harm-related internet sites than young men. When they compared people who had accessed such sites with those who had not, they found some striking results: those who had accessed such sites were substantially more likely to have self-harmed in the past, to have sought help for self-harm, and to describe a personal history of depression.

Such between-group comparisons raise interesting questions, but they have the major limitation that they can't tell us about the explanation of any association – how we are to understand cause. Are people who are depressed and prone to self-harm more likely to access internet sites about self-harm? Or does accessing such sites make people more prone to self-harm and low mood? Answering questions about causes requires a study that can generate a time sequence so that one experience (say, depression or internet use) can be seen as preceding the other; the preceding experience may then be regarded as an *exposure* and the later experience as an *outcome*.

Case-Control Studies

One important design used to get at the time element is the case-control study. Cases are people with a condition in which you are interested, depression say, while controls are people who come from the same population and don't have the condition. The logic is that if the numbers are big enough (to avoid chance findings) and sampling is unbiased, then the only differences between the groups should be those that might explain being a case. Having identified cases and controls, researchers then look backwards (these are called retrospective studies) to find experiences in the past, before the onset of the study condition, that differentiate cases and controls. Probably the most famous case-control study ever conducted showed that people with lung cancer [7] were more likely to have been smokers than people from the same population (in this case chest medicine clinics) who did not have lung cancer.

Example: A Chinese study [8] identified new cases of internet addiction among university students – defined as internet use that was disrupting education and had only emerged at least two months after starting university. Controls were students from the same university who did not meet the criterion for internet addiction. It was possible to identify exposures because all students had a standardized assessment on arrival at university, before the onset of internet addiction. In the 'case' group there were more students who reported symptoms such as depression and anxiety, and early difficulties adapting to campus life and learning, than there were in the 'control' group. Of course, these exposures are likely themselves to have earlier causes – the students were reporting problems so early in their university career that they probably came to university with such difficulties. The likely explanation is a causal chain or pathway – a series of related experiences each leading to the next and finally presenting with the problem being studied.

Most case-control studies suffer from the problem that exposures are identified retrospectively, and that can lead to biases – especially if the exposures are only identified by asking the cases and controls about their earlier life and experiences. In general, we might expect people who are cases (have a condition of interest) to search their past for explanations and therefore to be more likely to recall, accurately or not, something that we have introduced as a possible risk for their condition. The way out of the dilemma is to identify exposures before the onset of a condition of interest. This is how cohort studies work.

Cohort Studies

Cohort studies, when they are used to study the causes of conditions such as physical or mental illness, have the same primary aim as case-control studies – to compare exposures to key risks between people who are cases (however defined) and people who are not. However, rather than start with identified cases and controls and looking backwards for exposures, they work the other way round – starting with a knowledge of exposure in a group of people, they follow that group (cohort) over time to see who becomes a case. The two study designs are illustrated in Figure 6.3.

Cohort studies are therefore unlike surveys or case-control studies in that they involve following up a group of people (the cohort) over time, repeatedly measuring the outcomes in which the researchers are interested. Researchers undertaking cohort studies will want to undertake careful assessment at the first stage, when exposures are being recorded. Of course, this is necessary to ensure that participants are not already

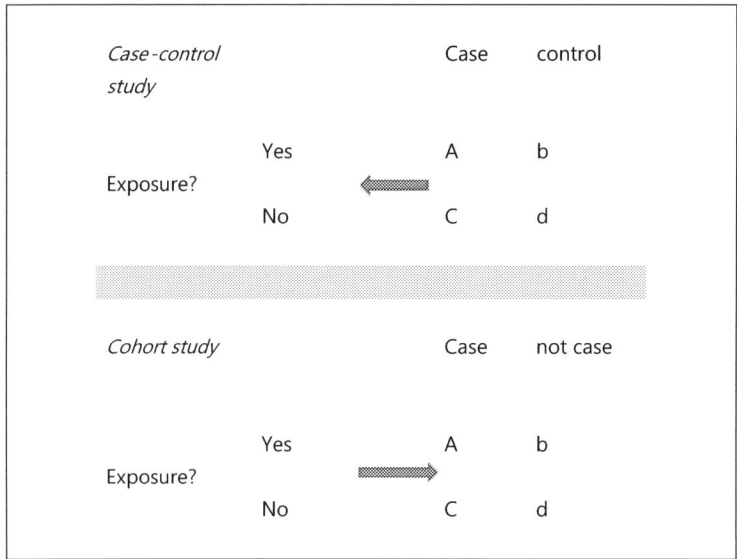

Figure 6.3 Schematic representation of the logic of case-control and cohort study designs

cases but it has another important function. Suppose the study finds that people who spend a lot of time on social media are more likely to self-harm than those who spend less time. We also know that people who are prone to depression and are socially isolated are more likely to self-harm and may be likely to use social media more. Could the association between social media use and self-harm be entirely explained by these other factors, so that social media use is only a marker for depression and social isolation rather than a risk in its own right? Factors that are associated with both an exposure and an outcome (like depression and social isolation in this example) are known as confounders or *confounding factors*. If we measure these two factors at the beginning of follow-up then we can take them into account, known as *adjustment* for potential confounders, so that we may be able to say whether or not social media use is an *independent risk* for self-harm.

Example: A study from North America [9] asked 126 12–15 year olds to complete self-report questionnaires about symptoms of depression and anxiety and about time spent using the Internet. All measures were repeated a year later. The question the researchers were asking was: does self-reported internet use at baseline predict the course of symptoms of depression and anxiety over the next year? They found (perhaps surprisingly to some) that internet use didn't affect depression symptoms but that anxiety symptoms at baseline were more likely to improve in those who spent more time online.

A real strength of cohort studies is that they measure exposures before the onset of the condition of interest, so identification of exposure can't be biased by knowing about outcomes. An important limitation is that it is difficult to adjust for all possible confounders, either because all the candidates aren't known or because there are too many to take into account – how much adjustment can be done depends upon the size of the study in proportion to the number of factors being measured. Cohort studies are also practically difficult; they are expensive and it is difficult to keep track of everybody especially if they are being followed for years, so that dropout (sometimes called attrition) is common – although recent developments that allow follow-up by obtaining outcome from electronic health records may, if feasible, overcome that difficulty.

Intervention Studies

Before-and-After Studies

Intervention studies are designed to assess the effect of intervening in a situation hoping to change it. Typically, they are thought of as testing the effect of a treatment in healthcare but they can be used to evaluate any intervention including changes that occur outside the setting of a formal experimental study. For example, they can assess the effect of a change in public policy. The simplest design is the before-and-after study, in which measurements are taken, an intervention is introduced, and then the measurements are repeated. We might want to know whether introducing restrictions on the showing of images of self-harm and suicide has an effect on self-harm or suicide rates among young people who use social media, and we could compare rates in the year before and the year after introducing the ban.

The trouble with a simple before-and-after design like this is that it doesn't take account of any changes that are happening already. If rates of self-harm are increasing year-on-year, then the effect of a reduction caused by the new policy might be hidden by the background increase so it looks as if there has been no change. On the other hand, if rates are falling then we might attribute to the new policy a change that would have happened anyway.

Interrupted Time Series

A more sophisticated example of before-and-after study is the interrupted time series. A time series is a set of data collected by repeated measurement over time; it can be 'interrupted' by introduction of a new policy.

Example: In 2017 the production company Netflix screened a TV series *13 Reasons Why*, which told the story of a young woman who had been the subject of a number of abusive experiences in her personal life and who eventually took her own life. The series was criticized for presenting suicide as a reasonable response to personal adversity and unhappiness, and for showing the protagonist's suicide in a way that made copying the method a possibility.

For our purposes, the screening can be considered an intervention and an interrupted time series analysis is one possible way of evaluating its effect on suicide rates. Researchers did exactly that in a study that used suicide data from the USA [10]. The results are shown graphically in Figure 6.4. Actual suicides are marked by dots up to the time of broadcast, represented by the shaded vertical bar, and after the bar triangles show what the suicide rate would have been if rates had not changed. Dots after the bar show the actual suicide rate, not the predicted one. The continuous line before the bar shows the suicide rate as a continuous time series, fluctuating because numbers are small; the two dotted lines after the bar show the rate as predicted (lower line) and as actual (upper line). The authors concluded that there had indeed been an increase in suicides after the series was broadcast.

One of the appeals of interrupted time series is that the results can be represented graphically, in readily understandable format. However, their meaning is not always

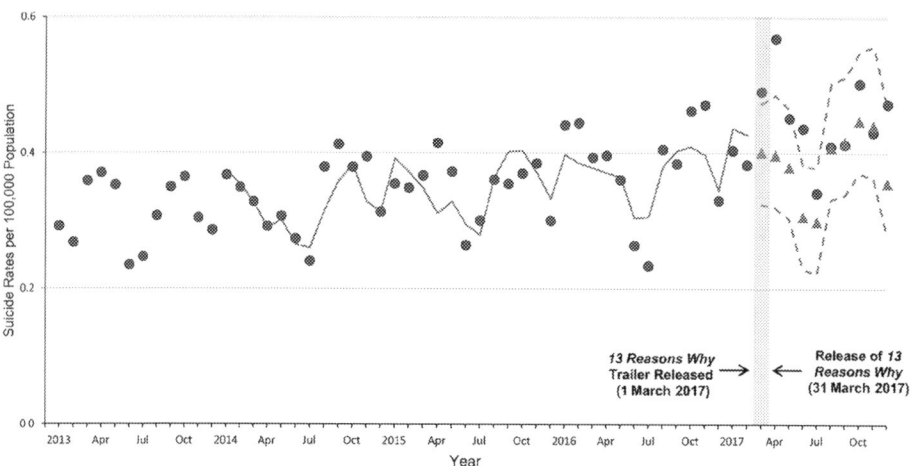

Figure 6.4 Interrupted time series showing suicide rates before and after broadcast of the series *13 Reasons Why* (dots) and predicted suicide rates after broadcast if there had been no change in rates (triangles)

clear. Many 'interruptions' do not occur at a single time point – for example, policy changes are often implemented in stages. A second challenge is posed by the decision about how long to monitor the key outcome in both before and after stages. In this case, suicides were noted for four years in the 'before' stage and less than a year in the 'after' stage. Can we be confident that any extra suicides would not have happened anyway, perhaps brought forward by watching the series, in which case subsequent rates might have fallen in the second and third years? To emphasize, this question isn't posed to imply an answer to this specific research question, but simply to illustrate one of the common problems about interpreting interrupted time series analysis.

Randomized and Non-randomized Controlled Trials

The usually accepted best design for a study evaluating an intervention is the controlled trial, in which individuals or groups are allocated (ideally at random) to receive or not receive the specified intervention. This design has transformed research in medical practice, but it is difficult to apply to questions posed about the effect of social media on mental health.

Example: Researchers in Austria were interested in whether viewing websites about suicide prevention was likely to encourage suicidal thinking or to make people better informed about suicide prevention [11]. They allocated undergraduate students randomly, after obtaining their consent, to look at online educational material about suicide prevention or to look instead at a website with no content about suicide or mental health in general. Afterwards they evaluated the students' knowledge about suicide and their own suicidal thoughts and mood. They found that knowledge improved, while changes in mood or thinking about suicide were transient.

Clearly an experiment like this does not accurately reflect the real world. The participants are not necessarily similar to those about whom we might be most worried; they are looking at a website chosen for them rather than by them, and their responses are likely to be influenced by the research context. This illustrates the problem with trials in this area – and indeed with trials in many areas outside technical medical treatments. The trial design helps avoid the bias and confounding effects found in other study designs, but at the expense of creating an artificial test that may not tell us much about what happens in real life. And yet it is difficult to see how more meaningful trials can be conducted – any trial will need to recruit and consent participants (and likely therefore exclude those who do not wish to share the nature of their own mental health problems); the intervention will have to be managed to ensure that it is delivered in a reasonably replicable way; outcomes will have to be measured in all or nearly all participants at standardized times for anything up to 12 months or more after the trial. These are tall orders and the challenges they pose explain why there are so few trials available.

The Study Sample: Participants in the Project

There are two other useful questions to ask when judging a particular piece of research, and the first is: exactly who is included (usually called the research participants) and how were they identified and recruited into the study? Occasionally it is possible to include in a study every case of relevance – for example, all hospital admissions or all suicides in a country with a national system for collecting such data. Usually, however researchers can't possibly study everybody who might be affected by a particular problem – all young people with mental health problems who use social media, for example – so they identify a subgroup who are likely to be representative of the whole group of interest, usually called a *sample*. The method by which they do that tells us how likely the sample is to be truly representative of the larger group or *population* they are taken to represent.

Convenience samples include those invited to participate, in a haphazard way because they are known to the researchers or readily available through a recruiting technique that involves self-selected participants [12]. Such sampling may lead to a highly atypical sample, but in ways that are not readily identifiable. *Systematic samples* include individuals selected on the basis of some regularly occurring and easily identifiable characteristic, such as first letter of surname, or every patient booked in to see a general medical practitioner. *Quota sampling* is a technique used in political polling or market surveys. It involves filling a predefined number (quota) of places in categories set in advance. *Random samples* can avoid potential biases – but if lots of people decide against participation once selected, we are left again with the problem of bias resulting from key (reluctant) people being missed.

Apart from the question of *how* participants were recruited, there is a question about *where* they were recruited from. We have already encountered examples of studies that included undergraduate students in a university class where the researcher worked, or people who responded to an advertisement. The other possibilities are legion: hospital case registers, people who contact a charitable agency, prisoners, and so on. Much research involves contacting and interviewing substantial numbers of people, which is expensive and time consuming and increasingly, therefore, studies recruit subjects and collect information from them online.

Although this chapter has talked about samples as if they always involve groups of people, it is perfectly possible to sample something else – for example, text or images posted on a social media site; search terms used on a search engine at particular times of day or during particular events such as a pandemic; or sites visited by unidentified individuals. It is possible now to undertake this sort of sampling by using computer-driven searching, which can be followed by automated analysis of the samples obtained. This use of digital science to collect and analyse samples is widely used in, for example, marketing and analysis for commercial purposes but has not been widely used to study mental health and social media use. One exception is the sort of network analysis noted already and another is described later in the chapter (sentiment analysis).

Regardless of the method of sampling or the source from which a sample is recruited, the same question is relevant: are the resulting participants clearly representative of a wider group to which we might want to apply the results, or could they be in some way unusual, so that it is risky to generalize the results?

For example, the Bristol study already noted was based on a large sample of people who have been followed since birth; at the time of the study the researchers sent a questionnaire to those they were still in contact with (about two-thirds of the original group) and just under half of them replied. It doesn't seem at all likely that those who replied were exactly the same as those who didn't, and the differences may be of a sort that biased the findings. The trouble is that we don't know what those differences are. Those for whom the questions held especial significance might be more likely to reply, inflating the result, or they might be less likely to reply (embarrassed or fearing disclosure for some reason) and therefore the result is an underestimate. Either of these influences on who responded is likely to have biased the results.

Example: In a US study [13], lesbian, gay, and bisexual (LGB) individuals were recruited to an online survey and asked questions about their LGB orientation, social media use, and depression. So, a sample that has been filtered three times: first, participants had to have seen details of the survey online which excludes those who didn't visit the sites where it was advertised; second, they had to be willing to answer questions about their sexual orientation; third, they had to provide information on their social media use and complete a depression self-rating questionnaire – meaning they were reasonably literate.

Research Measures: The Source of the Study's Results

Nearly all research involves collecting information from participants directly, using questionnaires or research interviews, or collecting information recorded for other purposes.

Questionnaires are a mainstay of research data collection. They are usually self-completed but can be read out to those who cannot read them for whatever reason. They have a big advantage that everybody is asked the same questions and expected to answer them in the same way – by endorsing a yes/no response or one of a limited number of standardized answers. The result is that analysis of large numbers of responses is easy. The big disadvantage is this very fact of the questions and answers being constrained by the format – it becomes impossible to explore and clarify details, and that can lead to misunderstandings.

Example: Two major research studies [14] asked young people about their experience of self-harm. The Millennium Cohort Study (MCS) asked one question in 2014: 'in the past year have you hurt yourself on purpose in any way?'. The Adults Psychiatric Morbidity Survey (APMS) in 2014 asked several questions: 'have you ever made an attempt to end your life, by taking an overdose of tablets or in any other way?' and 'have you ever deliberately harmed yourself in any way but not with the intention of killing yourself?', and then for each question they asked about method of self-harm if the initial response was affirmative. The MCS reported rates of self-harm in 14 year olds over the previous 12 months that were nearly as high as the APMS reported rates for 16–24 year olds over their lifetime to date. This difference may have been attributable to sampling but could also have been because the less specific question in the MCS in the 2014 survey elicited different answers. The structured questionnaire format makes the explanation uncertain.

Research interviews have the advantage that answers can be explored in more detail and uncertainties resolved, but they may require trained staff to deliver and are expensive when the sample size is substantial. They are often used in *mixed methods research* (see Chapter 5) to provide insights into the meaning of results from a quantitative study.

Natural language processing and related techniques can involve scanning text for words or phrases of interest to researchers. For example, in *sentiment analysis* content can be identified that indicates the emotional tone and content of posts on social media, in an effort to identify people with mood disorders or perhaps suicidal ideas. To date, the sophistication of the computer science involved has outweighed the sophistication of the analysis of mental states that can be undertaken using that technology, and these approaches have had little influence on understanding the association between social media use and mental health.

Sometimes it is possible to obtain the result researchers want by consulting data collected for other purposes. One common means of doing this is to consult clinical records collected as part of a healthcare contact rather than as part of a research study. There are significant ethical challenges to this approach which is becoming commoner as advances in the use of electronic health records make it more feasible.

Example: Researchers in Australia [14] wanted to know whether the implementation of a suicide prevention strategy was effective in reducing rates of suicide after attendance in the emergency department following attempted suicide. Even in this setting suicides are relatively uncommon so to overcome this problem of small numbers, they used further episodes of attempted suicide as a proxy. This information was collected routinely as part of clinical care in all those who reattended the emergency department in the study follow-up period.

Conclusion

No research study is perfect. The examples cited here are not presented in an attempt to criticize any study or its findings, but to illustrate the main types of research undertaken and to explain why, even after years of research on the topic, there remain so many uncertainties about the nature of the relationship between social media use and mental health problems. Critical appraisal involves, among other things, asking questions about the likelihood of chance, bias (systematic error), confounding, or measurement error. It does not require great technical expertise to pose most of these questions, which rest upon the idea that all most research can do is reduce levels of uncertainty rather than provide definitive answers to complex questions.

Further Reading

Bowers, D., et al., *Understanding Clinical Papers*. 4th ed. 2021, Hoboken, NJ: Wiley Blackwell.

Section 2

Social Media and Mental Health

Having set the scene, here we outline what is known about some of the more common mental health problems that have been associated with use of social media.

It is worth emphasizing that the descriptive or diagnostic terms used in the following chapters are ways of describing conditions, not people. In fact it is quite common for a person with any one of these problems to have in addition one or more of the other problems described. For example, mood disorders are common in people with an eating disorder, problem gambling, or a history of repeated self-harm. People with an eating disorder are more likely to self-harm than others of the same age and gender.

'Mental health' is an extremely general term that seems, when used in the news media, to cover everything from severe mental illness (psychosis) to anxiety induced by the COVID-19 pandemic and its social effects, to worry about work. To keep a focus on the most salient questions, we have chosen four important exemplars and asked our authors to discuss what we do and don't know about each. This isn't to imply that no other mental health issue is important, but in our view the benefit of concentrating on a few topics outweighs any disadvantages since many of the issues raised here can be applied equally well to other conditions.

This section of our book starts with a review of some likely mechanisms by which social media might affect mental health. Our contributors then review the four exemplars we have chosen, which are mood disorders, eating and body image disorders, gambling disorders, and self-harm and suicide. We have chosen these examples for three reasons. They are common and apparently becoming more so. They are the problems that social media have most frequently been implicated in causing; they can all be seen as subject to social influences in one way or another and are therefore plausible candidates for an effect of social media. And they are the most researched – not least because their frequency makes it easier for researchers to study their occurrence. Some common themes emerge from these reviews, and we have no reason to doubt that those themes are generally applicable.

Chapter 7

The Harms and Benefits of Social Media

Maša Popovac, Philip A. Fine, and Sally-Ann Hicken

Social media provide a range of opportunities to interact with others and to obtain information and support, which has considerable positive outcomes in terms of well-being. However, there are also a number of risks. While much of the debate has been focused on the negative aspects of social media use, it is important to have a balanced perspective so as to work towards harnessing the benefits and reducing the risks.

This chapter outlines the key issues and debates at present by first outlining three core risks of social media: cyberaggression and cyberbullying; sexting, coercion, and risky online interactions; and misinformation and interaction with harmful online groups. It then goes on to discuss three key benefits of social media: the benefits of information-seeking online; the sense of belongingness, social support, and social capital derived from social media; and the opportunities for identity exploration and self-expression.

Through discussing examples of risks and benefits that are of particular interest to current policy discussions, media, and research, we aim to provide an overview that sets the foundation for further engagement with these issues by researchers and practitioners, particularly via digital literacy and education.

Background

Information and communication technologies provide a multimedia environment that allows for a wealth of opportunities in terms of accessing content and interacting with others with ease. Social media are particularly interactive, with individuals connecting with other users in a variety of ways. The ability to share ideas and experiences, obtain information and emotional support, as well as to engage with others in a way that builds social support can lead to a range of positive outcomes. People can also freely express aspects of themselves online, sometimes more easily than offline, and this can have positive effects on well-being. However, there are also various risks to consider which can be detrimental to individuals, such as accessing harmful or misleading information, engaging in risky online sexual behaviours, or experiencing online aggression.

There are currently many debates around ways in which the benefits of social media can be harnessed as well as many concerns about the psychological effects of risky online experiences. One framework within which to consider these benefits and risks is Rheingold's (2010) social media literacy [1], a more specific form of digital literacy. He proposed a set of five interrelated literacies, described in Table 7.1, which users need to develop in order to engage with social media effectively and safely. Good social media literacy affords the ability to obtain the benefits we discuss through engagement with social media, whereas poor literacy can explain why some users fall prey to the risks outlined in this chapter.

Table 7.1. Rheingold's (2010) social media literacies and their relevance to the risks and benefits of social media engagement

Social media literacy	Description of abilities related to the literacy
Attention	Ability to attend to relevant information whilst ignoring others; relates to multitasking and the ability to ignore distraction, both from other aspects of social media platforms and from the real world
Participation	An appreciation of how to participate appropriately and constructively, for example commenting on posts; adding information to a wiki; relates to 'netiquette'
Collaboration	Social media require interaction between users and are collaborative, for example multiple authors create a Wikipedia entry; much information on social media is in the form of comments by multiple users
Network awareness	Technical knowledge related to platform use, for example an understanding of privacy settings, how to use advanced search boxes, etc.
Critical consumption	Also called 'crap detection'. Truth discernment ability using critical, deliberative thinking, such as asking 'is the source trustworthy?'; 'is the information supported by evidence?'; 'is it true or not?'

This chapter considers both the benefits and downsides to engagement on social media by outlining current trends and research issues. While numerous benefits and risks exist, we prioritize topics that are most widely discussed at present, both in empirical research and in broader debate. The chapter first highlights three core risks: cyberaggression and cyberbullying on social media; sexting, coercion, and risky online interactions; and misinformation and interaction with harmful online groups. It then goes on to discuss three key benefits of social media: the benefits of information-seeking online; the sense of belongingness, social support, and social capital that is derived from social media; and the opportunities for identity exploration and self-expression. Through discussing examples of risks and benefits that are of particular interest to current policy discussions, media, and research, we aim to provide an overview that sets the foundation for further engagement with these issues, ultimately facilitating the way forward in both research and practice.

Risks of Social Media Use

Aggression and Bullying on Social Media
What Are Cyberaggression and Cyberbullying?
Online aggression is widespread, particularly on social media. A recent UK survey reported that 62% of adults and 89% of adolescents had experienced a potentially harmful incident online, such as cyberbullying, threats, and abusive behaviours [2].

Cyberaggression refers to intentional harm delivered by electronic means to a target who perceives such acts as offensive and/or harmful. Cyberbullying is a form of online aggression, though not all acts of cyberaggression can be thought of as cyberbullying. Based upon the framework of traditional bullying, cyberbullying's three key attributes

Table 7.2. The seven types of direct and indirect cyberbullying behaviours described by Willard (2007)

Type of behaviour	Description of behaviour
Flaming	Rude and hostile comments that are made in a public forum
Harassment	Repeatedly sending cruel and offensive messages
Denigration	Demeaning and being disrespectful online by making derogatory remarks in an effort to damage someone's reputation
Impersonation	Similar to denigration but a person pretends to be someone else to post offensive comments
Outing/ trickery	Embarrassing an individual by tricking them into divulging personal information to then make it public
Exclusion	Leaving someone out of an online group
Cyberstalking	Creating fear by repeatedly sending threats of harm and offensive messages

are intentionality, repetition, and a power imbalance between the victim and the perpetrator. The repetitive aspect of cyberbullying is often the key distinguishing factor from potential one-off experiences of cyberaggression.

Cyberbullying refers to a set of online antisocial behaviours, shown according to Willard's taxonomy in Table 7.2 [3]. Whilst not exhaustive, this taxonomy encompasses some of the main forms of aggression that occur online. These can be perpetrated directly against the victim in the form of personal communication, or indirectly via public posts and comments. Features of social media offer a multitude of ways in which direct and indirect forms of aggression occur, particularly in relation to the available audience which can exacerbate the humiliation for the victim.

How Common Is Cyberbullying?

Different terms are used to describe aggressive online behaviours, including cyberaggression, cyberbullying, cyber-teasing, and cyber-harassment, which can make comparing prevalence rates across studies problematic. Indeed, it is difficult to gauge prevalence rates of cyberbullying with any degree of accuracy, often due to differences in definitions and operationalization of constructs. A review of literature between 2004 and 2016 reported prevalences for cyberbully victimization between 2% and 91%, perpetration rates between 1% and 54%, and witnessing between 36% and 69% [4]. Research also focuses disproportionately on adolescent populations, with fewer examining cyberbullying among adults or younger children. These issues over terminology and the population sampled, together with a lack of standardized measures, have hindered researchers' ability to estimate the actual extent of the problem. Despite this, the evidence suggests that cyberbullying is a serious global health concern across the lifespan.

The Roles and Risk Factors of Cyberbullying

Research has investigated the various cyberbullying roles and their dynamic complexities. The roles of perpetrator, victim, and witness mirror traditional bullying roles. However, instead of focusing on the perpetrator and victim in isolation, more attention is now being paid to the cyberbully/victim, defined as someone who is both the perpetrator and target of cyberbullying. In fact, some research reports that the cyberbully/victim is more common than the victim who does not themselves cyberbully [5]. One explanation is that cyberbully/victims are initially victims who then act aggressively online in retaliation or in search of revenge. Males appear more likely to be cyberbully/victims, as do minority group members, perhaps as a result of personal experiences of victimization offline as well as online. This is also the case for female victims of traditional bullying, who then find the online environment an easier medium for retaliation.

Broader research around risk factors of cyberbullying often highlights a combination of individual differences and contextual factors. As mentioned, minority group membership can lead to higher susceptibility of victimization in particular, but some inconclusive results have been indicated in relation to specific individual characteristics (such as race) and further research is warranted. A relatively new construct that has emerged is digital self-harm, also referred to as self-cyberbullying and self-trolling. It is broadly defined as posting or sharing negative content about oneself, such as derogatory photographs or self-deprecating comments. Motivations for self-directed abuse among adolescents may include it being a cry for help, wanting to be cool, or wanting to prompt compliments. Males tended to engage in digital self-harm as a joke whereas females reported they did so for sympathy [6]. This highlights the complexities and nuances of roles and experiences within an online context.

The Effects of Cyberbullying

A complex relationship exists between social media use and the effects of cyberbullying, which encompass psychological and emotional issues (internalizing) and behavioural and social issues (externalizing). More specifically, internalizing effects, such as depression and anxiety, and externalizing effects, including self-harm and suicidal ideation, have all been strongly associated with cyberbullying. These effects are similar for both victim and perpetrator and can have long-term impacts on quality of life.

Due to the place of social media in daily life, many individuals are unwilling to stop engaging with technological platforms despite experiencing cyberbullying. As social media are here to stay, it is imperative to educate across the lifespan about social media literacies and how to avoid and manage aggression online to reduce its potentially serious negative outcomes. Further research is needed, particularly with younger children and older adults, as less is known about their risk factors for cyberbullying and the impacts and effects such experiences may have.

Sexting, Coercion, and Risky Interactions on Social Media
Sexting

Even non-aggressive interactions with other users can still be risky, one important example being sexting. Sexting, the act of sending or receiving sexually themed and explicit images, videos, or comments via online communication, is widespread. A recent meta-analysis of 50 studies across 11 countries showed that 38% of emerging adults (aged 18–29) were sending sexts, 42% were receiving sexts, and 48% were engaging in reciprocal sexting [7]. Moreover, 15% of European 11–16 year olds had sent or received sexual messages online [8], highlighting that this behaviour also occurs among children.

Sexting is often a voluntary act that can be viewed as a normal modern form of interpersonal exchange within prospective or current romantic relationships. It may reflect natural curiosity and sexual identity exploration during adolescence but can also be motivated to gain approval from peers, thereby reflecting the role of subjective norms at particular developmental stages. However, sexting can also be coercive, which presents a serious concern in terms of online sexual solicitation.

Sexual Solicitation, Cybergrooming, and Coercion

Although social media present opportunities to expand one's social circle and can lead to deep and trusting connections with others, they also allow individuals to establish unique and private selves. Anonymity and invisibility afforded in online spaces create disinhibition and this allows people to establish false selves and use this to exploit the trust of others, including children. This can lead to general requests for personal information, images, or videos, but over time can also lead to sexting. Sexual solicitation occurs when an individual (adult or minor) attempts to interact sexually with a minor. This includes various forms of sexualized online contact such as sexting between minors and sexual solicitation of minors by adults, known as cybergrooming. Unlike a potentially isolated occurrence of sexual solicitation, cybergrooming involves the development of a trusting relationship with a minor to coerce them into sending sexual content; thus perpetrators often engage in online spaces popular among young people to initiate contact, including social networking sites.

A meta-analysis in 2018 showed that one in nine youths had experienced online sexual solicitation [9]. Some forms of sexual solicitation, particularly cybergrooming, involve manipulative techniques including threats, persuasion, deception, and bribes; this can lead to blackmail, extortion, and further cycles of abuse. Sexting material can also be distributed to a wider audience as is the case with 'revenge porn' (non-consensual sharing of sexualized content) and is used to cyberbully. Indeed, research has demonstrated the reciprocal and longitudinal relationships between sexting, online sexual solicitation, and cyberbullying at two time points [10], highlighting the interconnectedness of these online risks. In relation to revenge porn specifically, a meta-analysis shows that 15% of emerging adults experienced non-consensual sharing of sexting material, which can lead to serious psychological distress [7]. Non-consensual sharing of sexting material is often referred to as image-based sexual abuse that falls on a continuum of broader sexual violence, thus reflecting its severity.

Risk Factors for Sexting and Related Behaviours

Risk factors in relation to these behaviours have also been examined [11]. In addition to females potentially feeling more pressure to engage in sexting, contextual factors such as not being in a nuclear family, being a foreign national, or having homosexual or bisexual orientation were associated with higher risk of online sexual solicitation among adolescent females. Age is also a crucial variable, with older adolescents experiencing higher online risks in general, including higher engagement in sexting. Moreover, individual differences such as lower self-esteem and higher sensation-seeking were linked to both sending of sexts as well as non-consensual forwarding of sexts. Individuals lower in social media literacy may also be at greater risk of becoming a victim of cybergrooming or revenge porn due to a higher level of naïve trust and a poorer understanding both of network awareness and of the ease with which people can take on fake identities or share private material.

Societal-level factors are also relevant to online sexual solicitation of minors, including socio-economic status, availability of technological infrastructure, and cultural differences. Thus, a holistic approach to addressing these behaviours across multiple levels is needed (individual, home, family, and societal levels). A number of proactive approaches have been taken in some countries to address this among young people in school settings, including via improving the school social climate and empathy training. While such early intervention and prevention approaches are crucial, few strategies are aimed at adults. Nevertheless, adults also face psychological distress following such experiences, and further work is needed in this regard.

Misinformation and Harmful Groups on Social Media
Fake News on Social Media and Its Impact

In addition to cyberbullying, sexual solicitation, and other negative behaviours perpetrated online, another key risk on social media is misinformation and the extent to which it is perpetuated. The recent growth of fake news and distorted information online has become a major societal issue, coinciding with the increased prevalence of social media and the ease of communicating information. The term misinformation refers to false, inaccurate, or misleading information. For instance, wikis are crowd-sourced and not peer-reviewed, so the veracity of their information is often uncertain. Disinformation refers to false information deliberately fabricated in order to mislead. As information can spread easily on social media, it is often impossible to know whether the individual who originally created the information had deliberate intentions to mislead.

Fake news is a specific type of mis/disinformation, fabricated to mislead but designed to resemble legitimate news. Although the fake news author intends to deceive, the item may be shared many times by those who do believe it and thus perpetuated widely. Fake news is often politically motivated and could be considered as hyper-partisan 'spin': not entirely false but reporting events in a biased way. Recent prominent examples of fake news concern the 2016 and 2020 US Presidential elections, the UK Brexit Referendum, and facts about the COVID-19 pandemic [12]. This spread of COVID-19-related misinformation has been termed an 'infodemic' and highlights the importance of evidence-based information.

How Does Misinformation Spread?

Misinformation is rarely a problem unless it is shared with others, a behaviour central to many social media platforms. People share content for various reasons, including altruism, the pleasure of sharing information, and for entertainment purposes. Before sharing information, individuals usually decide whether or not it is true. Those with poor truth discernment have difficulty distinguishing between true and false news and may be more likely to share misinformation without being aware they are doing so. Somewhat surprisingly, people may still share misinformation even if they realize that a story is wholly or partly false. One reason is that aspects of social media (such as ads, pop-ups) distract them and so they still share the story without thinking, even though they recognize it as false. A study of COVID-19 misinformation sharing in Nigeria found that altruism was the strongest predictor of sharing, trumping the need to check the facts first [13]. Secondly, much fake news is political and partisan, and intentionally perpetuating disinformation through sharing is a way of proclaiming one's political leanings and group membership.

Why Do People Have Poor Truth Discernment?

Various individual differences affect how likely people are to spot fake news, including perceived credibility judgements, as well as their belief in conspiracy theories. One of the most important is people's predisposition to critical thinking. Dual-system models suggest that, broadly speaking, we have two ways of thinking: a fast, intuitive, gut reaction type of thought (system 1) and a slower, more careful, deliberative mode of thought (system 2). Critical thinking involves system 2, and those who tend to favour system 1 are more likely to accept what they read as fact without questioning it. A bias towards system 1 thinking is also indicative of poor critical consumption literacy – people believe what they are told without thinking about it.

When people make judgements and decisions, they tend to use mental shortcuts called heuristics. These make use of system 1 thinking, and though they generally save time and often lead to the correct judgement or optimum decision, on some occasions they lead to incorrect judgements. For instance, confirmation bias describes people's preference to seek out information that already fits in with their beliefs, even if false. Thus, online groups can function as echo chambers for one's own views. Myside bias is similar, but this describes a preference to evaluate information so as to fit with one's world view, rather than seeking confirmatory evidence. These heuristics tend to worsen people's truth discernment.

A further cue to the veracity of news is the perceived reliability of the source. Peer-reviewed publications, websites, newspapers, and blogs differ in their reliability and trustworthiness, both according to independent fact checkers and layperson ratings. Similarly, expert scientists, politicians, pundits, and personal friends vary in terms of how reliable their knowledge is. Greater credence should be given to news from informed experts and reputable publications. However, when information is shared on social media, it is often impossible to determine the original source and therefore know whether the item is likely to be reliable or not. A related issue is the misrepresentation of science in mainstream media (including social networking sites), whether through lack of understanding by a journalist or through twisting facts to better catch attention and increase website clicks.

Social Media as a Source of Harmful Information

Social media have a powerful influence on people's behaviour, particularly in the hands of those wishing to spread harmful misinformation. Though findings are mixed, social media can negatively affect both mental and physical health, particularly among young people. For example, vaguebooking, which refers to posting alarming but unclear posts to solicit attention, has been shown to act as a warning sign for suicidal ideation [14], while greater social media use during COVID-19 was associated with higher anxiety [15]. Social media also provide a forum for the discussion and promotion of risky health behaviours, such as eating disorders and self-harm. In some cases, discussion can allow these behaviours to become normalized, as well as potentially providing support. Social media have also enabled the spread of myths relating to COVID-19, some of which can have harmful consequences, such as those against vaccination.

As well as promoting risky behaviours and having negative effects on mental and physical health, information on social media can have negative societal effects, such as promoting hate, radicalization, and mobilizing groups for offline violence. Terrorist organizations use social media to raise funds, spread propaganda, and to radicalize, and misinformation on social media leads to an increase in domestic terrorism, mediated by increasing political polarization [16]. Social media can also be used to coordinate and mobilize people for protests and demonstrations, thus highlighting the powerful effects of these platforms on society more broadly.

Summary

These sections have outlined several core risks associated with social media which impact the daily lives of many people: cyberaggression and cyberbullying on social media; sexting, coercion, and risky online interactions; and misinformation and interaction with harmful online groups. As already noted, there are individual differences in people's susceptibility to these risks, including one's level of social media literacy. Towards the end of the chapter we note how some of these risks can be managed and addressed, such as increasing users' digital literacy through education. Before that, however, it is important to remember that engaging with social media also has benefits, some of which are discussed in the following sections.

Benefits of Social Media Use

Access to a Wealth of Information on Social Media

Information-Seeking Online

Despite the risks associated with the spread of misinformation, social media can be an excellent and convenient source of knowledge. People seek out information on social media for a variety of reasons. For example, a large-scale survey of Wikipedia users [17] documented motivations relating to work and educational assignments, in response to media coverage and current events, and for reasons of personal curiosity and boredom, demonstrating different behavioural patterns associated with each motivation. Related particularly to curiosity and boredom, information-finding is often incidental, for instance through following links or idle browsing. Indeed, social media is often designed so as to maximize incidental exposure to news.

Social media are an immense store of information on virtually all topics, and so their utility has broad reach. Students use social media to support their learning. Health information consumers search for information on diagnosing and treating disease, as well as lifestyle and well-being. Before making purchases, users often search both for information on the item or service in question and for reviews by previous buyers, on items from hotels and restaurants to electrical goods and books. Indeed, social media have become an extremely important platform for marketing; this has unfortunately led to an organized market for fake reviews. This is a clear case of disinformation for nefarious purposes, and even with a well-developed digital literacy for critical consumption, it is still very hard for social media users to spot fake reviews.

There are various factors affecting information-seeking on social media. These include, among others, the social media platform, the topic being explored, the credibility of the source, and individual differences in the information consumer, such as social media literacies, already discussed.

Health Information-Seeking Online

Social media are increasingly used to seek health-related information. Since 2010, studies across more than a dozen countries have established that over 60% of internet users sought health information online [18]. Health information is available on a range of social media platforms, including social networking sites, online Q&A forums, health blogs, and wikis. Users search for information about the symptoms and prognosis of illness and disease, often as part of self-diagnosis, both before and after speaking to medical practitioners. Individuals also explore possible treatments and their potential side effects, particularly surveying the experiences of others. In this way, health information-seeking can lead to key health-related decisions and social connections.

An important benefit of social media for health matters is the existence of online support groups and forums, for instance for cancer sufferers and those in chronic pain. This benefit relates both to fostering a sense of group belongingness and counteracting isolation as well as sourcing relevant information from others with similar experiences. For example, because routine oncological care was negatively affected during the COVID-19 pandemic, social media could be particularly important for cancer sufferers during lockdown in terms of providing both emotional and informational support. Indeed, social media were widely used for seeking and sharing information on the COVID-19 pandemic, not just on the practical and psychological effects of lockdown, but health-related aspects such as symptoms, contagiousness, variants, and vaccination. Online support groups and forums are available across geographical boundaries and at any time of day or night where support may be needed, unlike offline support contexts. This, together with aspects of the online environment such as invisibility and anonymity, can lead more individuals to engage with support seeking. For example, individuals with mental health issues may not seek help offline from professionals, friends, or family due to fear of stigma. Therefore, social media can be an important platform for individuals to share their experiences, to seek support from others, and to search for information about treatment.

Social Media in Education

Social media have become an important tool in education for schools and universities, as well as lifelong continuing professional development. This was strongly demonstrated during the COVID-19 global lockdowns when much formal education was shifted online. Social media are an excellent source of pedagogical material including YouTube videos and TED talks, blogs, lectures and presentation slides, and interactive educational resources.

Social media also provide a source of educational support through the use of online study groups, interactive online tutoring, and massive open online courses (MOOCs), facilitating formative assessment through these and other peer learning networks. As well as for teaching and formative assessment, social media can also be used for summative assessment through online quizzes and virtual learning management systems such as Blackboard and Moodle. All five of Rheingold's [1] digital literacies are relevant to educational engagement on social media, and indeed aspects of these literacies are now becoming more embedded into general education. Importantly, the interactive aspects of social media allow users to connect with one another which can promote learning and build a sense of community.

Belonging, Social Capital, and Social Support on Social Media
Social Capital and Social Media

Interpersonal communication presents opportunities to fulfil basic human needs, such as the need for belonging, social support, and the ability to enhance social capital. Social capital refers broadly to the connections formed with others that provide us with social resources. This includes bridging social capital (connections with distant others or 'weak ties') and bonding social capital (connections with close ties). Although much research has been conducted around offline interactions, online environments provide a space where both forms of social capital can be cultivated simultaneously. Social capital follows similar patterns online and offline, and a meta-analysis indicated that use of social networking sites was strongly associated with enhancement of both bridging and bonding social capital [19].

Social networking sites allow individuals to present themselves to others via online profiles and to accumulate friends or followers. This leads to interactions on each other's posts in the form of likes and other reactions, comments, or shares, which in turn can foster positive feedback and affirmation between users and promote further interaction and connectedness. Moreover, social media users can join online groups to share common interests, thus leading to the development of further connections across geographical boundaries. Although there are clearly opportunities to meet new people online which can lead to deep emotional connections, social networking site use largely fosters social capital via interactions with known offline contacts [19]; thus, social networking sites also enhance opportunities to strengthen existing ties.

Online Social Capital and Well-Being

Social capital has been empirically linked to a range of positive outcomes including physical and mental health, and internet use in general has positive effects on well-being; these have been attributed to an increase in online interactions. Positive online interactions can reduce loneliness and depression as well as increase one's perceived social support and self-esteem. Moreover, those who are more socially anxious may benefit from online environments and may self-disclose more in this context. This is potentially due to social networking sites lowering the barriers to obtaining social capital that may exist for individuals offline, where higher social anxiety and lower self-esteem may influence the extent to which individuals can connect with others face to face. Aspects of the online environment such as invisibility and not having to communicate in real time may make it feel more comfortable for some users. This maps onto the social compensation and social enhancement hypotheses, where online environments can be used either to compensate for a lack of social interaction or connection offline or to enhance an already-rich network of offline contacts. Thus, social media clearly provide additional opportunities for engagement with others which can positively affect well-being.

Individual Differences in Obtaining Social Capital Online

While obtaining social capital via social media may be a valuable tool in general, this can be influenced by various demographic and cultural factors. For example, a meta-analysis shows that the association between social networking site use and both forms of social capital were stronger for men, and that bridging social capital was stronger in individualistic countries [19]. This reflects potential differences in online activities or platforms used as well as differences in motivations for social networking site use in different groups. Further examining individual and social differences can help researchers unpick some of these nuances and develop a deeper understanding of the opportunities and limitations in relation to social capital across different populations.

Another aspect of these differences relates to social identity. Individuals derive belongingness and social capital from membership in a diverse range of groups based on identity characteristics such as age, political views, gender identity, race, or sexual orientation. Online spaces present opportunities to engage with similar others across geographical boundaries in a way that bolsters pride in one's social identity. Engagement on social media has been shown to be a source of support for refugees, ethnic minorities, and migrant communities [20] by facilitating their integration into a new society whilst enabling them to remain in contact with family members in their home country. Interactions on social media can also promote solidarity to particular causes and lead to civic action, although, as already noted, in the wrong hands such mobilization can be detrimental to society.

It is clear from these examples that social media have the potential not only to bolster social capital leading to positive outcomes, but also to influence social identity processes as well as social integration and cohesion more broadly. Harnessing this benefit of social media can, therefore, promote positive well-being of individuals and groups within society.

Identity Exploration and Self-Disclosure on Social Media
Online Self-Disclosure

Building on the idea of social identity, social media can be a safe place in which to explore 'possible selves' and reveal aspects of oneself which may not be easily expressed to others face to face. The sharing of personal information with others, such as feelings, thoughts, and beliefs, is referred to as self-disclosure. This can occur both publicly (such as status updates) or privately (in direct messaging), and the reasons for self-disclosure and information shared will differ across these two contexts.

Individuals will also be motivated to self-disclose for various reasons and to achieve different goals. Relational goals of self-disclosure include forming, managing, and maintaining relationships, building social capital, and demonstrating group affiliation and reciprocity within communities. Informational goals include sharing information to benefit others such as in the context of health communities. Both relational and informational goals have been discussed in previous sections. However, another motivation for self-disclosure is self-expression and self-presentation, which relates to identity development, attention seeking, and the need for social validation.

In comparison to self-disclosure offline, many people feel relatively at ease disclosing personal information via social media. For some individuals the pressure to be an active, interactive, and interesting sharer can be daunting. However, as already noted, online environments such as social networking sites can foster disinhibition. More specifically, social media can allow for more control over the timing and pace of interactions, a reduced emphasis on physical appearance, and easier management of social cues, affording users greater control over their content and the way in which they present themselves to others. This may enable individuals to feel more confident communicating online than offline, and thus to self-disclose more willingly. This in turn can lead to an authentic self being portrayed more easily and readily online, at least by some.

Online Authenticity and Well-Being

According to self-discrepancy theory [21], individuals possess three self-domains consisting of the 'actual self' (the abilities and attributes that we possess that form part of our self-concept), the 'ideal self' (the abilities and attributes we would like to possess, such as our hopes and aspirations), and the 'ought self' (the abilities and attributes that we or others feel we should possess that form part of our social roles and responsibilities). Congruence between one's actual self and the ideal or ought self demonstrates alignment and harmony of the self-domains, while discrepancies between one's actual and ideal self can lead to negative effects such as unhappiness, dissatisfaction, and self-dislike, and discrepancies between one's actual and ought self can lead to anxiety, personal inadequacy, and alienation due to pressure to fulfil social duties or expectations. Self-discrepancy theory is relevant to online authenticity as social media allow an individual to self-present in a way that may either be congruent with their actual self or may be more closely linked to their ideal or ought self.

Research has shown that self-disclosure on social media has a bidirectional relationship with subjective well-being and that being psychologically authentic online and feeling supported have positive impacts on subjective well-being; conversely, inauthentic self-presentation is associated with low self-esteem and elevated social anxiety [22]. Individuals with low self-esteem may attempt to self-present using inauthentic material to gain approval, and this can lower well-being and lead to depression. Moreover, presenting a 'false self' on social media may exacerbate any negative feelings of isolation and depression in individuals already distressed, meaning they are unlikely to benefit from self-disclosure in a public forum. Clearly, a greater gap between the authentic actual self and the ideal or ought self in online self-presentation can lead to negative effects.

Identity Exploration and Empowerment

The process of self-disclosure and self-presentation online, whether authentic or inauthentic, leads to audience feedback and interactions with other users. These interactions can help to form identity through self-discovery as individuals can explore parts of the self to gauge audience responses, sometimes expressing an actual self and at other times presenting more their ideal or ought self. During adolescence, identity formation is a key task which now also occurs via social media; a sense of self emerges by reflecting on feedback towards one's self-presentation that is received from online contacts. Social media play a significant role in enhancing connectedness. Thus, in order to derive positive feedback and to connect with others, certain levels of self-disclosure and self-presentation are required, and these will also be governed by different social norms. For example, research has noted a potential 'positivity bias' on social networking sites where there is an expectation that positive content will elicit greater audience feedback and support [23]. For individuals who have lower life satisfaction or poorer well-being in general, such norms may provide less opportunity for authentic (negative) self-presentation. This may well differ across social media platforms, particularly those where individuals can be more anonymous without links to offline contacts. For some individuals, such spaces may elicit greater opportunity for authentic self-disclosure with fewer consequences than in an offline context. Therefore, it is important to examine how different social media platforms and their associated norms alter self-presentation strategies as well as what impacts this has on individuals and groups.

Support provided via social media is particularly important to vulnerable groups and plays a key role as part of identity exploration. Indeed, social media can build a sense of community and open up opportunities for identity exploration among lesbian, gay, and bisexual individuals, impacting on the decision to 'come out', often difficult due to the tension created by concerns about being stigmatized by others and a desire to express one's authentic self [24]. Since psychological health and well-being can be negatively impacted by concealment of LGBTQ+ identity, such processes of identity exploration and the sense of group membership derived from online interactions can reduce stigma and enhance mental health. Online environments can feel safer and more non-judgemental, allowing individuals to more comfortably present an authentic self without the constraints or risks that may be faced offline.

This also applies to individuals with physical disabilities who, due to a pervasive narrative of difference, face isolation in face-to-face contexts. On social media, individuals with disabilities can control self-disclosure about their disability which opens up opportunities for social connection [25]. Social media use also has positive effects in terms of development of a social identity, self-esteem, and enjoyment for individuals with intellectual disabilities [26]. Clearly, social media provide an environment in which individuals can be free to explore and experiment without fear of reprisal. They provide a way to connect with others, and to forge and maintain relationships which are such an important source of support, ultimately leading to enhanced well-being. In this way, social media can be empowering.

Conclusion
The Importance of Digital Literacy

It is clear that engagement on social media can lead to negative experiences in the form of cyberaggression and cyberbullying, as well as potential risks associated with sexting and sexual solicitation. These experiences can have significant and far-reaching effects on mental health and well-being. Moreover, social media provide a space in which misinformation can spread readily, influencing attitudes, beliefs, and behaviours of both individuals and groups. However, social media also have important benefits. They provide a wealth of information, such as in relation to health or education, resulting in users having access to both support and resources. There is also ample opportunity for positive interactions with others online, resulting in enhanced social capital and sense of belonging as well as opportunities for self-disclosure and identity exploration. Such interactions have been shown to lead to positive effects.

While much media attention focuses on the moral panics of social media use, with a greater focus on its negative aspects, we believe that it is important to develop a more balanced view of the impact of social media. In this way, researchers and practitioners can work towards harnessing and enhancing their benefits and reducing their risks for users. A key aspect to this is building digital literacy and skills as part of specific prevention and intervention strategies and incorporating this into general education. Drawing on Rheingold's [1] social media literacies outlined at the start of this chapter, we propose some key opportunities to set the focus for research and practice.

Focusing firstly on **attention** and **critical consumption**, researchers can work towards understanding how individuals discern the veracity of information and the reliability of online sources, and the role of individual differences in this regard. Such understanding should assist the development of intervention strategies to enhance awareness and critical thinking, vital abilities in stemming the increasing tide of fake news and conspiracy theories.

In relation to **collaboration** and **participation**, researchers can further explore the ways in which individuals interact and build communities, the associated social norms and expectations, and the opportunities and risks inherent in different contexts and social media platforms. From an intervention perspective, this leads to working towards creating positive online spaces, fostering appropriate and inclusive social norms and 'netiquette', as well as improving empathy and conflict resolution skills. This can be beneficial in terms of reducing risks such as cyberbullying.

Finally, understanding the limitations of **network awareness** is key to reducing a range of risks while maximizing the benefits of social media. Network awareness promotes the use of security features such as privacy settings and blocking as well as safer practices, for instance in the context of online sharing behaviours. Together with better critical consumption and a healthy dose of wariness, network awareness can also help guard against such risks as cybergrooming.

Overall, given the rate of technological development across social media and the Internet more generally, there is an urgent need to enhance users' digital literacy through education, particularly younger users who are more vulnerable to the risks inherent in social media. With this in mind, there is ample opportunity for researchers and practitioners to work towards a holistic approach to online safety and to acknowledge and strengthen the benefits of social media going forward.

Social Media and Disorders of Mood

Allan House

'Mental health' is a catch-all term used to describe a wide range of conditions – from emotional states such as worry about academic progress or distress due to relationship problems or social challenges such as poverty, through to psychosis and other severe mental illness. To start, therefore, this chapter will outline the definitions of some common terms used to describe those disturbances of mental health that are usually called emotional or mood disorders, and what might define mood disorders that are severe enough to be considered an illness. It will review what can be said with some certainty about social media use and disorders of mood, in a field where there is in truth a great deal of uncertainty. It will consider the common causes of mood disorders in general and what features of social media use might therefore lead us to be concerned that in any association between social media use and mood disorder, the former explains the latter. It will conclude with pointers to the research that needs to be done if the situation is to be clarified.

Defining and Identifying Disorders of Mood

It is helpful to think of three types of emotional disturbance – a loss of sense of emotional well-being, a state of personal distress, and a mood disorder that can be thought of as a form of illness.

Loss of a Sense of Emotional Well-Being

The World Health Organization defines health as '[a] state of complete physical, mental and social wellbeing and not merely the absence of disease or infirmity'.[1] For our purposes what this means is that there is more to being mentally healthy than simply being free of symptoms. Typically, definitions of being mentally well include ideas like life satisfaction, having a sense that life is worthwhile, and being able to feel happiness and a sense of pleasure in some aspect of life.

We can therefore think of loss of emotional well-being as an indication that things are not going well for somebody and indeed loss of a sense of pleasure in life has attracted its own name, *anhedonia*. Although not regarded as evidence of mood disorder when they are the only changes in feelings, loss of positive aspects of emotional state can still be important.

---

[1] www.who.int/data/gho/data/major-themes/health-and-well-being

States of Personal Distress

States of personal distress are typically labelled by the predominant emotion – such as depression or anxiety – but they have other components. They are usually accompanied by changes in ways of thinking, sometimes called cognitive symptoms; for example low mood can be associated with negative thoughts about oneself or pessimistic thinking about the future, while anxiety can be associated with fearful thoughts about things that might happen in the future. These emotions and ways of thinking can be accompanied by physical or somatic symptoms like sleep disturbance or loss of appetite. The fourth component of states of personal distress and the one by which we frequently identify them in others is changing behaviour. For example, depression may be accompanied by withdrawal from social contacts while anxiety may bring frequent requests for reassurance.

Mood Disorders as Illnesses

We often label states of personal distress as depression or anxiety, and yet these are also words used to describe what are varieties of mental illness. What is the difference between states of personal distress and mood disorders as illness? After all, they typically share the same symptoms. The answer lies in one of two main areas:

First, the *severity* of emotional change as defined for example by the number, intensity, duration, and intractability of symptoms or their disruptiveness – which may go beyond what could reasonably be expected given the person's circumstances. In this situation the emotional disorder is perceived as in some way not understandable by the person themselves or those close to them.

Second, there may be indications from the *specific form and content* of symptoms, so that they *aren't* entirely typical of personal distress. Depressive symptoms may reach a level where the individual thinks of themselves as completely worthless or their future as hopeless. They may come to think that suicide is the only option. Rarely, these thoughts may develop as delusions in so-called psychotic depression: for example, one encounters (as a psychiatrist) people who are convinced with unshakeable conviction that they are dying of an incurable disease or are being punished for past wickedness. Anxiety may lead to such severe avoidance that all normal activity is curtailed.

While much research relies on identifying depression from questionnaires that pick up on the *number* of depressive symptoms experienced (see later in this chapter), in clinical practice one sees people whose mood state is a worry by virtue solely of certain *individual* symptoms – a strong sense of hopelessness, for example, or preoccupation with death or suicide, is likely to be treated as a mood disorder even if emotional distress is not an explicit part of the picture.

In truth it isn't always easy to distinguish between mood disorders that are illnesses and states of personal distress that are entirely understandable as responses to recent life experiences and that will resolve with the passage of time or as circumstances change. Much research in this field provides a snapshot of how somebody is feeling at a particular time but doesn't allow a timeline to emerge, or identification of major events that may have occurred recently to explain symptoms. This uncertainty is reflected in writing about mood disorders, which are sometimes described as depressive symptoms or symptoms of depression, sometimes as depression, and sometimes less specifically as mental illness or mental health problems. All these states are important. Loss of a sense of well-being, of pleasure in the company of others, in music or in other shared activity, takes away one of the important motivators of social participation and this can start a spiral of withdrawal and worsening mood. Personal distress is just that, distress, and distressed people deserve our support and help. Mood disorders are an important cause of loss of quality of life and can be associated with social disability and an increased risk of physical illness.

The main reason to differentiate between these different states is to help in thinking about the most appropriate response – to avoid medicalizing states where the best form of response is not intervention by the mental health services, and to target specialist help at those most in need of it. It is worth bearing this question in mind when considering the effects of social media use; we want to avoid overzealous intervention in what may be self-limiting states of distress while at the same time making sure we do not miss states that might benefit from professional help.

How Do We Identify Who Has a Disorder of Mood?

In day-to-day life, if we want to know how somebody is we usually ask them an open question like 'how are you feeling?', perhaps followed up with more specific and closed questions like 'you seem rather low at the moment?' or 'are you worried about anything?'. When we are talking with somebody who is comfortable in sharing their feelings with us this is usually the best approach, but for research purposes it has disadvantages. Because the questions (and therefore the answers) aren't standardized, we can't compare different people according to their responses, or follow changes over time. We can't judge severity, and questions that are important to a researcher or mental health professional may not be asked at all if it is left largely an informal exchange.

These drawbacks of non-standardized questioning account for the popularity of standardized questionnaires asking about mood symptoms, and there are many of them – including examples available online.[2] They usually cover a number (about 5–20) of symptoms and ask if the person filling in the questionnaire has had those symptoms in (say) the last week or month, and if so how often and how persistently. Each response is allocated a score and the total score is taken as an indication of current mood problems. Scores for several of the more commonly used questionnaires have been benchmarked against clinical judgement or research interviews, so that it is possible to estimate on the basis of a total score how likely it is that somebody has a mood disorder of illness severity.

Example: A recent study [1] explored the relation between social media use and depression in two groups of young people from Ontario, Canada: one of school pupils and one of university undergraduates. Participants were contacted annually for up to six years and were invited to complete a self-report questionnaire, the Center for Epidemiologic Studies Depression Scale (CES-D), which has 20 items each scored 1–5 according to how much of the time each symptom was experienced [2]. This questionnaire has been used in research for nearly 50 years now, to identify people with depressive symptoms that might be of illness severity. In this study, however, the researchers were not interested in that question but in a different topic, which was whether there was

---

[2] See for example www.nhs.uk/mental-health/self-help/guides-tools-and-activities/depression-anxiety-self-assessment-quiz/

evidence that the emergence of new depressive symptoms was related to social media use earlier in the study (they found that it wasn't). In this case then, the standardized questionnaire was being used not for its so-called case-finding properties, but because it has been shown to be a reliable (repeatable) way of picking up symptoms that would be widely accepted as depressive.

There are disadvantages to the use of questionnaires. Summing all responses to produce a single score makes for simplicity, but the same score may be achieved in different ways. For example, a score of 10 on a given scale may mean that 10 different items have been endorsed but only at a severity level of one, or 5 items have been endorsed at a level of two. It isn't possible to get an exact picture. Sometimes researchers respond to this challenge by using not just the total score but also noting whether a single particularly important item has been endorsed; for example, a depression questionnaire may yield a total score and also an observation about how many respondents endorsed a question about suicidal thinking.

There are two ways to explore these more detailed aspects of mood. One is to ask respondents to complete a much longer and more exhaustive questionnaire, which few are willing to do. The other is to undertake a standardized research interview – which provides the most detailed and interpretable information if done properly but which is both expensive to do and difficult to deliver in studies that require large numbers of participants. For these reasons, most research into the effects of social media on mood has relied on, and will continue to rely on, the use of standardized questionnaires [3].

Social Media Use and Mood Disorder

There is no shortage of research aimed at answering, in one way or another, a question about the relation between social media use and mental well-being or mood disorder. One recent review [4] identified 42 relevant studies published up to the beginning of 2019, while another, using slightly different criteria in its search strategy, identified 62 studies [3]. A review of these reviews found there had been 25 such reviews on how social media use affects adolescent mental health [5].

Under the circumstances, it comes as something of a surprise to discover that there isn't a definite answer to the question of whether social media use can cause disordered mood, and especially depression. Some studies have reported no association at all [6, 7] and the authors of one much-quoted study suggested that any effect was small and had been sensationalized, the health risk being no greater than comes from eating potatoes [8]. On the other hand, there are studies, including longitudinal (follow-up) studies, that suggest social media use is indeed associated with the onset of depression and that this association is not restricted to adolescents and young adults [9, 10]. How can we explain these apparently conflicting findings?

There are a couple of rather obvious explanations for inconsistency in findings from social media research. One is that not all researchers take trouble to define and measure carefully what they mean by social media use, or mental health [5]. Another is that different results are likely to reflect, at least in part, variation in the groups of people being studied. Why should we expect high school students, university undergraduates, and respondents to online surveys to be sensitive in the same ways to what they encounter online? If some people, perhaps a minority who are vulnerable for some reason, are harmed emotionally by their use, some are benefitted, and for some there is no real impact, then looking for global effects across a whole study group is likely to underestimate the impact on the minority vulnerable group. Perhaps the correct answer is that social media use is harmful for some and beneficial for others, so that averaged out it does not look very important.

This last observation now informs much research into the effects of social media, which increasingly explores more specific questions about what types of social media use are beneficial or harmful for which people under what circumstances.

The Importance of Type of Social Media Use

Following this line of thinking, one line of inquiry has been to ask if there are special features of how social media are being used which explain an association with mood problems for subgroups of users.

Quantity of Social Media Use

It has long been an axiom of health research that *a dose–response effect* is a useful sign that a particular exposure is a cause of illness. For example, if two people have hypertension the person with very high blood pressure is more at risk of complications than the person whose blood pressure is only slightly raised. A person exposed to a high dose of radiation is more likely to become ill than somebody exposed to a low dose, and so on.

'Dose' of social media exposure can be thought of in several ways. The most obvious is *duration* – how much time each day is spent on social media sites, or how often is each site checked? A second measure is *intensity* of use – for example, how emotionally invested is a person in their social media presence, working at and worrying about their online identity, concerned about being there (one example of fear of missing out, known colloquially as FOMO). A third indication is *intrusiveness*. There is of course a wide range of what we might think of as normal use of social media defined in these terms – we all know people who seem unable to hold a conversation without holding their phone at the same time, or to share a meal without their phone on the table. In extreme cases, however, problematic social media use takes on features of a sort that have been likened to addiction: an individual can spend hours a day (more than six hours a day is by no means rare); other activities can be foregone to spend time online; use of social media has a compulsive quality making it difficult to resist; and social media use can intrude into and disrupt work or study.

Although the evidence isn't watertight, the indications are that within quite a wide range, simply the amount of time spent on social media isn't a big risk for depression [1]. A stronger suggestion is that problematic (addiction-like) use is associated with depression, although even here some caution is needed not to exaggerate the size of the effect. In a recent study [11] of just under a thousand young people in the USA, just under one in seven, 15% (the heaviest users) were engaged in some way with social media for more than five hours a day, while about a third, 31% (the lightest users) were using social media for less than two hours a day. The heaviest users were just over 2½ times more likely to have developed depression than the lightest users during follow-up in the study, as defined by their score on a self-rating questionnaire. This sounds dramatic but in fact 80% of the heaviest users did not develop depression by the study's criterion, and the absolute numbers of young people implicated was quite small, less than 20. Given the problems with the study – only just over a half of the original sample were available for follow-up, the duration of which varied considerably – what this study does is add weight to (rather than prove conclusively) what common sense would suggest to us, which is that very heavy use of social media is, for some people, not good for their mental health as measured by self-reported depression.

The Quality of Social Media Use

There are other ways to characterize social media use. For example, we can ask how many social media platforms somebody is using, with how many identities. This may be thought of as a reflection of how important social media are in a person's life, as judged by a willingness to explore different aspects of the experience. On its own, however, the use of multiple platforms doesn't tell us much – it might be a sign of enthusiastic engagement in the online social world or on the other hand it might suggest an individual who is ill at ease, moving from place to place while they search for somewhere to feel comfortable.

We need more information on how individuals are using social media, and another recent approach has involved a distinction between active and passive use. Active use involves a more 'social' engagement with the media – interacting with other users, posting and responding to posts, while passive use entails a more detached browsing, reading only.

There is some evidence that depression is associated with multiple platform use [12] and with more passive approaches [13]. On the face of it these two associations might seem contradictory but they would be compatible with the idea that multiple platform use represents unsatisfactory, perhaps rather unengaged and marginal, involvement with social media environments rather than meaningful participation which does not therefore obtain any of the potential benefit from the social, interactive aspects of social media.

Content of the Social Media Experience

There is a third question, beyond the *how* and *how much* of social media use, and its associations with depression. The third question is about *what* – that is, the content of what is being accessed or posted on social media platforms. We might think of the content of social media use on a desirability–undesirability spectrum, as follows.

Not all social media content is undesirable or potentially harmful. Many people find social media a useful resource for seeking help in the form of practical advice, getting encouragement from others, and making supportive contacts.

There is a great deal of social media activity that is hardly touched on in writings about social media use and mood disorders. Users share personal and family news, and swap ideas and opinions about music, fashion, sport, films and so on. These activities appear emotionally innocuous, unlikely to offer much insight into the question at hand, and yet they account for a great deal of the popularity of social media. They should perhaps be thought of as one of its main benefits for the sense of social involvement they bring. There is, however, even with these apparently positive or harmless activities, an inevitable element of social comparison: social media comment, and especially images, can present an idealized and unrealistic view of the world which can lead to a sense of failure or low self-worth.

Some sharing is about matters that are more usually withheld in offline social interactions – such as disclosures about mental health problems, self-harm, or concerns about body image. Such activity has uncertain online results – it may lead to words of support and advice or it may provoke criticism and ridicule.

More unambiguously undesirable are risky behaviours such as talking with strangers, sharing personal information about drug use, or sharing sexual content either personal (sexting) or impersonal (pornography).

There is no real ambiguity or debate about certain sorts of content – ridiculing or abusive posts, bullying or harassing other posters, posting violent aggressive or pornographic content are all highly undesirable. In fact, in a survey of 9–16 year olds from Europe [14], it was these three topics (pornography, bullying, violent content) that were nominated as most upsetting, a long way ahead of topics such as self-harm or other mental health problems.

The evidence on the relation between depression and these aspects of the content of social media experience is as one might expect: disturbances of mood are associated with exposure to more undesirable content, with bullying and harassment the most consistently reported risk. It has to be said that the evidence in this area comes almost entirely from cross-sectional studies, making it impossible to be sure which is cause and effect – whether people with or prone to depression are more likely to use social media in certain ways, or whether social media use of certain sorts can lead to depression.

Some Theory about Common Causes of Mood Disorder

Another way to look at the problem is to pose an entirely different question. Rather than asking about research evidence we can ask – do we have theoretical grounds, based upon what we know already about the causes of depression, to consider social media use as a risk for mood disorders?

A standard way of describing the causes (and treatment) of health conditions is to use the so-called *biopsychosocial* model, which takes into account biological (physical) causes and psychological (individual) and social (including interpersonal) factors. In relation to depression *biological* factors might include genetic influences, especially in relation to the more severe forms of mood disorder such as bipolar illness. *Psychological* factors can include negative ways of thinking about the self (worthlessness or low self-esteem, for example) or about the future (such as hopelessness). The impact of *social* factors is felt through adverse life events and difficulties, and especially those involving loss. Since social support is a strong protective influence against life adversity, then lack of social support is an important risk for depression. Do these ideas help us think about the likely status of social media as a cause of depression?

The most obvious candidate for a physical effect on mood is that social media use has an effect on sleep [15] – as time spent online increases, especially in the evening, then time spent asleep decreases. This is likely to be because the time for sleep is eaten into by time online, and there may also be an effect of screen light on sleep, mediated by its effect on melatonin levels. Sleep disturbance is a predictor of depression [16], either because it is an early (precursor) symptom or as a direct cause. There is likely to be an iterative effect here – poor sleep leading to depression leading to worse sleep.

The social effects of social media come from two sources. First, heavy use can have a disruptive effect on offline (face-to-face) social interactions, leading to or exacerbating a sense of alienation and isolation. The type of social support available online is different from that which may be available offline [17]. The former is more readily available and comes from others who (at least seem to) share the same experiences, but it is not the same as face-to-face support, which may be harder to come by but is more likely to come from somebody with whom the individual can have an intimate or trusted relationship. Second, social media can be a source of adverse personal experience and especially bullying, abuse, and harassment.

The psychological impact of social media use arises mainly from its social characteristics: an effect of bullying and related experiences is to prompt negative ideas about self, a sort of self-denigration or low self-esteem; online social comparisons may prompt negative judgements about self-worth, or envy [18]. A more direct effect may arise from sustained immersion in unhappy online content, a so-called mood-induction effect [19]. There is an obvious analogy between passive use of social media and passive approaches to problem-solving more generally, which may be important given the mood-related benefits of therapies aimed at enhancing active problem-solving skills [20].

Conclusion

We will start with a tentative summary. There is something like a consensus in the literature now, which is that most social media use is not terribly harmful to mental health but that certain sorts of social media use can be: spending many hours a day preoccupied with visiting social media sites, to a degree that affects other aspects of life; social media use that is poorly regulated and passive in nature rather than actively managed by the individual; accessing content that is bullying or undermining.

The picture is complicated by the fact that it is individuals with existing mood problems, or who are prone to develop them, who are most likely to use social media in these harmful ways. So an iterative loop can develop: low mood leads to harmful patterns of social media use, which then exacerbate the mood problems. The few longitudinal studies in the field are troubled by small numbers and the biases that come from not achieving high follow-up rates (see Chapter 6) but they tend to confirm this picture. Most of the resulting mood disturbance is at the non-severe end of the scale with loss of sense of well-being, or mild/moderate depressive states rather than the more severe disorders that might suggest mental illness.

Other authors in this book discuss the question of how to develop interventions that enhance healthy use of social media while helping to reduce unhealthy use. Any success in that direction is likely to be helpful for those experiencing or at risk of mood disorder. However, research suggests that more focused help is needed for those who are already depressed or already drawn into the loop of depression leading to unhealthy social media use leading to depression. In providing this help, we should be aware that a number of dilemmas may arise.

Interventions here might be educational or informational – giving guidance on practices that are likely to be unhelpful, for example – as a part of supporting self-management. There is a need always to balance the desire to reduce harms with the recognition that for many people access to social media also brings benefits. Too great an emphasis on demonizing social media may lead to withdrawal and loss of opportunity to provide support.

If supportive friends or family are available it may be helpful to draw them into providing assistance – encouraging a turn towards face-to-face contact. Again there is a balance to be struck between supportiveness and intrusiveness, a judgement that can only be made with knowledge of each individual's circumstances.

Such a judgement may also be needed when an individual is in a therapeutic relationship with a professional. Is social media use something to be explored in detail, or is it a separate private matter, of concern only to the individual who has decisions to make about boundaries with a therapist as much as with others in their life?

Finally, there is a question about gender. We know that when we compare females and males, patterns of social media use are different and so are risks for and rates of depression. And yet we know almost nothing about how gender-specific we should make any help we might offer.

Further Reading

Tacchi, M.J. and J. Scott. *Depression – A Very Short Introduction*. 2017, Oxford University Press.

Chapter 9

Social Media Use, Body Image, and Eating Disorders

Rachel Rodgers and Katherine Laveway

In this chapter we review how social media affect body image and eating behaviours. In asking how visual images, text messages and the like alter attitudes to the body, we review evidence from experiments and observational studies. We consider whether social media produce clinically severe eating disorders or exacerbate existing ones, and whether social media can be a positive resource for people suffering from eating disorders. We discuss the options for prevention or treatment of eating disorders and body image concerns using social media or other digital resources.

Social media are now ubiquitous with especially high usage by youth. Similar to traditional media, a number of aspects of social media including their preoccupation with bodily health and appearance make it a relevant context to examine in terms of their potential influence on body image and eating disorders. Moreover, social media possess a number of aspects that are specific to them, including their interactive nature, and possibility of user contributions, that may also be important elements in terms of their relationship with body image and eating disorders. This chapter will present an overview of the ways in which social media may be related to body image and eating disorders, a review of the available evidence for these different pathways, as well as a consideration of how social media may also promote positive body image and eating behaviours and facilitate access to and the dissemination of resources and interventions.

Body Image, Eating Disorders, and Social Media

Body image refers to the thoughts, feelings, perceptions, and behaviours related to one's body and experience of embodiment, that is, the experience of inhabiting one's body. Negative body image includes a range of preoccupations, anxieties, and dissatisfaction regarding appearance, related to rigid beliefs regarding appearance standards, often accompanied by efforts to avoid situations in which these uncomfortable experiences arise, or to change appearance. Positive body image, in contrast, is characterized by a flexible and accepting approach to the body that values dimensions broader than appearance.

While the way in which an individual relates to and experiences their body can be conceptualized as an internal process, a number of external or social and cultural factors play an influential role. Examples of these factors include social constructions of race, gender, beauty, health, and self-worth, to name just a few.

Body image concerns are recognized as one of the key risk factors for eating disorders, as well as a variety of forms of disordered eating. Eating disorders are serious mental health conditions that are characterized by a lasting disturbance of eating or eating-related behaviour that results in impaired psychological functioning. The term disordered eating refers to problematic eating patterns or behaviours (such as skipping meals, eating to regulate emotions, loss of control eating, purging behaviours, or eating only certain foods). Individuals engaging in these behaviours may not meet the full clinical criteria for an eating disorder, as they are less frequent and severe than in someone with an eating disorder. However, these behaviours can be greatly impairing, and individuals engaging in disordered eating are at greater risk for later developing an eating disorder.

A number of elements of social media make it an important context to consider as related to body image. First, images on social media typically represent individuals whose appearance is close to appearance ideals and whose images are frequently digitally edited so that they portray an unrealistic and very narrow range of appearances. Second, social media platforms offer commercially created content as well as user-generated content. The distinction between these two is not always clear, which may lead users to believe that the images they are seeing are of individuals who are closer to them socially than images of celebrities or professional models. Third, social media are interactive environments where individuals can provide feedback and comments (often appearance related) on content posted by others. And lastly, social media rely on underlying algorithms that are designed to maximize user engagement through machine learning. This has been described as leading to an 'echo chamber' effect where content offered to users may become increasingly narrowly focused on a particular topic (for example appearance).

Some Theoretical Considerations

Efforts to investigate the relationships between social media use and body image, disordered eating, and eating disorders have successfully been framed within several theoretical frameworks – primarily sociocultural theories, objectification theory, and uses and gratification theory. In addition, newer theoretical frameworks on the development of critical body awareness may better account for the relationships between body image and social media from a developmental and dynamic perspective.

Sociocultural theories (such as social appearance comparison and thin-ideal internalization) have highlighted how the narrow and unrealistic range of appearances presented on social media, exacerbated by digital modification, may lead individuals to internalize a very thin and lean body type as a personal standard to strive for [1]. This internalized standard, coupled with appearance comparisons with the images posted by others on social media, likely increases body dissatisfaction and may then lead to disordered eating behaviours in attempts to modify one's body and bring it closer to the unattainable social ideal.

Sociocultural theories also describe how the importance of pursuing unrealistic appearance ideals is relayed by other interpersonal agents such as peers. On social media, the explicit feedback provided by peers, as well as the more implicit messages conveyed by the types of content and images posted, may therefore also contribute to an individual's body image through appearance comparisons and the reinforcement of appearance as a core element of identity.

Objectification theory emphasizes how objectifying messages and practices may increase body image concerns. Objectification refers to a social practice by which an individual is viewed as an object, rather than as a person. Repeated exposure to this process is believed to lead to self-objectification, whereby an individual internalizes the perspective of being observed and appraised by others, which can manifest in the vigilant monitoring of one's appearance. Thus, objectification theory posits that individuals in Western society, and particularly women and other minorities, are socialized to view their bodies in the third person, in other words as objects, often sexual objects, whose value is derived from how they appear to others. This self-surveillance may lead to body shame and anxiety, which in turn may increase the risk of developing negative body image and engaging in disordered eating behaviours. On social media the act of creating and posting self-images takes place within a context in which posting is largely motivated by financial or other types of gain (such as increasing social capital) and this has the effect of influencing the mobility of an individual in a social hierarchy [2]. These acts have been described as essentially self-objectifying, and therefore likely to be associated with body image concerns.

Uses and gratification theory poses media users, and here social media users, as active agents of media use and consumption [3]. The theory posits that differing motivations will lead to different types of social media use, which, coupled with proposed content derived by machine learning, will lead to individualized social media environments. Individuals with body image concerns may therefore find themselves in a cycle of actively seeking out appearance-related content, which would then increase the amount of appearance-related content proposed by the platforms. In contrast, individuals with other interests or motivations for social media use might be protected from appearance-related content to some extent.

Together, these theories suggest the value of *critical awareness* of the processes described. That is, it may be protective against harmful influences of social media on body image and disordered eating behaviours if users are more aware of the unrealistic nature of social media images, the discrepancy between online self-presentation and real life, the commercial and personal interests of those posting content, and the ways in which the social media environment may be reactive to user behaviours [4]. Critical awareness skills, which can be defined in this context as social media literacy, are believed to disrupt the damaging pathways posited by sociocultural and objectification theories and provide individuals with the knowledge and skills to engage with social media in value-consistent and protective ways.

The Theory of Development of Critical Body Awareness: Although useful, the preceeding theories fail to account for the ways in which users' body image, motivations for social media use, and social media literacy likely evolved together in an interactive process that may be moderated by other factors. Thus, individuals for whom appearance is an important factor (for example due to certain personality traits, potentially coupled with appearance-focused environments and personal history) may be more likely to experience negative effects of social media use on body image. These individuals may be more likely to engage in unfavourable appearance comparisons, to strive for unattainable appearance ideals, and to therefore use social media as a source of information and support regarding how to modify their appearance to bring it closer to appearance ideals, as well as curating their online self-presentation to most closely resemble those ideals. For such individuals, social media may be a constant reminder of their failure to meet unrealistic social standards and exacerbate their body image concerns and potential disordered eating behaviours.

However, the individual should be seen as an active agent in their use of social media, with the capacity to change. The presence on social media of some content aiming to deconstruct appearance ideals and point to the contrived and curated nature of social media content, and the increasing distress associated with unsuccessful efforts to modify the body, may progressively lead such individuals to question the utility of pursuing unattainable appearance ideals. At this point, individuals may become more attuned to the unrealistic nature of social media content and its impact on their own body image and may start to look for ways to improve their body image rather than changing their appearance. Although body dissatisfaction, appearance preoccupation, and disordered eating may decrease, this may continue to be a time of tension between a desire to experience less pressure to achieve unrealistic standards and the effortful need to continue to actively remind themselves of their unrealistic nature.

Over time these efforts, in conjunction with actively seeking to modify the personal online space through searching for content that is supportive of positive body image and healthy behaviours, may lead individuals to engage to a greater extent with content that actively seeks to deconstruct appearance ideals and to promote diversity and broad conceptualizations of beauty. Individuals may become actively engaged in the promotion of this stance by following or posting body positive content and other forms of appearance activism. Individuals may experience heightened body appreciation and acceptance, as well as appreciation for their bodies' functionality. This body positivity may lead to an embracing of body liberation, that is a broader activist stance that recognizes the importance of promoting inclusivity, body autonomy, and size diversity. Body liberation emphasizes the importance of all individuals being able to live in safe ways within their bodies and separates a person's self-worth from their body and appearance.

Finally, for some individuals, continued experiences of positive body image and a shift away from body-centering social media may lead to decreased investment in the body, and a stance of body neutrality that is viewing the body through a neutral lens and acknowledging that body love may not always be realistic or attainable. At this point, engagement with social media is no longer effortful or activist as related to appearance, and other interests may lead to individuals being exposed to very little appearance-related content, be it promoting the thin-ideal or diverse conceptualizations of beauty. Importantly, while some may reach this stance through a personal journey of increasing awareness of social media effects on body image and effortful and active engaging in skills to reduce them, others may start out with low investment in appearance and high levels of protective factors that might shield them from body image concerns and help them to sustain a stance of body neutrality.

In sum, various theories have described how highly visual social media may be detrimental to body image via different pathways and how different types of social media may vary in their potential for positive or negative effects on body image depending on individuals' characteristics and their position in the model of the development of critical body awareness.

Social Media, Body Image Concerns, and Disordered Eating: Empirical Evidence

Body Image and Disordered Eating

A growing body of evidence supports the relationship between the use of social media, principally highly visual social media, and body image concerns and disordered eating

[5]. In their meta-analysis Saiphoo and Vahedi [5] examined behavioural aspects of body image disturbance, which included measures of disordered eating behaviours separately from more cognitive and affective indices. Cognitive dimensions of body image include one's thoughts and beliefs about one's body, while affective dimensions include how someone feels about their body and the emotions that accompany evaluating their appearance (for example, appreciation, dissatisfaction, disgust, or confidence). While the effects for behavioural variables were found to be lower than cognitive or affective variables in this meta-analysis, they still emerged as significant. In other words, strong evidence exists for a small but robust relationship between exposure to highly visual social media and poorer body image. The study also examined the cumulative evidence from extant longitudinal work and reported that social media use revealed a small-size relationship with poorer body image over time [5].

In addition, a growing body of experimental work, and a small number of longitudinal studies, have provided additional support for causal relationships at play. A recent meta-analysis of experimental studies confirmed that exposure to thin-ideal images revealed a moderate-size negative effect on body image, noting that these images were also found to be more harmful to body image as compared to other types of social media content [6].

These two recent meta-analytic studies, in addition to the wider literature, provide strong support for the fact that the use of highly visual social media, and, more specifically, exposure to images promoting unrealistic appearance ideals, is harmful to body image and related disordered eating behaviours.

Mechanisms and Moderating Individual Characteristics

As described, the relationship between social media use and poorer body image has been well documented [5, 6]. Understanding the mechanisms underlying these harmful effects is important for identifying modifiable intervention targets, so additional work has sought to examine such mechanisms. As predicted by sociocultural theories, engaging in in-the-moment appearance comparisons with the images presented on social media has received support from experimental studies as one of the important mechanisms. In addition, qualitative work has pointed to the importance of peer feedback in the effects of social media on body image [7]. Moreover, integrated models of the relationship between social media use and disordered eating and muscle-building behaviours among mixed-gender adolescents have provided further correlational support for these pathways.

In addition, support has been found for the pathways proposed by objectification theory, such that a relationship has been found between social media use and increased self-objectification across a variety of platforms. For example, in their 2017 study examining mediators of the relationship between Instagram use and self-objectification, Feltman and Szymanski [8] found that greater Instagram use increased both upward and downward appearance comparisons, comparisons that were respectively unfavourable and favourable. However, only upward appearance comparisons (in which individuals engaged in comparisons to individuals they perceived to have 'better' bodies than their own) were positively associated with self-objectification. This finding provides evidence that engaging in this upward comparison is the mechanism through which an individual adopts an observer's perspective of their own body [8]. Furthermore, support has also emerged for the ways in which different motivations may orient individuals towards different types of social media use, and how this may be related to different exposures that might then affect body image differently [9].

Although the content being viewed on social media plays an important role in its effects on body image, with idealized imagery being most harmful [7, 10], individual characteristics may also play a part in these effects. One dimension that has received attention is age. Indeed, younger adolescents present a number of specificities as a group that may render them particularly vulnerable to the negative effects of social media on body image, including the fact that this is a time when many are transitioning through puberty and is an important time of identity development. In addition, young adolescents are in the process of developing cognitive understandings of marketing intent and media literacy skills which may also make them particularly susceptible to the effects of social media.

Given the usefulness of sociocultural and objectification theories in grounding research focusing on exploring the relationships between social media use and body image, and the role that appearance pressures and oppressive social processes such as objectification play in the pathways put forth by these theories, groups holding historically marginalized identities are also of particular interest. Together these theories would predict that those whose appearance is furthest from appearance ideals, and who are least represented, would likely experience some of the greatest negative effects of social media on body image.

Consistent with this, for example, gender differences have been found in the relationships between social media use and body image, although the gendered patterns in these relationships still warrant further elucidation. Similarly, some evidence has suggested that the relationship between social media use and body image concerns may be strongest among sexual minority men as compared to heterosexual men. Thus, individuals who experience the most pressure to conform to appearance ideals, and for whom greatest emphasis is placed on the importance of appearance, may be most vulnerable to the effects of social media on body image.

Furthermore, cultural context is also important to consider in these relationships [5]. Cultural context may impact the types of social media an individual is exposed to, and cultural values may also moderate the relationships between social media use and body image concerns and disordered eating. Although cross-cultural research in this area is still nascent, the extant data suggest that these cross-cultural differences, both in content and in the ways in which social media use and exposure may be related to individuals' body image and eating concerns, do exist.

Finally, consistent with the developmental theory of critical body awareness outlined earlier, it may be that the most useful way of conceptualizing the ways individuals may be affected by different types of social media content is to consider both the nature of the social media content and their individual characteristics together. Thus, for example, individuals who are highly adherent to appearance ideals may find content that starts to challenge those and highlights how most individuals fail to meet those standards to be most helpful, and in contrast idealized content most harmful. As individuals gain critical skills and move towards positions of body positivity, body liberation, or body neutrality, other types of social media content may be more helpful, and the likelihood of idealized content having a negative impact might be reduced due to both less exposure and the buffering protective skills of these individuals. In this way, an intersecting approach of *which content* and *for whom* might be most useful when considering moderating factors of the effects of social media on body image.

Clinical Eating Disorders

To date, less is known regarding the capacity of social media to exacerbate or maintain clinical-level eating disorders. One of the ways in which this might occur is through the presence on social media of content and communities that cast eating disorders as life choices rather than mental health concerns and encourage individuals to maintain or increase their eating disorder patterns. Such content has existed in online spaces for many years and has been shown to lead to increased eating disorder symptoms [11, 12]. While many social media platforms have instituted policies to limit such content, it remains difficult to monitor and regulate. In addition, for individuals who are recovering from eating disorders, social media and online spaces may be both critical places of support and validation during the process, as well as a place in which unhelpful or triggering content may be always present. Navigating these spaces while working on recovery with its inevitable hurdles may be a particular challenge.

Social Media as a Medium for Intervention and Support

In view of the documented harmful effects of exposure to idealized highly visual social media on body image, it has been suggested that other types of content may be more helpful for body image. Furthermore, it has been proposed that social media may also constitute a useful environment for the dissemination of intervention and prevention efforts and resources.

Body Positive Social Media Content

Body positivity has gained ground as an important online movement over the past years. Rooted in fat activism, the body positive movement eschews normative and oppressive appearance ideals and seeks to increase representativeness and inclusivity in media. Although it has been criticized for its own lack of diversity and over concerns that it is subject to its own commercial influences, body positive content has been proposed to be helpful for body image by increasing the diversity of bodies represented, by normalizing images of non-idealized bodies, and by promoting and modelling stances of body acceptance, body love, and body pride. In this way, it is anticipated that exposure to body positive content would be protective of the harmful influences of idealized social media content by reducing unfavourable appearance comparisons with unrealistic images and reducing pressures to pursue appearance ideals. Overall, the empirical evidence has provided some support for this, with content portraying individuals of average body sizes and content without images emerging as most helpful for body image [6]. More research is needed to better understand how social media can help to support positive body image and for whom different types of content might be most helpful.

Social Media as a Platform for Prevention and Intervention

Social media have been identified as a potential tool and platform for the dissemination of prevention and intervention resources in several ways. First, as a space to which individuals who may have heightened appearance and eating concerns come to gain information related to these concerns, it may offer opportunities for early identification of concerns and connecting individuals with helpful resources (that could be online or offline). For example, eating disorder recovery accounts can serve as important community spaces where survivors offer perspectives and insights on the process of recovery. Second, social media provide a medium for the dissemination of such resources in an effective and low-cost manner that may circumvent some of the barriers related to access to care typically experienced by individuals with appearance concerns and disordered eating.

Regarding the identification of individuals who would benefit from support and resources related to appearance concerns and disordered eating, screening programmes (for example, in higher education institutions) and machine-learning detection tools (based on online activity) have emerged as approaches with high potential for success. Connecting individuals with resources at the appropriate level is a critical element in access to care and social media offers important avenues for doing this.

In terms of the delivery of resources and treatment, the last few years have seen a substantial increase in the number of e-mental health resources available that target appearance concerns and disordered eating [13]. Some formal organizations, like the National Eating Disorders Association, have a presence on social media, providing access to screening tools, helplines, and information about local treatment providers [14]. While findings are promising, improvements are needed. Considering design features as well as the personalization of content may help to increase retention and uptake as well as the efficacy of such interventions. With such improvements, effective social media-based interventions have a very large potential as useful interventions.

Conclusion

In sum, evidence points to the harmful effects on body image of idealized images on highly visual social media. While these effects may vary across individuals, they are concerning given the disproportionate number of youths who are the most active social media users. In addition, social media may pose particular risks for those with existing eating concerns and who engage with content specifically designed to maintain and exacerbate such concerns. Nevertheless, some content may also be supportive of positive body image. Moreover, social media hold promise as a means of aiding with the identification of individuals who might benefit from resources and connecting them with appropriate levels of care. Interventions that can be disseminated via social media warrant further development and evaluation given the benefits in terms of reach and accessibility of e-mental health interventions. Additional research is needed aiming to clarify the mechanisms underlying the effects of social media on body image and disordered eating, as well as the intersections of types of social media content and individual characteristics.

Further Reading

Rodgers, R.F., Media and body image in children and adolescents, in *Educational Research and Innovation Education in the Digital Age: Healthy and Happy Children*, T. Burns and F. Gottschalk, Editors. 2020, Paris: OECD Publishing. p. 98–112.

Chapter 10

Social Media and Gambling

Thomas B. Swanton, Sascha Callaghan, Nicola C. Newton, Vladan Starcevic, and Sally M. Gainsbury

For many people, gambling is a form of entertainment and a social pastime – perhaps playing table games at the casino or enjoying a day at the races. Many people engage in gambling occasionally. However, some people develop problems with gambling and experience difficulties controlling the amount of time and money they spend gambling. Excessive gambling can result in serious harms for the gambler, as well as for the people around them. Gambling might have become a means to cope with life stresses, an escape from feelings of sadness and worry, a way to experience temporary feelings of pleasure and reward, or perceived as a way out of debt and financial problems. Gambling can become unaffordable and impulsive, resulting in significant problems across multiple domains of a person's life, including in their relationships, work or study, physical and mental health, and financial well-being [1].

Technologies, such as the Internet, smartphones, and social media, have radically changed the gambling landscape in recent decades. The online sphere has dramatically increased the accessibility of gambling, allowing people to place bets at any time of the day or night from wherever they happen to be – whether the office, the dinner table, the bathroom, or bed. Activities that traditionally took place in brick-and-mortar venues, such as clubs and casinos, are now easily accessed in private. Although gambling is a highly regulated activity in many jurisdictions, people can access gambling websites online that may not hold local licences and may have few safeguards in place to protect consumers from experiencing harm.

Digital technologies allow advertisements for gambling and other addictive products to be targeted to customers in highly personalized ways. This is a new phenomenon that was not possible with traditional media. Elements of gambling have also appeared in new

---

Disclosure statements: Thomas Swanton has received a PhD scholarship through the NSW Government's Gambling Research Capacity Grants programme, funded by the NSW Responsible Gambling Fund, and supported by the NSW Office of Responsible Gambling. He has received honoraria for research advisory services from GambleAware, an independent UK charity that seeks to minimize gambling harms and which receives voluntary donations from the gambling industry.
 Nicola Newton is supported by an NHMRC Career Development Fellowship (APP1166377).
 Sally Gainsbury has received research funding and worked with various government, community, and industry organizations to deliver presentations and reports with the aim of reducing gambling harms. A list of funding sources is available at www.sydney.edu.au/science/about/our-people/academic-staff/sally-gainsbury.html#collapseprofileassociations
 Acknowledgements: The authors are grateful to Garner Clancey for his constructive feedback on an earlier version of this chapter.

contexts, such as within games, often blurring the distinction between what gambling is and what it is not.

In this chapter, we look specifically at the role of social media in connecting people with gambling-related content and facilitating engagement with gambling. We consider how these factors may impact a person's risk of experiencing harms associated with gambling, especially those in vulnerable groups such as young people and those already experiencing gambling problems. We then consider what needs to be done to reduce the risk of social media contributing to gambling harm. First, however, we provide some background on online gambling and gambling-related problems.

The Rise of Online Gambling

Since its introduction in the late 1990s, online gambling has grown at a rapid pace. In 2020, market research firms estimated the market to be worth US$59.6 billion worldwide, forecasting it to more than double in size by 2027. This growth is driven by increasing penetration of high-speed internet connections, greater use of smartphones and mobile devices, and liberalisation of online gambling regulations in many countries. In the United Kingdom, which has a relatively liberal approach to online gambling regulation, nearly one in four adults report having gambled online in the past month. In the United States, the National Council for Problem Gambling estimates that 15% of adults have placed a bet online in the past year despite online gambling being illegal in most states. This statistic reflects one of the main challenges for regulating online gambling. Customers can easily access gambling websites from their computer or smartphone regardless of what local restrictions or legislation may be in place.

Several studies have observed higher rates of problem gambling among people who gamble online compared to those who typically gamble in brick-and-mortar (land-based) venues [2]. Initially, this led to the perception that online gambling might be inherently more harmful than offline gambling. However, research has since found that the link between online gambling and higher rates of problem gambling is largely explained by someone's overall gambling involvement. In other words, it is the overall amount of time and money someone spends gambling, combined with the intensity of their gambling and breadth of product use, that predicts their risk of experiencing problems with gambling, rather than simply whether they gamble through online or offline channels.

Nonetheless, proliferation of internet and smartphone use has increased people's opportunities to gamble. No longer are people constrained by opening hours or distance to their local venue, which in any case tends to provide a relatively small range of gambling games. Technology has facilitated all-hours access to seemingly countless gambling products from wherever someone happens to be, whenever they want it. This uncurtailed access makes it easier for people (who might already be at risk) to gamble more frequently and intensely than ever before.

Around the world, between 1% and 6% of adults are affected by problem gambling each year [3]. A smaller proportion meet the diagnostic criteria for gambling disorder, the more severe variant [1]. However, the harms associated with gambling are far-reaching, affecting many people beyond the relatively small group of individuals experiencing severe problems controlling their gambling. Research shows that for every person experiencing a severe gambling problem, another six people are affected by gambling-related harms – most often, members of the gambler's immediate family [4].

> **Defining Some Key Terms**
>
> *Gambling* is a strictly regulated activity in many jurisdictions and involves placing a bet (a monetary outlay) on the outcome of a predominantly chance-based event for the possibility of winning a prize of monetary value. Outcomes on most gambling activities, such as slot machines and lotteries, are determined completely by chance (the gambler has no influence on the outcome). Other gambling activities, such as poker and wagering, may involve an element of skill as individuals actively select which bets to place. Gambling activities involve a house advantage (essentially, the price of playing the game). This means that, even though wins are possible, it is highly likely that people who gamble persistently will lose money over time.
>
> *Gambling-related harms* are negative consequences associated with gambling. Harms occur across a variety of domains, including financial (such as debt), psychological stress, physical health (such as disruption to sleep), social (such as relationship breakdown), disengagement from other activities (such as reduced engagement in other hobbies), reduced performance at work, and critical events (such as criminal activity, bankruptcy, and suicide). Harms lie on a spectrum of severity, ranging from relatively mild to severe. Gambling-related harms affect not only the individual engaging in gambling but can be experienced by their loved ones as well as people in the broader community.
>
> *Problem gambling* refers to a pattern of gambling behaviour in which an individual has difficulty controlling how much they gamble and experiences negative consequences (harms) as a result of their gambling. A person can vary in their level of risk of problem gambling based on the degree to which they are experiencing negative consequences from their gambling. Someone who gambles recreationally and on occasion might experience little to no negative consequences and is said to be at low or no risk of problem gambling. In contrast, someone who gambles regularly, spending large amounts of time and money relative to their personal situation, might experience severe negative consequences and have trouble controlling their gambling. This person is said to be engaging in problem gambling. Problem gambling can also occur when a person's gambling patterns result in harms being experienced by another person (such as a family member).
>
> *Gambling disorder* is a formal diagnosis under international classification systems for psychiatric disorders published by the American Psychiatric Association and World Health Organization. The diagnosis is applied by a registered clinician, such as a psychologist or medical doctor, based on a person meeting specific diagnostic criteria. The defining features of gambling disorder involve the person feeling unable to reduce or stop gambling despite trying to do so and experiencing severe negative consequences (harms) as a result of their gambling. A person experiencing gambling disorder becomes so focused on gambling that it takes priority over other activities and interests in their daily life. Even though the person experiences negative consequences from gambling, they typically keep gambling at the same rate or with even greater intensity, resulting in a downward spiral. Gambling disorder denotes a more severe pattern of hazardous gambling and is a narrower term than problem gambling.

How Do Gambling Problems Develop?

Gambling involves an interaction between a person and a gambling product within a broader environmental context. The person's individual characteristics, the product's core features, and the broader environment in which they interact all play a role in the development and maintenance of gambling problems [1, 5].

A range of biological, psychological, and sociodemographic factors can increase a person's risk of experiencing problems with gambling. Differences in functioning of several brain regions and neurotransmitter systems have been linked with the risky behaviours characteristic of problem gambling. People experiencing problem gambling are frequently affected by multiple psychiatric conditions with an estimated 58% affected by substance use disorders, 38% by mood disorders, and 37% by anxiety disorders [6]. Although more longitudinal evidence is needed, comorbid mental health problems are thought to be both a potential cause and consequence of problem gambling. In other words, pre-existing mental health problems may contribute to someone's likelihood of developing a gambling problem, and problem gambling may exacerbate existing mental health problems or play a crucial role in causing new psychiatric disorders.

Sociodemographic risk factors for problem gambling generally include being of male gender, non-white ethnicity, lower educational attainment, and lower socioeconomic status. However, risk factors vary based on the main type of gambling activity a person is engaged in. For example, problems related to sports betting are more prevalent among young men, whereas problems related to slot machines tend to occur among older women, often engaging in gambling as a way to cope with psychological distress.

On the product side, gambling activities are designed in specific and intentional ways that frame our decisions about how we engage with them [7]. Slot machines and casino games, for example, employ persuasive design features that play on biases in the way we think. One of these biases is commonly referred to as the gambler's fallacy. After a series of losses, it is common for people to believe they are 'due for a win'. This thinking is flawed because every time the lever on the slot machine is pulled or the button is pressed, the outcome is determined completely at random. Whether the previous game resulted in a win or loss has absolutely no influence on the outcome of the subsequent game. Outcomes of recent games are often displayed at roulette tables in casinos despite this information being irrelevant to the outcome of future events. Structural features of gambling products can distort a person's understanding of their chances of winning and strengthen irrational thoughts about gambling, which are a central feature of problem gambling.

Finally, the broader environment in which the person and the gambling product interact plays an important role in the development of gambling problems. Environmental factors extend beyond situational characteristics related to the gambling website or venue in which a person gambles to the broader sociocultural, political, and regulatory context. Problem gambling and gambling-related harm are more prevalent in geographical areas where gambling is more accessible and available. Family and peer networks have a powerful role in shaping young people's attitudes towards gambling and their perceptions about what is normal, as do advertising and marketing of gambling in traditional and social media. Prevention of gambling-related harm focuses on addressing these environmental factors through a combination of strategies, including the provision of consumer protection tools, education and awareness programmes, and the design of more effective legislation and regulation [1, 8]. In the next sections, we look more closely at the role of social media in exposing people to gambling and consider what needs to be done to reduce risk of harm.

The Role of Social Media in Gambling

Gambling-related content is prevalent on social media, particularly through advertising and promotion of gambling and gambling-like products, including games. Recent research using big data analytics found that more than 41,000 children in the UK follow gambling-related accounts on Twitter [9]. Young people and those already experiencing gambling problems are especially vulnerable to promotion of gambling on social media. Exposure to and engagement with gambling-related content can influence people's attitudes towards and perceptions of gambling, the way that they gamble, and their risk of developing a gambling problem and experiencing gambling-related harms [10].

Marketing and Advertising of Gambling on Social Media

Social media are one of the main channels through which gambling operators engage and communicate with potential and existing customers. As consumer activity has increasingly moved online, gambling operators (like many other businesses) have shifted the focus of their marketing activities from traditional media to online channels, including social media. For example, UK gambling operators spent an estimated total of £1.5 billion on marketing between 2014 and 2017, and nearly half of this amount was spent targeting consumers online (five times more than was spent on television) [11]. Operators tripled the amount spent reaching consumers through social media during the same period.

Research shows that gambling operators use a range of marketing strategies to engage with their customers on social media, including paid advertising (such as banner advertisements), posting content and communicating directly with customers via corporate social media accounts, and endorsements from influential third parties, such as celebrities [12–14]. Marketing strategies may be leveraged to elicit a relatively immediate response from the customer, such as by using limited-time promotional offers that directly link customers through to the operator's website to place bets. More fundamentally, strategic marketing (from an operator perspective) is intended to influence consumer behaviour over the longer term, for example, by enhancing consumer awareness of the operator's brand. The gambling industry's marketing practices may influence people's attitudes and perceptions of gambling over time, potentially indirectly influencing their propensity to gamble in the long term.

The interactive nature of social media enables gambling operators to engage in marketing in fundamentally different ways to traditional media. Whereas traditional media provide a one-way channel of communication for businesses to broadcast advertising messages to potential customers, social media facilitate a two-way communication between businesses and their customers. Gambling operators use corporate social media accounts to post content that users can interact with through liking, commenting, or sharing functions on the platform. Humour, memes, and celebrity endorsement are frequently employed to frame gambling as a fun activity and to enhance the shareability of posts. Operators often seek to engage users in topical discussions about gambling-related events (most commonly related to sport), such as by using polling functionality or hashtags to promote their content within trending topics. Much of the content posted by operators through their corporate accounts is generated with the intention to build brand awareness and appeal rather than to advertise specific promotional offers.

> **Two Key Features That Distinguish Gambling Marketing on Social Media from Traditional Media**
>
> **Delivering Gambling Advertisements in a Highly Targeted Manner:** Social media companies possess troves of data on users' demographic characteristics and browsing history that allow them to offer advertising that is highly targeted to an individual's predicted interests [14]. This enables gambling operators to deliver paid advertisements to potential customers who, based on their predicted interests, are more likely to interact with the advertisement (and ultimately, more likely to spend money gambling on their websites). Consumer advocacy groups have raised concerns about the potential for unethical use of targeted advertising towards vulnerable groups, such as minors and people who are already experiencing problems with gambling. The increasingly personalized nature of gambling advertisements creates challenges for researchers investigating gambling marketing practices as individual users may be delivered different advertisements [13]. Sharing of industry data (such as click-through conversions from specific advertisements coupled with player behavioural data) may facilitate a better understanding of the links between gambling marketing, gambling behaviour, and harm.
>
> **Marketing of Gambling through User-Generated Content:** Social media platforms have created new avenues for gambling operators to promote their products within content posted by third parties, such as influencers and tipsters [14]. This practice, known as affiliate marketing, blurs the distinction between paid advertising and user-generated content, meaning it may not be clear to consumers that the content posted has been intentionally placed and sponsored by a gambling operator. Individuals are more likely to follow and interact with content posted by influencers on social media in comparison to posts made through a gambling operator's corporate social media account, so advertisers typically adopt different communication strategies for different channels. An analysis of Twitter posts in 2019 found that affiliates of British gambling operators tended to be much more direct in promoting specific bets than the operators themselves [15]. In contrast, gambling operators adopted a brand awareness strategy through their corporate social media accounts, typically sharing posts incorporating humorous content and sports news. Another study found that more than two-thirds of tweets made by British tipsters and bookmakers were not compliant with gambling advertising regulations [9].

Simulated Gambling Games on Social Media

Social casino games are free-to-play online games that involve simulated gambling or gambling-related themes [16]. Since their emergence around 2012, social casino games have transitioned from being browser-based games played mainly on Facebook to stand-alone mobile apps. These games simulate gambling activities (such as slots, casino games, and poker) and are free to play (as players are given free chips or credits to start); however, players can choose to purchase additional credits to continue playing beyond their free allocation. Credits have no real-world value and cannot be redeemed for currency, but some games are linked with reward programmes that offer real-world opportunities. Social casino games are often owned by parent companies that also offer real-world monetary gambling; however, social casino games are not always linked to these products. As a result, social casino games have been examined by gambling regulators in some jurisdictions. In numerous court cases (primarily in the USA), it has been alleged that these games offer real-money gambling; however, the legal outcomes of these cases have been mixed.

One of the main concerns about social casino games is that access to the games is typically unrestricted. This means that children and adolescents, as well as those vulnerable to experiencing gambling harms, may be exposed to gambling themes and gambling-related products, potentially encouraging a transition to real-money gambling (a gateway effect). Given the lack of restrictions on advertising of social casino games, advertisements often include offers of 'bonus' credits and are targeted towards young people and those with predicted interests in gambling. From a psychological perspective, playing social casino games is very similar to gambling. Games are visually and mechanically akin to online gambling and include similar elements of risk and reinforcement (the 'highs' and 'lows' of winning and losing). Social casino games may have vastly different payout rates to gambling, and the positive experience of winning might cause players to believe that they are more likely to win if they were playing real-money gambling games (a behavioural modification effect). Research suggests some players use social casino games as a way to 'practise' their gambling skills. There are also concerns that the structural, visual, and auditory similarities between social casino games and gambling may increase urges to gamble in individuals vulnerable to experiencing gambling problems, and that the games themselves may result in harms if individuals spend excessive time or money engaging with them.

Social casino games, like social media more broadly, are highly dynamic and research on their impacts is still emerging. A review concluded that it is not yet clear whether or how exposure to simulated gambling during youth is related to increased risk of experiencing problems with real-money gambling later in life [17]. Whether engagement leads to later experience of gambling problems likely depends on a range of individual-level factors (for example, whether the person experiences peer pressure to gamble), as well as the structural features of the simulated gambling games played (for example, whether they involve misleading payout rates that inflate a person's confidence about their chances of winning in real-money gambling). Some stakeholders have hypothesized that social casino games could have a positive impact by allowing people to engage in simulated gambling at much lower costs than actual gambling, or that they could be a way to manage urges to gamble without actually gambling [16, 17]. As such, social casino games remain an important area of consideration in terms of the relationship between social media, gambling, and gambling problems.

Gambling-Related User Engagement Mechanisms on Social Media

Social media platforms have been popularly likened to slot machines in their ability to keep people 'hooked'. Indeed, both social media platforms and slot machines are designed using fundamental psychological principles from reinforcement learning, such as providing users with unpredictable rewards to motivate continued engagement. Many of these engagement mechanisms are subtle and have relatively little to do with gambling aside from broader similarities with reward-seeking behaviour. However, there is evidence that some social media platforms incorporate engagement mechanisms that bear a much closer resemblance to gambling (although usually not meeting strict legal definitions of gambling). This reflects a broader trend towards the incorporation of elements of gambling in strategies used to generate revenue in online environments, such as by the video gaming industry [18]. Gambling-related engagement mechanisms are of particular relevance here as users may be exposed to gambling-related content and activities in situations that might otherwise be completely unrelated to gambling.

For example, chance-based elements and gambling-related themes are found in strategies used by streamers to engage their fans on Twitch, one of the world's leading live-streaming platforms [19]. The top streamers attract very large audiences and can use these strategies to generate revenue from the content they broadcast. Viewers can wager virtual currency to take part in minigames offered by streamers that closely resemble elements of gambling activities like lotteries, roulette, slots, and parimutuel betting. To make a wager, the viewer typically has to type a command into the chat. Commands needed to play these minigames often make clear references to gambling (such as !gamble, !bet, !bingo, !roulette, !slot). Streamers set the probability of winning rewards, which often take the form of loyalty points or social recognition (for example displaying the donor's username on a leader board).

Similar to social casino games, gambling-related engagement mechanisms on social media platforms are not regulated as gambling activities, meaning no specific consumer protections are in place. Little research has investigated the scope or impacts of gambling-related engagement mechanisms on social media as these types of features have only recently begun to emerge. Given the success of gambling-related monetization strategies in contributing to growth of other industries operating in the online environment (such as the gaming industry), it seems likely that this trend will continue in various forms. It remains unclear how exposure to and engagement with these mechanisms might have downstream impacts on people's propensity to engage in real-money gambling and their risk of experiencing harm.

Gambling-Related Communities on Social Media

The final aspect we consider in this section relates to the use of social media platforms to facilitate connections and interaction among gamblers. These communities tend to function either as discussion forums for people interested in gambling as a recreational activity, or as peer support forums for people affected by gambling-related harm [12, 20].

People with shared interests in gambling may gather on social media to discuss their experiences with gambling, as well as to share tips and 'strategies' for how to win. Discussions in these forums generally reflect positive attitudes towards gambling rather than problems associated with gambling. Participation in this type of online community is especially common among young men and has been linked with greater likelihood of experiencing gambling problems (although there is some evidence to the contrary for forums specifically related to online poker). Online forums may be important to recreational gamblers as part of their shared social identity; however, participating in them is thought to play a role in reinforcing irrational beliefs about gambling and normalizing risky gambling behaviours.

Peer support forums, on the other hand, provide an important support for people affected by gambling harm (both gamblers and their friends and family). Discussions in these groups usually focus on stories of emotional and financial harms experienced as a result of excessive gambling, as well as strategies and resources to aid recovery. Forums can provide a sense of identity and community that helps people to cope amidst the feelings of loneliness, guilt, and shame commonly experienced by those affected by gambling harm. The anonymity offered by online forums may facilitate open sharing of personal experiences. However, many forums are not moderated by qualified treatment professionals, which means that their helpfulness is likely dependent on the accuracy of information shared between users. Overall, the efficacy of online peer support forums for long-term recovery from gambling problems remains unclear.

What Is the Place of Social Media in Gambling Harm Reduction?

Gambling harm occurs within a complex system of interactions, both within the individual (for example biological and psychological factors that drive someone to gamble) and between individuals and their environment (including social interactions with other people and institutions, including gambling companies and regulators) [8]. In this environment, lessons can be learned from public health. At their best, public health strategies look at entire ecosystems in which harms are generated with a view to regulating systemic factors, including the social determinants of gambling harm.

Historically, strategies to address problem gambling have focused on treating individuals already experiencing problems, largely failing to recognize and address the systemic forces that drive gambling harm. Treatment interventions, such as psychotherapy, are crucial for helping individuals experiencing problems with gambling to change their behaviour; however, these interventions have relatively little value for preventing harm from occurring in the first place [21]. Greater focus is needed on designing policy and regulation that are effective in addressing the systemic factors that contribute to gambling harm, including promotion of gambling on social media and utilization of these platforms to reduce harm.

Multiple stakeholder groups are involved in the gambling ecosystem, including individuals engaging in gambling (who may be experiencing varying degrees of harm), their family and friends (who may also be affected), the broader community, treatment and welfare providers, researchers, industry organizations that profit from gambling (either directly or indirectly), and government bodies [22]. These stakeholder groups have various roles to play in reducing gambling harm and have unequal capacities to effect change. Some groups, such as government and industry stakeholders, have much greater power and resources available to shape the environment in which harm occurs [8]. Online gambling operators, for example, shape the environment by investing vast sums of money marketing their products on social media to attract customers to spend money on their websites. Some individuals, such as those already experiencing gambling problems, may be particularly vulnerable to content encouraging continued gambling. In many jurisdictions, existing advertising codes are outdated and largely ill-equipped to deal with novel strategies used by social media marketers, such as the use of data analytics to deliver highly targeted advertisements, which were not possible in traditional media [14]. Governments and regulators need to review advertising codes in light of emerging marketing practices, adopting a precautionary approach as needed to minimize risk of harm.

In addition to gambling companies themselves, ancillary organizations that facilitate gambling are increasingly recognized as stakeholders in the system. As such, they too attract a share of responsibility for harms and can play a strategic role in gambling harm reduction. For example, financial services firms facilitate payments between a gambler and a gambling operator. As an example of harm reduction strategy, financial services firms can give individuals the ability to set spending controls at the bank level (rather than with each gambling operator). This means spending limits are in place closer to the source of funds and are effective across the various gambling websites used by an individual.

Social media platforms are another type of ancillary organization that function primarily as a means for gambling operators to promote their products to consumers. Some platforms have introduced restrictions on gambling content, such as limiting the delivery of gambling advertisements to users over the minimum legal age. However, many age verification systems can be easily circumvented. Stronger government regulation and enforcement are clearly needed to restrict promotion of gambling on social media, especially given the potential impacts on vulnerable groups. For example, in Spain, rules introduced in 2020 mean gambling operators are only allowed to advertise on YouTube between the hours of 1am and 5am, can only share advertisements with followers of their social media channels, and are required to use age-gating technology to minimize exposure of minors to gambling-related content.

Greater awareness is needed among social media companies and the advertising industry about their role in shaping the environment in which gambling harms occur. As regulatory change is typically a lengthy process, stakeholders can take proactive steps towards harm reduction, for example, by preventing gambling advertisements from being targeted to vulnerable users.

> **Five Recommendations to Reduce the Risk of Social Media Contributing to Gambling Harm**
>
> 1. Regulations must be updated to be fit for purpose in an era when gambling advertising and marketing increasingly occur through social media instead of traditional media. Regulations should attribute responsibility not only to the advertisers (for example gambling operators and affiliates), but to the social media platforms that trade advertising space and develop the digital technologies used to deliver advertisements in highly targeted ways [14]. Greater transparency requirements are needed to ensure marketing of gambling through user-generated content can be clearly identified by consumers as advertising [9].
> 2. Strict enforcement is needed to ensure compliance with regulatory standards. The recent finding that more than two-thirds of gambling-related tweets made by British affiliates are non-compliant suggests current enforcement action is inadequate [9].
> 3. Social media platforms and advertising industry stakeholders should utilize their strong digital capabilities and advertising technologies to minimize delivery of gambling-related content to social media profiles predicted to belong to vulnerable individuals, such as minors or individuals accessing content related to help-seeking for gambling problems [11].
> 4. A precautionary approach should be adopted when insufficient evidence exists to guide policy decisions. This approach is especially relevant in cases where gambling-related activities or features (including social casino games and gambling-related user engagement mechanisms) do not meet legal definitions of gambling, yet they reasonably resemble elements of gambling and it seems plausible that they may contribute to harm.
> 5. Gambling marketers should share data with researchers to reduce reliance on self-report measures of behaviour and to facilitate a better understanding of the causal relations between gambling marketing, gambling behaviour, and harm. This is important in the digital environment where marketers can deliver targeted offers and advertisements to consumers based on their individual user profiles as these specific interactions are otherwise challenging to study.

Conclusion
- Gambling-related content is prevalent on social media in a variety of forms, including paid advertising, endorsements and product placement in posts made by influential third parties, simulated gambling games, gambling-themed engagement features, and discussion forums.
- Exposure to content promoting gambling can influence a person's attitudes towards gambling and their perceptions of what is normal. This could increase their risk of experiencing problems with gambling, but more research is needed to confirm this relationship.
- Social media have an important role in shaping the environment in which gambling harm occurs. To protect people from harm, regulators need to ensure standards are fit for purpose in the rapidly changing technological environment.

Further Reading
GambleAware UK provides guidance on ways consumers can limit gambling ads on social media: www.begambleaware.org/limiting-gambling-ads-online

Gainsbury, S.M., et al. Reducing Internet gambling harms using behavioral science: A stakeholder framework. *Front Psychiatry*, 2020. **11**: p. 598589.

Chapter 11

Social Media, Self-Harm, and Suicide

Cathy Brennan and Allan House

In this chapter we review the research evidence on the relationship between social media use and self-harm. There is much discussion about the possible role of social media in rising rates of self-harm, seen especially in young girls, a discussion that is accompanied by a worry that there may be an associated increased risk of death by suicide. It is beyond the scope of this chapter to go into detail about current understanding of why some people self-harm and some die by suicide – suffice to say that reasons for both are complex and multifactorial. Here we focus specifically on what we know about any potential role of social media and discuss possible mechanisms of action towards harm or benefit in relation to self-harm content.

Defining Self-Harm

The World Health Organization defines self-harm as 'an act with non-fatal outcome, in which an individual deliberately initiates a non-habitual behaviour that, without intervention from others, will cause self-harm, or deliberately ingests a substance in excess of the prescribed or generally recognised therapeutic dosage, and which is aimed at realising changes which the subject desired via the actual or expected physical consequences'.

In the UK, the National Institute for Health and Care Excellence (NICE) has simplified this to define self-harm as an act that is intentional and involves 'self-poisoning or self-injury, irrespective of the apparent purpose of the act'.

Within professional discourse a number of subdefinitions of self-harm exist. They tend to make distinctions based on method of harm (for example, distinguishing self-injury from self-poisoning), its potential lethality, its frequency (one-off crisis response or repeated), and any perceived intent to end one's life associated with the act.

In relation to intention, we have chosen to use the term self-harm in this chapter in line with the NICE definition, to encompass all acts irrespective of purpose. Self-harm thus refers to acts that include an intent to die and acts without such intent, as well as acts where any intent is unclear. We use this definition for a number of related reasons. First, it is not always possible to attribute intent to an act of self-harm. This is especially so on social media where you may have to infer intention of a described act from the nature of the content or associated hashtags. But it is also often difficult for the person who has harmed themselves to attribute intent to an act; many people when questioned after an episode can be ambivalent about the presence or not of suicidal intent. Second, whilst it may be possible to attribute intent to a particular *act* of self-harm, at the level of the *person* distinctions between suicidal behaviours and non-suicidal self-harm are often less clear. For example, self-harm even when not explicitly identified as attempted suicide is often accompanied by suicidal thinking. Third, there is a common underlying aspect to any act of self-harm which is about expression of distress, regardless of whether the act is accompanied by a wish to die.

What are excluded from these definitions, although common in non-specialist discussions, are other actions that are sometimes described as self-harm because they may result in physical harm, but which are not undertaken with that primary purpose. Such actions include deliberate starvation or binge eating (as in eating disorders), excessive alcohol consumption or use of recreational drugs, and reckless risk-taking.

The Reality of Self-Harm

Estimates of the prevalence of self-harm vary depending both on the context of the population under study and from where and how the estimates are obtained. For example, studies that use attendance at emergency departments as cases tend to be lower than those that use community samples as not everyone will attend an emergency department or indeed seek any professional support following an episode of self-harm. Notwithstanding the context of the data, self-harm is a major, global health concern with even lower estimates of life-time prevalence (the proportion of the population who have self-harmed at some time in their lifetime) of around 6% of a population and higher estimates at about 18% of a population [1]. Rates of self-harm are generally higher in females compared to males across all ages, but this difference is most marked in those under 24 years [2]. In recent years there has been a notable upwards trend in the rates of non-fatal self-harm, particularly in young teenage girls [3].

Across Europe and in the USA self-poisoning is by far the most common method of self-harm in those accessing services, accounting for about 80% of reported episodes. Self-injury (predominately cutting) is the next most common method [2, 4]. In community surveys the relative proportions are reversed, with self-injury predominating especially in younger people. It is important here to make two important points about method of self-harm. The first is that it is wrong to assume that any individual will use only one method if they repeatedly self-harm – only cutting or only taking drug overdoses, for example. In fact switching methods between episodes is common, and even doing both at the same time is not rare [5]. The second point is that method of self-harm should not be taken to indicate the degree of suicidal intent or suicide risk. There is a tendency, particularly in the US, to use the diagnostic term *non-suicidal self-injury* (NSSI). We discussed the difficulty of attributing intent to acts and the person to some extent earlier and here add the observation that lifetime suicide risk is actually greater in those who have a history of what is often labelled NSSI.

The Relation between Self-Harm and Suicide

Suicide is one of the leading causes of death worldwide with over one in every 100 deaths the result of suicide [6]. Most deaths by suicide occur in low- and middle-income countries; however, the highest age-standardized rate (accounting for population size and age structure) is in high-income countries, where the rate in 2019 was 10.9 deaths per 100,000 people. In contrast to non-fatal self-harm, rates of suicide are consistently highest in males, who are about three times as likely to die by suicide as females.

Self-harm, even without the presence of suicidal thinking, remains the biggest risk factor for subsequent death by suicide; for example, the risk of death by suicide in the year following hospital attendance for an episode of self-harm is over 40 times the risk of suicide in the general population [7]. It is tempting therefore to think of a continuum of 'suicidality' from thoughts about suicide to self-harm with some degree of suicidal intent to determined attempts at suicide (attempted suicide) to suicide itself. Each link in this chain is however only weakly tied to the next. For example, thinking about suicide may occur in anything up to 5% of people in any one year, which makes it about 500 times commoner than suicide. The relative risk of suicide after self-harm is high, as noted, but even so the great majority of people who self-harm (95% or more) never go on to take their own lives.

Of course self-harm is worth our attention in its own right as a sign of personal distress, and intervention to prevent it or reduce its frequency is therefore a worthwhile activity regardless of the link to suicide. However, we need to be cautious about drawing conclusions from self-harm research and applying it directly to thinking about suicide. Interventions that reduce the frequency of thoughts of suicide or of non-fatal self-harm may or may not have an effect on suicide.

Self-Harm on Social Media

What Does a Self-Harm Search Find on Social Media?

Self-harm content on social media will often include behaviours excluded from clinical definitions, such as disordered eating or substance misuse. For example, a study we undertook to explore the nature of images tagged as self-harm on three social media sites found that over half the images did not explicitly represent or refer to the act of self-harm although tagged as such. Distress, however, was commonly represented in the content with over a third of the images expressing feelings such as sadness, anger, loneliness, or hopelessness. There was also a noticeable overlap in the imagery between disordered eating and self-harm with many posts tagged as self-harm but documenting extreme thinness [8].

Even when self-harm is the main focus, distinctions between self-harm without suicidal thinking and with suicidal intent are often unclear. A key feature of social media is user-generated content and this rarely conforms to the boundaries set by professional discourse. There is some content that can certainly be placed in a particular category – for example, streaming of live suicides and using groups or platforms to create suicide pacts. However, the nature of much of the content is not so easy to disentangle. Posters will often use a generic tag of self-harm to identify content that is about distress in general and the presence or absence of self-harm or suicidal thinking is not always evident.

Where content on social media does explicitly represent an act of self-harm, this seems to be predominantly referencing self-injury and especially cutting. The impression given on social media of the nature of self-harm is therefore different to that we have from data on hospital attendance where self-poisoning is by far the predominant method of self-harm. It is unclear why this is this case but may be a consequence of the visual nature of much of social media; it is arguably more challenging to produce image-based representations of self-poisoning. It may be that self-injury is something that is talked about more on social media even if it is not the most common method. Some of the content posted is about seeking help with wound care or scar management, for example.

It could also be that those posting content on social media differ significantly from the population who seek professional help following an act of self-harm. We know that population surveys suggest that self-injury is more common in younger people and there is an 'iceberg' effect where many acts will not result in hospital attendance [9].

The Nature of the Content Found on Social Media

Not all content is about distress. In our study on the nature of images, fewer than a third were about negative feelings. Much of the content was offering messages of hope or celebrating recovery. These findings are replicated across other studies exploring the nature of content; common hashtags for self-harm will find content that is diverse in nature and not simply graphic content or that which references anguish. Indeed, many studies find that searches can often identify more helpful content than content that is potentially harmful [10]. None of these studies however can realistically replicate the content that a particular person might experience as this will be influenced by how they curate their own experience, those they are connected to on different platforms, as well as by previous activity.

There is certainly content found on social media that is recognized to be harmful and is likely to contribute to acts of self-harm or maintenance of behaviour. For example, posts that are focused on verbal encouragement of self-harm, posts that include explicit discussion of methods, using social media to organize suicide pacts, and the spreading of challenges or games that include elements of self-harm. There is also much content that, while not explicitly encouraging self-harm, may implicitly encourage it through suggestion that it is linked to particular identities or subcultures or that it is desirable in some way; in our study we found that some of the images incorporated text that implied that self-harm was positive – for example, talking of scars being cute or reflecting on positive feelings after cutting as something to be celebrated [8].

There is other content that is likely to be harmful because of the specific distress it can cause to users. Content of this kind includes baiting, jeering, or active encouragement to proceed in response to expression of thoughts or acts.

Much of the content though is that which is not necessarily harmful in its own right, but its potential impact is dependent on context. Opportunities for mutual support are created through the sharing of stories and feelings via social media. Research exploring the experience of using social media to engage with content about self-harm suggests it can be helpful to read other people's stories as it reduces feelings of isolation and shame. However, it is also the case that it can sometimes be a 'heavy burden' to be immersed in emotive accounts of distress; this can be particularly problematic for those who are feeling at crisis point themselves [11].

Images of self-injury are often thought to be especially harmful content with much focus on the role of so-called graphic depictions of self-injury in triggering urges to self-harm or images of cuts and scars in normalizing self-harm as an accepted response to distress. However, the research suggests that it is not necessarily the nature of the visual content itself that is harmful but the context in which it is being posted and viewed [10]. For example (as noted in Chapter 5), there is not one clear definition of what is meant by graphic imagery; images of deep wounds and fresh blood are generally classified as graphic, although some studies suggest that any images even of healed scars, or images of paraphernalia that are intended to be used in self-injury, should be classified as such.

Some social media platforms have instigated content bans on such content. However, research exploring the use of images suggests a much more nuanced picture: images of fresh wounds can be used in posts seeking immediate help or advice on wound care; many pictures of healed cuts and scars are associated with posts documenting recovery and hope; and some people have reported using imagery of self-injury as a way to resist their own urges to self-harm [10, 11].

Who Might See Self-Harm Content on Social Media?

One of the challenges of understanding the who and why of social media is that it is difficult to establish with any certainty the characteristics of those posting and interacting with content. Nonetheless we can draw some general conclusions.

It is likely that much of the user-generated content on self-harm is posted by people who are *thinking about self-harm or have self-harmed recently or in the past*. These groups are also actively interacting with content – responding to posts, engaging in conversations, and making connections. A further group of users are those who may be *feeling distressed and isolated but have not had thoughts of self-harm*. There is a lot of overlap between the content that is about distress and that which is explicitly about self-harm; posts will often have multiple labels or tags that reference general mental health difficulties as well as self-harm. It is likely that young people in distress will be exposed to content about self-harm although may not be actively looking for that specific type of content, particularly given the use of curation algorithms that suggest similar content to users [12].

What we don't know much about is the nature and extent of *incidental, or unintended, exposure* to self-harm content on social media in those who are not actively searching for content or browsing general mental health content. A survey on exposure to self-harm content on Instagram among 1,262 young adults in the USA found that 18% had seen content but only once and 25% had seen content more than once. Of those who had seen content, only 20% reported actively searching for content [13]. So, in this study about a third of respondents had been exposed to content through Instagram without any intention on their part and over half reported feeling emotionally disturbed by this content. The authors labelled this accidental exposure, although it is likely that most of this exposure was from content posted by friends or connections. People may be unsure how best to respond to content of this kind from those they are connected to. In Chapter 12 the authors outline guidelines that equip young people to communicate safely online; this includes how to respond to friends who may be thinking about harming themselves.

The Experience of Self-Harm Content on Social Media

Most research on understanding the impact of self-harm content on social media focuses on active users and suggests that social media can provide an opportunity for expression of feelings and for many are considered safe spaces for voicing worries about distressing feelings or thoughts of self-harm. What is valued is a non-judgemental space and one that is easily accessible in times of crisis. Using social media can reduce feelings of isolation, help manage urges to harm, and be a forum for help-seeking [10]. It is not necessarily that social media displace other forms of help seeking; only a minority seek professional help following an episode of self-harm and many people are not in contact with services. Some report turning to social media after negative reactions from friends or family to initial disclosures. However, many people who self-harm have never talked about it with anyone and social media can often be the first, and for some the only, forum for self-disclosure [11]. So, used in this way social media can be an important place for conversations about self-harm that may not happen elsewhere.

This is not to say that accessing social media is always a positive experience for those who are actively using them to engage with self-harm content. Some report that the experience can exacerbate their feelings or entrench their own self-harm; they report using images posted on social media as part of their own rituals, or being triggered to harm themselves by witnessing the distress of others. Some users report that connecting with others for support may sometimes lead to more extreme acts of self-harm as they feel they need to compete to show they need support [10, 11].

The expectation that you reach out and get a supportive response may lead to disappointment for some. It is difficult to control the reactions of others to social media posts and responses such as baiting or jeering to expressions of distress can make a poster feel even more isolated. The experience of posting feelings and getting no response may also be distressing and lead to further feelings of isolation and alienation.

How Do Social Media Cause Harms and Benefits?

There is, as yet, no reliable evidence to tell us to what extent, if any, incidental exposure to self-harm content on social media is a stimulus to initiate self-harm in those who have previously had no thoughts or are not experiencing poor mental health. Interviews with people who have actively accessed content on social media suggest that they tend to go online to find information about, or make sense of, existing thoughts [11]. However, with the ubiquity of social media in everyday life and the overlap of content with that of general mood disorders, exposure to content about self-harm is likely for many people, especially if they are seeking connections because of low mood or other mental health difficulties.

Some Mechanisms of Harm

For most content it is not always possible to attribute harm arising from the content itself but it may be harmful to some depending on the context in which it is accessed [10]. However, some mechanisms of harm are easy to understand and recognize. They are recognizable in the overt or explicit harmful content of posts:

- explicit verbal encouragement to act or to escalate severity of actions (including that found in 'games' or challenges);
- online self-harm or suicide pacts;
- circulation of manifestly disturbing content (such as live streams);
- offering detail of methods; and
- trolling or abusing posters who are expressing personal distress.

Less clearcut is content where the effect may be less well established or may depend very much on context – an ambiguity that arises because posts do not contain the explicit messages outlined above but may carry similar implicit messages. We include:

- the likelihood of copycat behaviour, sometimes called spreading by contagion;
- the role of posts (texts or images) about self-harm in normalizing or glamourizing – that is, presenting self-harm as a natural or desirable, even chic, response to circumstances; and

- the role of images in reawakening impulses to self-harm, sometimes referred to as triggering with the assumption that such impulses are already there but somehow suppressed or inhibited until a new image is presented.

More indirectly, social media posts about self-harm and related emotional problems may induce a lowering of mood, especially when exposure is prolonged and repeated – immersing the viewer to the exclusion of other social cues. It is this *mood induction* mechanism that lies behind the effect of certain types of social media experience on depression (see Chapter 8).

Some Mechanisms of Benefit

Responses from those who self-harm can tell us of a number of benefits from accessing self-harm content on social media:

- using forums to talk as a means of clarifying and sharing a personal story in a non-judgmental environment; this provides a sense of relief and reduces stigma;
- exploring and defining an identity;
- seeking and offering practical advice; online access to good quality advice and support is important given that self-harm and suicidal thinking are often difficult to talk about directly;
- vicarious experience online may reduce direct personal urges to harm; and
- receiving emotional support and recovery messages from people who have (or at least are perceived to have) the same experiences.

Harm or Benefit? A Difficult Judgement

Psychologist Thomas Joiner has proposed three crucial risks for suicide – thwarted belongingness, perceived burdensomeness, and acquired capability. These risks, or protection from them, can be seen as reflected in three aspects of social media – a way of thinking that emphasizes the ambiguous nature of the exposure:

- In terms of belongingness the 'social' in social media can mean more connectedness and support, but more exposure to unhealthy content and contagion, less real-world social support.
- The 'emotional' side of social media can increase or reduce a sense of burdensomeness, generating a greater sense of acceptance or exposing the user to bullying and ridicule.
- The 'attitude or knowledge' side of social media can influence the individual's capability – giving a stronger sense of personal control and useful information but risking the introduction to methods to do more harm, which may be normalized or glamourized.

Can We Minimize the Harms in Social Media While Maximizing Their Benefits?

It is in understanding the uncertainties and ambiguities around the question of the effects of social media that we can respond to the challenges posed by self-harm content. It is not in content or person or place alone that the effects reside but the interplay between them. Even so, there are certain interventions that are surely desirable and ought to be the focus of immediate action, needing no further debate.

In the *management of harmful content* the most obvious need is to restrict or suppress entirely the content we have already described as explicitly harmful. However, in managing this explicitly harmful content, care needs to be taken to ensure that we don't restrict content that is likely to be helpful for many as this could lead to increasing stigmatization of self-harm and increasing feelings of shame and low worth in those posting content. Where content is suppressed due to established risk of harm then thought needs to be given to those who have posted the content initially. Many will not be posting content to intentionally cause harm and blocking of content from those already in distress without thought to how this may be perceived can be harmful.

In the *management of process* there needs to be immediate modification of algorithms that push self-harm content to users, even those who have started their own contact in a search for self-harm or suicide content. Helpful modifications could be to restrict, or remind users to limit, the amount of time spent viewing self-harm content, both in a single session and on repeated visits.

Explicitly *helpful content* should be made more readily available, whether searched for or not. However, care needs to be taken when promoting resources. It is the user-generated nature of social media that is one of its most valued characteristics, and much officially generated material can be seen as uninteresting, impersonal, or even unhelpful, especially to younger people [14]. Examples of the types of resource being generated to tackle this problem are reviewed in Chapter 14.

Education and support for social media users should also be aimed at *empowering people* to manage their own experience safely. This means talking to young people about how to navigate content safely and how to respond to content that they find disturbing.

Other interventions are less clearcut – there is a balance to be achieved in restricting exposure to what might be harmful for some people without blocking access to what others might find helpful.

Two recent policy suggestions have emerged in the UK. Following a recent high-profile inquest into the death of teenager Molly Russell, who had accessed a great deal of online material about self-harm, depression, and suicide before taking her own life, the coroner issued a prevention of future deaths report, in which he said:

> I recommend that consideration is given by the Government to reviewing the provision of internet platforms to children, with reference to harmful on-line content, separate platforms for adults and children, verification of age before joining the platform, provision of age specific content, the use of algorithms to provide content, the use of advertising and parental guardian or carer control including access to material viewed by a child, and retention of material viewed by a child.[1]

Multiple charities with an interest in the mental well-being of young people wrote a letter to the then prime minister in October, in which they attempted to unpack the idea of harmfulness in a constructive way:[2]

---

[1] 'Regulation 28 Report to Prevent Future Deaths', 2022-0315, HM Coroner Mr Andrew Walker, 13 October 2022. www.judiciary.uk/wp-content/uploads/2022/10/Molly-Russell-Prevention-of-future-deaths-report-2022-0315_Published.pdf (last accessed 26 October 2022).

[2] www.papyrus-uk.org/wp-content/uploads/2022/10/Online-Safety-Bill-Rt-Hon-Elizabeth-Truss-MP.pdf (last accessed 26 October 2022).

We are writing to urge you to ensure that the regulation of harmful suicide and self-harm content is retained within the Online Safety Bill ... [defined as]
- Information, instructions, and advice on methods of self-harm and suicide
- Content that portrays self-harm and suicide as positive or desirable
- Graphic descriptions or depictions of self-harm and suicide.

The first two criteria look as if they ought to be amenable to careful definition, whereas 'graphic' is more problematic. One person's clear and vividly explicit detail is another's matter-of-fact account. Or does it mean any image (depiction) at all, that is not shaded, pixelated, or whatever – descriptions of how to look after or conceal your wounds, for example?

More debate is needed about what principles to use when drawing the line, a debate that would be helped by more rigorous attention to the definition of terms like normalizing, glamourizing, and even encouraging, so that decisions can be more evidence-based.

Conclusion

There are three areas of activity that need to be informed by and changed by our understanding of the double-edged nature of social media for those who self-harm. In clinical practice the task should be easiest: those offering help to people who self-harm need to be comfortable in leading discussions about social media for the individual – both previous experience and approaches to managing future use. In public health intervention the main challenge is to develop and disseminate online resources that are both likely to be useful and likely to be used by their target populations. In the legal and political arenas the challenge is greatest, because debates about regulation take place in in an arena where there are competing commercial and cultural influences. It is in this situation that our lack of clarity about what exactly is harmful or beneficial is most likely to impede successful action.

Further Reading

Brennan, C., et al., Self-harm and suicidal content online, harmful or helpful? A systematic review of the recent evidence. *Journal of Public Mental Health*, 2022. **21**(1): p. 57–69.

House, A., *Understanding and Responding to Self-Harm: The One Stop Guide: Practical Advice for Anybody Affected by Self-Harm*, 2019, London: Profile Books.

Section 3
Social Media as a Resource

So much attention has been directed towards the discussion about harms from social media use that it is easy to forget a simple truth. If social media have the reach and potency to do harm, then by the same token they should be able to do good.

We know that people who are struggling with their mental health are likely to turn to social media – a signal that other resources, including other online resources, are insufficient or unavailable and also that we need to concentrate on how to make social media as useful as we can.

In this final section some of the leaders in this field outline recent initiatives in the area. Contributions from the USA, Canada, and Australia remind us that since social media are global in their coverage, then so can be research and intervention. Embracing the technology and using it to help those who access it is surely likely to be a more productive strategy in the longer term than attempting suppression, and these chapters provide a welcome positive note upon which to finish.

Chapter 12

Safely Navigating the Terrain:
Keeping Young People Safe Online

Jo Robinson, Louise La Sala, and Rikki Battersby-Coulter

Introduction

This book has provided a broad overview of both the challenges and opportunities that social media present when it comes to mental health. This includes consideration of a range of potential harms and benefits across diagnoses, including the provision of (mis) information about different disorders, information about sources of healthcare services, and the role of peer support in the context of online social networking. It has also included discussion relating to some of the specific challenges that social media may present when it comes to communication regarding suicide and self-harm, in particular the issue of 'contagion' and how some types of communication about suicide or self-harm may inadvertently increase risk among other users.

We have also heard a lot about some of the potential levers for creating and maintaining a safe and healthy online environment for users. These include legislative approaches, the responsibilities and capabilities of the platforms themselves, and educational approaches in which users are provided with the information and agency to optimize their online experience, and each of these has a role to play when it comes to improving online safety.

In this chapter we will provide some practical information regarding the ways in which social media platforms can create and maintain safe online spaces when it comes to mental health, and in particular suicide prevention. This will include: 1) a brief overview of *policy approaches and frameworks* adopted in some countries; 2) a discussion of *the role of platforms*, including their own policies, and the provision of tools and resources that can be accessed by users to improve safety; and 3) a case example of how one *educational approach* designed to facilitate safe online communication about suicide was developed, delivered, and evaluated, with a view to considering how this approach might be applied to other topics. Finally, we will argue that the best results are likely to be achieved when all three approaches work together in concert.

National Policy Approaches

Governments around the world are becoming increasingly concerned about the ways in which social media platforms operate. This includes concerns relating to privacy and the use of individual data, as well as the ways their functionality may be detrimental to the mental health of their users, in particular younger users.

Our work primarily focuses on the ways in which social media platforms manage content related to self-harm or suicide, with policymakers often calling for social media companies to take increased responsibility for the content that is shared and distributed across their platforms. This is partly the result of a small number of high-profile suicides that have occurred where it is believed social media may have played a role; for example, in the case of Molly Russell in the United Kingdom [1]. Situations such as these have led to high levels of community pressure on governments to impose greater regulations on the types of content that can be posted and shared on social media platforms. In some countries this has led to specific online safety policies to address these concerns and although these policies vary across countries, the intent remain the same: to develop legislation that attempts to give consumers more control over their data and minimize access or exposure to harmful content.

For example, at the time of writing, the United Kingdom is debating an Online Safety Bill that seeks to regulate social media and technology companies. In its current form, the Online Safety Bill imposes a 'duty of care' on providers of regulated services, with the national communications regulator, the Office of Communications (OFCOM), to issue codes of practice relating to legislated duties. This imposed duty of care works towards protecting users from harmful content, including scams, the sharing of non-consensual sexual images , and the promotion of violence against women and girls, with penalties to be brought against violators by OFCOM. As part of these 'duties of care', technology and social media companies would be mandated to offer identity verification tools to dissuade anonymous 'trolls' and give users the ability to block accounts where the user has not verified their identity. The Online Safety Bill also calls for companies to take 'reasonable steps' towards protecting children's online safety, specifically in relation to cyberbullying and content that encourages self-harm.

Similarly, in the United States of America, two pieces of legislation exist to safeguard against 'toxic' online content. The Children's Online Privacy Protection (COPPA) rule was originally passed in 1998 and was last amended in 2013 to reflect the changing landscape of social media use and misuse. Specifically focused on regulations to protect children under 13 years of age, COPPA introduced compliancy rules regarding the regulation of unfair or deceptive acts or practices with the collection, use, and/or disclosure of personal information from and about children on the Internet. This also included obtaining parental consent before collection, use, or disclosure of personal information from children and parental consent to any material change in the collection, use, or disclosure practices to which the parent had previously consented. COPPA also includes provisions for the right of parents to access content shared online by, or about, their child, the prohibition against conditioning a child's participation in a game, and the confidentiality, security, and integrity of personal information collected from children. Further, and currently being debated, is the Kids Online Safety Act. If passed, this would apply to any app or service that could be used by any young people aged 16 and under. Under this bill, platforms used by young people would have a duty to prevent the promotion of certain harmful behaviours, including suicide and self-harm, eating disorders, and substance abuse. Additionally, it would give parents and users the ability to opt out of potentially problematic algorithmic recommendations and would prevent third parties from viewing the data of minors. Finally, it includes provisions regarding platforms' disclosure policies and advertising system and is written with the intent of providing a safeguard to protect users against problematic content.

Perhaps one of the most recent advancements in online safety policy is the approach taken by Australia. The Online Safety Act is new legislation brought about in 2021 to strengthen the existing laws for online safety. It was established to improve and protect online safety for all Australians by making it an offence to produce and/or distribute: cyberbullying or cyber abuse material; offensive and/or violent content; and non-consensual sexual images. For the first time, a clear set of expectations have been delivered to online providers (including social media companies) making them accountable for the safety of their users and to protect them from online harm. To facilitate the implementation of this legislation, an eSafety Commission was established led by an eSafety Commissioner. This role includes promoting online safety, administering a complaints system for cyberbullying targeted at any Australian individual, administering the online content scheme described by the act, and coordinating activities across Australian government departments and agencies relating to online safety.

The eSafety Commission also developed a Best Practice Framework for Online Safety Education [2] in order to help educate young people about their rights and responsibilities as digital citizens. It was developed using a robust co-design process and a youth advisory council to assist with its implementation has recently been established. The development of the eSafety Commission and the engagement with young people is an important step towards involving young people in the legislation that impacts them. For instance, Australia has positioned its approach towards online safety within the human-centric principles of Safety by Design [3]. These principles articulate clear and actionable approaches to be taken by platforms to ensure the safety of their users and include: 1) service provider responsibility; 2) user empowerment and autonomy; and 3) transparency and accountability, and collectively they underscore the ways in which Australia expects social media companies to operate. This youth-informed vision includes giving young people control of their own online safety and experiences, providing clear guidance that is easy to read, providing users with helpful safety tools and functions, imposing restrictions or sanctions on those who violate those rules, and ensuring that users are not exposed to inappropriate content.

National policies, such as those listed here, are necessary broad-brush approaches towards regulating platforms. Essentially, they serve to protect social media users by providing guidance to platforms on how they should operate safely, and imposing fines or penalties on companies that do not comply. However, because social media platforms transcend geographical boundaries, national policies can be hard to implement, and as such, will only ever be able to go so far in protecting the well-being of their citizens. For this reason, increasing pressure is being placed upon the social media companies to develop and implement their own industry standards and safety frameworks.

Platform-Specific Approaches

As already mentioned, social media have been identified as playing an important role in the distribution of suicide-related information. However, suicide-related information is just one example of harmful content that social media companies are under increasing pressure to remove quickly, with other harmful content including nudity, violence, harassment, false information, hate speech or bullying, and content that encourages acts of terrorism. While there seems to be consensus in relation to many of the topics that can be harmful or distressing, approaches to managing that content are less consistent and are continually evolving as platforms' safety functions become more sophisticated. Further, as new platforms come to market, or functions within existing platforms are created, users are increasingly being offered new ways of creating and curating their online environments. While each platform (very) slightly differs in the safety tools that it offers their users, their main objective is to keep their online communities safe and provide a way for users to escalate, report, and remove content that may be unsafe or distressing. This section looks at some of these safety features embedded within four of the most popular social media platforms used by the young people we work with: Facebook, Instagram, Snapchat, and TikTok.

Safety Advisory Boards

One of the ways social media companies have demonstrated their commitment to online safety is through the establishment of their own safety advisory boards from whom they seek advice on policy, content, and platform moderation. The purpose of these advisory boards is to gather feedback on new policies, tools, and resources designed to keep users safe online and bring together academic and industry leaders in online safety. For example, the Facebook Safety Advisory Board was established in 2009 with independent representatives from leading organizations from around the world, including India, the United Kingdom, the United States of America, Brazil, New Zealand, Europe, and Australia. Board members are called upon for their advice, expertise, and perspectives on a wide range of internet safety issues, including but not limited to mental health and suicide prevention. Snapchat also gathers advice and expertise from a wide range of safety experts as part of its Trust & Safety team, as well as its Trusted Flagger Programme. This programme facilitates the reporting of content that violates its community guidelines. TikTok has what it describes as 'Safety Partners' who provide guidance in relation to fact-checking, media literacy, digital well-being, and family education.

In addition to the safety advisory boards, these companies also have specific subject matter advisory groups who meet regularly to provide more nuanced advice on the specific issue at hand. For example, Facebook has a global Suicide and Self-injury Advisory Group that meets quarterly to provide advice on new policies, content, and safety features. Similarly, TikTok has recently established a Content Advisory Council which provides advice on matters relating to suicide and self-harm via the International Association for Suicide Prevention.

These partnerships also provide the opportunity for social media companies to receive updates on new and emerging evidence regarding online safety and well-being, which (in theory) should better equip them to update their safety policies and functions (see next subsection).

Safety Tools and Functions

Platforms also have several safety tools and functions that provide users some level of control over the type of content that they are exposed to. Across all platforms, these safety tools are offered via in-app reporting (as the user is engaged with the platform and currently online) and provide the option for users to notify the platform of content that they wish to report, remove, or see less of. We now describe some key safety features of each of the platforms.

Facebook and Instagram

Facebook has developed the Facebook Help Centre [4] where users can receive step-by-step instructions on how to control the content they are exposed to and report content that they do not wish to see. For example, they can: 'hide' posts (if they wish to see fewer posts of a particular nature); 'snooze' the page/user for 30 days (if they wish to temporarily stop seeing posts by a particular user); 'hide page/user' (if they wish to stop seeing posts by a particular page/user altogether); and 'report' posts (if they are concerned about the content of a particular post). If a post is reported Facebook asks users to indicate what that post was about, which then informs the platform's response. For example, when reported content relates to suicide or self-harm there is a specific Suicide Prevention Help Centre that helps the user report the content to a trained member of the safety team who will identify the post, the user, and their location (if necessary). If required, Facebook then contacts emergency services to assist the user. Other tools help users manage their accounts, monitor their privacy, safety, and security, and locate the policies relating to Facebook's community standards.

Instagram's approach towards online safety is similar to that of Facebook (unsurprising given they are both owned by Meta). However, arguably, Instagram communicates more overtly with its users about building a 'safe and supportive community'. In contrast to Facebook, the Instagram help centre [5] is also more visual with videos and short tutorials to help educate users about certain safety features. There are also step-by-step guides for dealing with pages versus individual posts. This likely reflects its younger user base and the ways in which they engage with the platform. Although the tools remain the same (i.e. reporting content, unfollowing users, etc.) the differences in the support provided to users largely represent the visual content that is mostly shared via Instagram, in contrast to the text and visual communication offered by Facebook. Given that Instagram is built on the sharing of images, there is also a specific set of safety resources dedicated to dealing with images, including those relating to self-harm and suicide.

In addition to the in-app tools described, both Facebook and Instagram also provide content warnings to their users and blur potentially distressing or harmful images. Meta also provides users with ways of holding themselves accountable when it comes to time spent online and digital well-being. For instance, across its platforms, it allows users to view their daily activity, set daily reminders or time limits, mute push notifications, and, on Instagram, hide their like counts. A recent development from Meta includes the 2022 launch of its Family Centre and Parental Supervision tools on Instagram and Virtual Reality (VR). This centre is designed to offer intuitive supervision tools so that parents and carers can support their young people to stay safe online. The intent is for it to evolve as new technologies enabled by the Metaverse and VR technologies are brought to market.

Snapchat

Snapchat also houses a Safety Centre [6] and a range of resources targeting the user, as well as adult stakeholders, such as parents and educators. Most recently, Snapchat has launched 'Safety Snapshot' – a digital literacy programme aimed at educating users on online safety, privacy, and security. It also has a search tool titled, 'Here for you' which lets users search for specific information relating to mental health, stress, suicidal thoughts, grief, and bullying. Similar to other platforms, users also have access to in-app reporting tools that let them monitor the content that they see. If they would like to escalate or report certain content, users can press and hold on the user or specific 'snap' that they wish to report, and they will be asked to let Snapchat 'know what's going on'.

TikTok

TikTok recently conducted an overhaul of its Safety Centre [7] in response to claims that more than a third of its US-based users were under the age of 14 years. Given that they host some of the youngest social media users, TikTok has developed a series of guides for parents and families to help them better support their young people to keep themselves safe online. When users open the Safety Centre, they are directed to dedicated sections on a range of issues including eating disorders, online challenges, bullying prevention, well-being, suicide, and self-harm. The Safety Centre is split into three main sections: safety controls (providing users with information about keeping their account secure and being aware of their online presence); community controls (helping users define who can interact with their content); and content controls (helping users manage the content that they see in-app). While using TikTok, users can press and hold on a video and select from the options: 'not interested' (notifying TikTok that they wish to see less of this type of content) or 'report', where they are prompted to provide a reason for reporting that content.

As discussed throughout this section, platforms put a lot of effort into keeping their users safe via a number of resources, tools, and functionality. However, as in the case of national policy approaches, platform safety measures can only go so far when it comes to keeping users safe. For example, the reporting functionality will only be effective if young people use it and if the platforms then act on the reports that they receive in an appropriate and timely manner. We also know from our work with young people that they may not always want to use the functionality or resources provided, and sometimes they will actively choose to use platforms that are not moderated as well as those already described, in order to be able to communicate more freely about topics such as suicide and self-injury without fear of being blocked or reported. Appropriately engaging with these functions also requires a certain element of self-regulation and knowledge, which will be influenced by users' age and mental well-being. For these reasons, safety policies and functions offered by the platforms will always be limited. As such, it is also important to educate users so that they have both the knowledge and skills to look after themselves (and each other) online.

Educational Approaches

Educational approaches to online safety involve better educating and equipping users to navigate their online worlds safely. This is important across the spectrum of mental health issues; however, arguably it is critical when communicating about suicide and self-harm where there is significant potential for harm. There is however also the potential for social media to be beneficial, with our own research identifying their capacity to reach large numbers of people quickly at relatively little cost, their acceptability (in particular to young people), and their potential therapeutic value [8–11]. Therefore, it has been important to develop an approach that can capitalize on the benefits that social media offer when it comes to communicating about suicide whilst simultaneously minimizing the risks. One such example is the #chatsafe initiative, described next.

Case Study: The #chatsafe Initiative

The #chatsafe initiative was specifically developed to better equip young people to communicate safely online about suicide [12]. It comprises a set of evidence-informed guidelines, a suite of social media content to help disseminate the guidelines to young people [8], plus a set of resources designed to help the adults in a young person's life (such as resources targeting parents and families, educators, and community agencies). Next we provide a brief description of the #chatsafe initiative and the evidence demonstrating the ways in which it has helped educate young people about online safety.

The #chatsafe Guidelines

The #chatsafe guidelines are the first evidence-informed guidelines in the world specifically designed to help young people communicate safely online about suicide. They were developed using the Delphi expert consensus methodology [12] and include the following sections: 1) Things to consider before posting online about suicide; 2) How to share your own thoughts and feelings safely; 3) Communicating about someone else who is affected by suicide; 4) Responding online to someone who may be suicidal; and 5) Operating memorial pages and closed groups safely. The guidelines are freely available on the #chatsafe website. They have also been translated into 11 languages to better support young people from across the globe. However, because young people are unlikely to read lengthy guidelines, or read detailed information on a static, professionally run website, the guidelines were brought to life via a national social media campaign that was co-designed with young people.

The #chatsafe Social Media Campaign

The development of the #chatsafe social media content has been described in detail elsewhere [9], but in brief the initial suite of content was developed via a series of co-design and co-creation workshops conducted with 134 young people from across Australia. The initial campaign was delivered over a 12-week period via Instagram, Facebook, Snapchat, Tumblr, and YouTube and reached 1.5 million young people [10]. It focused on the different sections of the guidelines and, in addition to content specific to suicide prevention, it also provided advice on the safety functions offered by the different platforms (see earlier in the chapter). Figure 12.1 provides an illustration of some of the #chatsafe content that was created with young people.

Evaluating #chatsafe

Because of its innovative nature and the sensitivities associated with communicating about suicide on social media, it was important to ensure that the #chatsafe social media campaign was safe and acceptable, as well as potentially efficacious, for young people. For this reason, the campaign has been evaluated in two separate studies.

Study 1 (N = 189) targeted young people from across three jurisdictions in Australia [11]. In this study all young people were eligible to participate regardless of the presence of suicidal thoughts or behaviour. In contrast, Study 2 (N = 207) targeted young people who had recently been exposed to a suicide or suicide attempt, and as such, may have been at elevated risk of experiencing suicidal thoughts and feelings themselves. In both studies the primary aim was to determine whether the #chatsafe campaign was able to improve online safety by increasing a young person's confidence and capacity to communicate safely online about suicide, as well as increasing their willingness to intervene if they saw suicide-related content online. Because the intervention was so innovative, and because of the potential for certain types of suicide-related content to inadvertently cause harm, we also assessed safety and acceptability. The findings from the first study have been reported elsewhere [11] (the second study is in preparation at

Figure 12.1 Examples of the #chatsafe social media content

time of writing), but in short, these studies saw increases in participants' willingness to intervene against suicide, and their perceived internet self-efficacy, confidence, and safety when communicating on social media about suicide. These studies also showed that the #chatsafe campaign was both safe and acceptable. Indeed, one young person told us:

> I'm just emailing to say a huge thank you. The work that you have done has truly impacted my life and those of my friends. A couple years ago, we lost a friend to suicide. Participating in this campaign has given me a great sense of closure and I feel that I have taken part in something that is sure to save lives.

Taken together, this suggests that the #chatsafe initiative certainly has the potential to educate and equip young people to communicate more safely online about suicide, and that social media presents a unique opportunity to reach young people with suicide prevention information.

There is often a tension when trying to improve online safety for young people between approaches that advocate for greater parental controls and those that equip young people to have greater autonomy, and the #chatsafe initiative is clearly an example of the latter. However, it stands to reason that the impacts of such an approach will be greater if both young people and the adults in their lives are operating in concert. To date, our adult-facing resources have been downloaded ~200,000 times [13]. When combined with the findings from the research, this suggests that there is a significant need for these types of resources across the community.

A Real-World Approach

#chatsafe is a clear example of an initiative that has been developed by researchers, in partnership with young people, that has significant real-world applicability. In addition to being housed on its own website and rolled out via a series of social media campaigns, the guidelines and associated resources have been embraced by the platforms and they can now be accessed via the Facebook and Instagram Safety Centers, thereby making them accessible to their 1.1 billion+ users globally.

In addition, the #chatsafe campaign is now regularly used as part of a 'real-time response' following the suicide of a young person. It is well established that young people who have been exposed to a suicide in their community or social network are at elevated risk of experiencing suicidal thoughts themselves [14] and certain types of communication about the suicide may increase this risk [15]. Therefore, an intervention that can promote safe communication about the suicide and can be delivered quickly, has the potential to form an important part of a suicide prevention response.

On 15 occasions to date, the #chatsafe team have been notified of a suicide by a local health department or agency. We have then deployed a social media campaign lasting 4–6 weeks targeting both young people and adults across that community. Together these campaigns have reached over 750,000 people for relatively little cost and have been perceived by community stakeholders as an important part of their response to the death.

Co-designing with End Users

There are many possible reasons for the apparent success of the #chatsafe initiative. However, we believe one important reason is that the entire programme of work was fully co-designed with end users. Social media moves quickly and users themselves are the real experts in the ways in which they use their online worlds to manage their own mental health.

UX, or co-design, is common in the technology industry, including in the development of mental health apps, but it is less common in the area of suicide prevention, possibly because of concerns that partnering with young people may cause distress or exacerbate pre-existing suicidal thoughts. However, our previous work suggested that it can be safe to co-design and develop online suicide prevention interventions with young people [16]. Therefore #chatsafe was co-designed with end users from start to finish and not only did this lead to an acceptable, youth-friendly intervention, but the co-design process was also beneficial in and of itself, with participants reporting feeling better able to respond to suicide risk in their friends both on- and offline [8].

#chatsafe also has its limitations. For example, whilst it has had some success and become embedded in both Facebook and Instagram, young people use several platforms including smaller and less visible ones. As such there is room for broadening this work in order to ensure it reaches all the right people across all of the spaces that they communicate in. For instance, gaming platforms or massively multiplayer online games also need to be considered. Similarly, our work to date has focused on older adolescents and young adults, therefore an obvious next step is to examine how initiatives such as #chatsafe could be safely adapted for younger children and adolescents.

We have used #chatsafe as a case example of an educational approach to enhancing online safety when communicating about suicide and whilst this is just one example, there is no reason to assume that a similar educational and partnership approach could not be applied to supporting online safety when it comes to other mental health issues or disorders. It is also important to note that the support of the #chatsafe initiative by Facebook and relevant policymakers was core to the success and reach of the campaign and resources, highlighting the need for policy, platform, and education approaches to work together to provide the best outcomes for all social media users.

Conclusion

This chapter has identified that policymakers, platforms, and end users all have a role to play in creating and maintaining online safety in the sensitive area of mental health and suicide prevention. It also suggests, via the case study provided, that the best effects are likely to be achieved when all three approaches are working in concert. The issues addressed within this chapter, although specific to suicide prevention at times, could be applied to mental health challenges more broadly. The lessons are in the co-design process and partnering with end users and relevant stakeholders to really understand the needs of young people and to create solutions that are age-appropriate and have impact. Such approaches lend themselves to the development of online safety education initiatives much more broadly, but also in addressing other mental health challenges with young people.

Further Reading

#chatsafe website: www.orygen.org.au/chatsafe

#chatsafe guidelines (international translations also available): www.orygen.org.au/chatsafe/Resources/International-guidelines

Chapter 13

Technological Interventions for Adolescent Mental Health

Arjuna Ugarte, Renee Garett, and Sean D. Young

Introduction

The burden that mental illness has on adolescents has become increasingly apparent in recent years. Approximately 1 in 10 people younger than 18 years old have been diagnosed with a mental illness [1], although estimates vary greatly by country and social characteristics. Over the past 30 years, child and adolescent mental health diagnosis has shown an upward trend in symptoms of depression and anxiety throughout the world [2]. While there is currently a lack of research regarding rates of mental illness in lower-income countries, it is evident that mental health struggles are present and problematic in these countries, too. For example, in a report by UNICEF on Jamaican youth, 35% of the 3,471 evaluated students reported suicidal ideation in their lifetime. Of those, 25% reported suicidal ideation in the past year [3].

Medical professionals and academics have worked to identify potential long-term solutions that can quickly reach large numbers of adolescents. One potential solution may be to use technological interventions to help reduce symptoms and provide treatment to adolescents. Technology is already a part of many adolescents' daily lives, with 96% of adolescents in the UK aged 12–17 having access to a cell phone [1]. In the USA, the Common Sense Census reported adolescents spend an average of 7 hours and 22 minutes daily using various technologies [4]. Engaging adolescents through a medium that is comfortable to them and that they can access on their own terms will be an important part of the solution. Technologies such as mobile apps, online/mobile games, texting interventions, online therapy, and health web platforms are being used more as a tool to help assess, treat, and provide support to adolescents struggling with their mental health.

Furthermore, the COVID-19 pandemic has increased the need for remote work in many industries, including in mental health treatment. The way we communicate, educate, work, and live will be impacted in the longer term by the pandemic and the pandemic itself has been a source of the increased mental health burden. During the initial part of the pandemic, schools were suspended in 188 countries and over 90% of enrolled learners (1.5 billion youth) worldwide were out of education [5]. This experience has taken a toll on adolescents emotionally and led to a rise in adolescent mental illness and adolescents seeking mental health services due to the pandemic. Even worse, when schools closed, many students lost access to mental health services they were previously receiving at school [5]. This makes it even more important to discover better methods of providing mental health services that are accessible to all youths.

It is clear that technology has reshaped the way we interact in the world and is fully integrated into our daily lives. Media and technology use among youth aged 8–18 have doubled in the last year [4]. In the USA, by age 11, 53% of 11-year-olds have their own smartphone and 69% of 12-year-olds have individual phones, making mobile phone and computer-based programs as well as social media and texting programs an ideal tool for improving mental health [4].

Adolescent Mental Health

As part of the Data for Children Collaborative with UNICEF,[1] a literature review exploring adolescent mental health and technological interventions was conducted to create a basis for their Phase I workshops. This chapter builds off that (not yet published) literature review and goes in more depth into the outcomes and conclusions.

Of the current studies involving a technological intervention for adolescent mental health, the mental health symptoms targeted by those technological interventions were primarily depression and anxiety (44%). While depression and anxiety are distinct symptoms, most of the current studies found that depression and anxiety overlapped and so combined them. Of the remaining studies, 28% involved ADHD, 12% focused on self-harm and suicide ideation, 4% targeted medication adherence, 4% focused on general well-being, 4% involved drug and alcohol use, and the remaining 4% focused on psychosis.

This is also in line with the current prevalence of mental health disorders in adolescents, with the most common being anxiety, mood, attention, and behaviour disorders [6]. Furthermore, suicide is the fourth leading cause of death in adolescents aged 15–19 years old [7].

Types of Technologies

Multiple types of technologies have been studied for efficacy in the treatment of adolescent mental health including mobile apps, computer programs and games, texting programs, and social media. The most common technologies used (84%) were mobile apps or online computer-based programs. For the remaining studies, 8% used texting, 4% used gamification, and 4% used social media.

Next we present examples of some of the interventions explored in these research studies.

Mobile Apps and Online Computer Programs

Mobile apps or online computer programs were used for various applications including providing mental health treatment, providing advice and guidance, providing education and resources for coping, and detecting changes in mental health.

Some apps delivered CBT-based interventions such as the MEMO intervention, which included 15 key CBT-based messages such as, 'You can take control of this.' Messages were delivered using a variety of mediums to engage the users such as video clips [8].

Apps like WeClick were loaded with features to provide adolescents with a variety of tools to meet their needs and help them build positive coping mechanisms, learn about problem solving, goal setting, and conflict resolution, and build healthy relationships [9].

---

[1] www.dataforchildrencollaborative.com/

Other apps focused on resources for self-care and coping and had access to immediate help in the form of suicide hotlines or parental involvement [10]. For example, one app had a skills section that was divided into four main topics: option to call a trusted adult, demonstrations of relaxation techniques/music the user finds helpful, a laugh section with personalized videos and images, and a personalized list of activities to engage in [10].

To increase engagement even more, some apps detected changes in mental health and gave users feedback on things like their moods and emotional states [11].

Texting Programs

Texting is also a popular medium among adolescents and a means to provide complete or supplementary treatment. The iDove texting intervention included an initial in-person CBT session followed by eight weeks of a texting intervention, also based on the principles of CBT and motivational interviewing [12].

Furthermore, technology provides the foundation for integrating self-help interventional content for adolescents with social media. One study concluded that treatment programmes could be developed to target social impairment of teens with ADHD on various online platforms that they utilize [13]. For example, social training interventions for teens with ADHD, such as the Interpersonal Skills Group, which gives real-time feedback to support teens meeting their social goals, could be adapted for an online platform [13].

Social Media

Social media are also ingrained into everyday adolescent lives. A lot can be learned from social media about a person and monitoring social media engagement can give insights into how it relates to their mental health [13]. Despite this, only 4% of the examined studies used social media as an intervention. Possible reasons for this are that analysing social media data involves a variety of skills, including technical skills to collect the data, as well as additional technical skills to analyse the various forms of data, such as text and images. For example, analysing changes in mental health states based on social media text involves natural language processing skills that might be unfamiliar to many health research teams. In addition, social media collect a lot of information, including information that might be sensitive, that might deter adolescents from joining a social media-based research study. Adolescents may also not want other sensitive information linked to their social media accounts. Furthermore, with all the information that can be collected, independent ethics review may be much stricter than for an app that just provides an intervention, especially for populations under the age of 18. The most popular social media among adolescents is also always changing, with Facebook use currently declining and other social media sites like Snapchat gaining more popularity [13]. Information on social media like Snapchat is also much more temporary compared to other social media sites, making interventions on those platforms more challenging for research.

Gamification

Turning therapy into a game can be fun and engaging. The REThink therapeutic game featured a main character, RETMAN, who is a superhero who helps children to think rationally and have functional emotions [14]. The binary model of distress is composed of functional and dysfunctional negative emotions. Whether an emotion is functional or dysfunctional is based on subjective experience, cognitions, and behavioural consequences. A functional emotion (like sadness) is associated with a negative experience, rational beliefs, and adaptive behaviours. A dysfunctional emotion (like depression), however, is associated with a negative experience, irrational beliefs, and maladaptive behaviours. In the game, RETMAN gives players missions of increasing difficulty such as identifying people's emotions as positive, negative, or neutral and if they are functional or dysfunctional [14]. In later levels, players will be tasked with identifying people's irrational beliefs and providing them with a potion to change the thought into a rational version. The REThink game was designed to help children and adolescents, between the ages of 10 and 16 years old, to learn healthy strategies for coping with things like depression, anxiety, and anger. Other apps already mentioned may have also utilized some kind of gamification, for example, answering questions within the app.

Locations

Technological mental health interventions have been studied in various places around the world including the United States, Australia and New Zealand, and the United Kingdom. Studies have also been done in other parts of Europe, as well as parts of Africa and Asia.

While there is a lack of research regarding technological interventions to improve mental illness in many lower-income countries, mental health struggles are present and problematic in these countries, too, and could potentially be helped by similar interventions. To explore this, grey data, which includes theses and dissertations, government reports, and content from non-profit organizations, were also looked at.

For example, UNICEF's findings from U-Report (2020), provided insight into engagement in mobile messaging services among youth in Jamaica. This social messaging tool, which was created by UNICEF, utilized bots for interactive questions and answers, live chat, and short polls, which helped provide real-time mental health information about youth in Jamaica. This highlights the potential usefulness of a texting-based intervention to provide education about health and wellness, prevention, identification of mental health issues, and subsequent referrals when more help is needed [15].

As another example, in conjunction with UNICEF, the Ministry of Health in Peru addressed the mental health concerns, due to COVID-19 changes, among adolescents. Its cross-sectional study during a portion of the lockdown in Peru contained 4,531 children and adolescents who had previously been identified as at risk for psychosocial problems. Approximately one-third of the children showed a high rate of mental health problems because of the lockdown including emotional problems, behavioural problems (generally due to the stress and anxiety from emotional problems), and difficulty focusing. As children transitioned to online classes and remained at home with parents and siblings, approximately 10% of children were regularly disciplined and 20% of households were exposed to violence at home including sexual violence. These findings highlight the serious need for technological interventions to reach children who may be stuck at home without advocates [16].

Outcomes: Some Reported Benefits

Overall, the majority of studies which utilized technology with the goal of improving mental health reported a positive correlation between technology and improved adolescent mental health, although such claims should be treated with a certain amount of caution (see chapters 5 and 6 for discussion of research challenges in this area).

Global coverage and treatment for adolescent mental health remains a critical issue [2]. Treatment, however, can be delivered through technological interventions. For example, apps have been used to prevent body image problems through a game that helps combat distorted thoughts [1]. Users would rate the model's weight status, from extremely thin to extremely big, and could try again until the correct answer was chosen. The feedback from showing what a 'normally' weighted body shape looks like and getting a reward screen stating 'This is the correct answer' helped build self-esteem and body satisfaction leading to protective effects when seeing 'ideal' body portrayals in the media. One girl even noted that she 'learned that our view on models differs from reality'. Furthermore, valuable information was gained about the opportunities for future development of apps targeting body image in adolescents.

Other apps delivered CBT-based treatment for eating disorders through self-monitoring of meals and symptoms, setting goals, providing coping mechanisms, education about meal plans, rewards and affirmations, and social support [1]. Overall, the majority of apps provided some way to teach coping skills and offered resources and support for their target symptom: anxiety, depression, providing opportunities for education about mental health, creating connections with other users, and giving access to potentially helpful resources.

The therapeutic game REThink improved emotional symptoms among 46% of the participants and improved depressive mood among 84% of participants [14]. Furthermore, the game helped 64% of adolescents to regulate their emotions and gain emotional awareness while 69% were able to control their emotions more effectively. This further shows that technology is an effective tool in building emotional resilience, providing adolescents with the tools they need to be emotionally aware, and encouraging positive mental health.

Not only can apps provide users with engagement and enrich their lives but they have the potential to save lives, helping to reduce suicidal ideation and depression among recently discharged adolescents and their parents [10]. Adolescents reported feeling supported in managing their thoughts of self-harm [1]. Furthermore, a statistically significant number of participants were comfortable using the app during a crisis and approved of the manageability, personalized content, ease of use, and accessibility of the app.

Technological interventions also serve as a source of education. In countries like Uganda, girls out of school have an increased risk for HIV, risky behaviours, and poor mental health but involvement in Suubi4Her offered educational resources for them and education about risk behaviours and mental health were successfully provided to these at-risk girls [17]. Self-management education can also be provided through these apps to empower users, promote lifestyle changes like medication adherence, and build a sense of agency [18].

Monitoring symptoms can also be done through technological interventions. Mood tracking proved particularly useful for participants and some apps helped reduce depression among engaged participants [1]. Over eight weeks, daily self-reported moods and smartphone sensor data were collected and had a prediction accuracy of 88% for mental health, 90% when parental evaluations were included [1]. Some apps sent automatic alerts to users at specific mood levels to encourage help seeking [19]. Engagement with the app improved depressive symptoms and users enjoyed tools where they could write about potential mood influences, record events, and see a visual representation of how those events might influence their mental health [19].

Data collection within the app of mood, coping efficacy, and mental health problems revealed that 45% of users never talked about their problems [11]. Negative emotions throughout the day, as rated by users, were significantly, positively associated with distress, as measured by the short version of the Depression Anxiety Distress Scale (DASS-21). The app concluded that adolescents with a low sense of connectedness and belonging have a positively correlated range of negative emotions (worry, stress, anger, or sadness). Those participants with high coping mechanisms, however, recorded more daily happiness. This highlights that coping mechanisms and knowing how to deal with negative emotions are essential for good mental health. Supplementary text message responses in between in-person meetings with mental healthcare professionals, led to a reduction in the severity and frequency of depressive symptoms [12]. The Check Yourself app/website tool provided real-time feedback for health-related behaviours such as drug and alcohol use. Results indicated those who engaged in habitual drug or alcohol use wanted to change but didn't know how. At the two-month follow-up, overall frequency and quantity of alcohol consumed were reduced in those who had used the Check Yourself app [20].

Outcomes: Some Reservations

Although 98% of the studies in our review examining technology for adolescent mental health have concluded that technology has shown a positive impact on mental health, not all studies were successful and finding the right medium to engage adolescents will be important. For example, the MEMO study showed no statistically significant improvements over the 12-month intervention [8].

As mentioned in some of the studies, *engagement* is an important aspect and generally the more engagement correlates with better outcomes. In discussing their results, the MEMO researchers noted other longitudinal studies that had similarly shown a lack of statistical improvement but measurements of engagement were not accounted for in the study. A shorter study found that increased engagement had a direct correlation on feelings of usefulness of the app, highlighting the importance of engagement [21]. Similar apps can potentially predict mental health problems, especially when combined with emotional/mood tracking, and provide self-help resources to intervene early. Users reported that the more they used the app, the more normalized it became to seek help for mental health [21].

There are some *gender differences in medium preference*, with boys favouring games and videos and girls favouring social media and reading [4]. Some apps offered a variety of tools to cater to activity preferences: text, pictures, audio, animations, quizzes and games, etc. Users could utilize what worked best for them to help identify triggers and promote emotional well-being, leading to less depression and anxiety [22].

Digital Exclusion

While some places like the USA and UK have high rates of cell phone access among adolescents, that may not hold true in all countries around the world. A report by UNICEF showed that approximately two-thirds of youth under the age of 25 did not have access to an internet connection at home [23]. Those without access to cell phones or the Internet may be part of some of the most vulnerable populations. Digital interventions may also be more challenging to implement in developing countries. Places like Jamaica have begun to create Teen Hubs where adolescents can access the Internet and other resources [24] and libraries are also a good resource for internet access, with some libraries even loaning out mobile devices. While this is a great start, these solutions are temporary and dependent on those places being open to be able to utilize the resources. Being public places also reduces the privacy of users and so may not be ideal for mental health interventions. Another solution would be to provide adolescents with cell phones through a school, clinic, or governmental programme. In the USA there are programmes like the Lifeline Program that can provide cell phones at low or no cost to those in need.

Conclusion

Overall, the evidence suggests that technology can be used for good to support adolescent wellness, promote good mental health, and help prevent poor mental health outcomes.

Technology like social media can provide a way to integrate self-help interventions into an online environment. Engagement on these platforms can also lead to better outcomes like improved medication adherence. Managing medication for more serious illness is imperative to overall health which includes mental health [18]. Mobile apps also have the potential to intervene early and reduce the risk of depression or anxiety through education and coping skills. By offering tools like coping mechanisms through apps and other technology, adolescents can develop the skills they need to maintain positive mental health.

While general information can help target mental health overall [21], the more specific the information is to the user, the more likely the outcome will improve [19]. Also, as mentioned, the more engaged the user is, the more benefit they receive from the intervention. Furthermore, educational apps and online tools can provide adolescents with actionable information such as when behaviour is risky, when their emotional state can lead to risky behaviours, and what they can do to cope or find help. Finally, the current studies have shown high feasibility and usability among apps that utilize mood tracking and self-monitoring [12, 19, 20].

Key Points

- Adolescence is a crucial time for developing and maintaining both social and emotional habits that are important for good mental well-being but approximately 20% of adolescents globally experience a mental health disorder.
- Addressing this problem has become even more of a concern due to the COVID-19 pandemic.

- Technology is already ingrained into adolescent daily life, with approximately 96% of adolescents aged 12–17 having access to a cell phone in places like the USA and UK.
- Technological interventions can help to reduce symptoms and provide treatment to adolescents quickly and efficiently.
- Current literature suggests that technology can be used to support adolescent mental health and well-being.

Chapter 14

Online Outreach and Support Provision
An Empirically Informed Approach and Case Illustration

Stephen P. Lewis

As should be clear by this juncture of this volume, the use of the Internet and social media can represent a double-edged sword for a range of health concerns such as eating disorder behaviours, suicide, and COVID-19. This notwithstanding, there is arguably significant potential to harness online platforms, including social media, as accessible and powerful mechanisms of support provision. Commensurate with this, online initiatives can be used to offer helpful resources and related health information. Indeed, the Internet and its venues have become central to how people across the globe connect with others and retrieve information. Moreover, for many health concerns (such as self-injury) and within particular demographic groups (such as adolescents), the use of online technology represents a preferred means of support and information obtainment; for a review see Lewis and Seko, 2016 [1].

Following this, the current chapter offers an empirically informed approach that utilizes the Internet and social media to provide support and resources for health concerns. The topic of self-injury[1] will be used as a case illustration throughout. To this end, initiatives aimed at supporting and offering outreach for people with lived experience of self-injury as well as key stakeholders who can play key support roles will be presented. By the end of the chapter, readers will be able to reflect on how these various considerations can be drawn upon when planning their own outreach efforts aimed at providing support and informational resources for a range of health concerns via the Internet.

Online Outreach: Key Considerations

When embarking on online outreach initiatives, several considerations merit discussion. These are summarized in Table 14.1 and then discussed. Naturally, the nature and relative import of each will vary across different health concerns and one's intended outreach aims. For example, some topics may have especially poor-quality health information online (for example, misinformation woven into discourses on social media). Correspondingly, attention geared towards dispelling myths may be essentially salient in such instances. In other cases, certain forms of online content may be harmful to certain populations; examples include reporting methods of suicide in anti-suicide initiatives

---

[1] In line with much of the cited research throughout the current chapter, self-injury is used as a general term that includes non-suicidal self-injury. It is acknowledged that other terms, such as self-harm, may also be used in the broader literature and across disciplines.

Table 14.1. Empirically informed considerations for online outreach

Outreach consideration	Brief description
Identifying intended audiences	• Consider broad-based approaches intended to reach a wide audience (including people with lived experience and others who may benefit from outreach) • Consider specific stakeholder groups, including historically marginalized and stigmatized people
Determining the content of outreach work	• Identify existing outreach efforts for a topic of interest to guide one's efforts (for example, to minimize redundancies, clarify and address gaps) • Also consider broader online communication for a health topic to ensure relevance of outreach work (such as platforms to use, media formats to draw on)
Factoring in motives for online communication	• Consult relevant literature and draw on various research methodologies (including analysis of online communication, surveys with stakeholders) as needed to determine and verify stakeholder needs
Accounting for the impact of online material	• Identify whether online content related to a health topic carries risks and/or benefits • Work to minimise risks and maximize benefits in ensuing online outreach work
Understanding the quality of health information online	• Determine the overall quality of health-related information (such as treatment recommendations) across health websites • Also consider the relative accessibility of health information (for example, via major search engines)
Evaluation of outreach work	• Conduct ongoing evaluation to ensure outreach aims are met; typically, this involves use of various website and social media analytics • Also consider involvement of key stakeholders to further evaluation and inform ongoing outreach
Enhancing outreach work: additional considerations	• Drawing on participatory approaches may enhance outreach work and empower stakeholders involved • Make use of professional networks, media, and other forms of dissemination to maximize reach and impact

and sharing imagery that promotes a thin ideal when engaging in advocacy for individual with lived experience of an eating disorder. In these instances, outreach activities would need to avoid such content in their dissemination efforts. Although all forms of online outreach and support will need to be tailored for several reasons, including the health topic being addressed and the social media venues most relevant to a specific demographic, readers are encouraged to consider the relative utility of each consideration we discuss in the early and ongoing stages of their outreach work.

Identifying Intended Audiences

When using the Internet for outreach purposes, attention to the intended audiences of any planned activities is essential. On the one hand, online outreach efforts may not have a specific target audience such as a particular age group, or individuals in support roles, and thus will aspire to provide a general suite of resources or broad-based support including basic health and treatment information, sharing encouraging and hopeful messages, or offering interactive support with trained staff. Often, these approaches are warranted and can go a long way in providing many people with needed resources and support. On the other hand, there may be a need to narrow efforts to particular groups, such as caregivers, who may be uniquely impacted by a specific health concern. Similarly, there may be utility in centring efforts on underrepresented groups, for whom online support and resource provision is limited or historically overlooked, such as a marginalized racial group or a group that has been especially stigmatized in relation to a health concern.

By and large, most outreach work will focus on individuals with lived experience of a particular health concern (people diagnosed with cancer, individuals who have lived experience of self-injury, or people with a history of depression). In many cases though, expanding the lens of what constitutes lived experience to also – or, at times, instead – include stakeholders who play key supportive roles (family, friends, or romantic partners), as well as health and other professionals (educators who interact with students, first responders, nurses, physicians, or psychologists) will be warranted. By reflecting on which audiences to target, individuals involved in outreach work will be better positioned to ensure their efforts meet the needs of intended stakeholders.

In the case of self-injury, there is ample evidence to indicate that stigma associated with the behaviour and people who engage with it is long-standing, significant, and widespread [2]. Unfortunately, such stigma carries many serious consequences in that it foments social isolation, marginalization, and reluctance to seek support [2, 3]. As a result, researchers have found that the Internet represents a highly relevant and appealing mechanism for many people who self-injure to connect with like-minded others as well as to obtain support and resources [1, 4, 5]. Unsurprisingly then, a primary target group in many online outreach efforts are individuals with lived experience of self-injury. For example, the website for Self-injury Outreach & Support (SiOS: www.sioutreach.org), an international non-profit outreach initiative, allows site visitors with lived experience to read and share their self-injury stories and words of encouragement, which are also shared through various social media channels. Additionally, SiOS offers empirically informed coping strategies and treatment information, intended to help individuals combat urges to self-injure and enhance their coping efficacy as they work on their own recovery. Many other sites have likewise been created to reach people who self-injure and to offer coping and other practical guides such as the Self-Injury & Recovery Resources (SIRR) website from Cornell University (www.selfinjury.bctr.cornell.edu). While there are numerous sites specifically for self-injury, outreach also occurs on broader platforms, including communities intended to help and support people with health and mental health difficulties. One such example is the online Self-harm Recovery Guide by the website The Mighty (www.TheMighty.com). As discussed in other sections of the chapter, social media channels are also commonly used to reach people who engage in self-injury.

In as much as it is imperative to reach people with lived self-injury experience, this is not the only key stakeholder to focus upon. Due to the aforementioned stigmatization of self-injury, many individuals report that upon knowing they have self-injured, people in their lives have responded in inappropriate and invalidating manners including shaming/blaming or responding with anger or recoil [2, 3]. Understandably, this can worsen shame, self-worth, and isolation, rendering it especially difficult to disclose self-injury in the future [3]. Hence, it is important that these stakeholders have access to resources that can foster understanding about self-injury as well as increase the likelihood that interactions about self-injury are responded to supportively.

Several online initiatives have been launched to reach a variety of stakeholders who can play supportive roles for people who self-injure. This includes efforts geared towards parents and caregivers, peers and romantic partners of people who engage in self-injury, stakeholders in schools and on university campuses, as well as an array of health and mental health professionals. For instance, the websites mentioned earlier (SiOS and SIRR) offer helpful resources for a wide array of stakeholders. Although a detailed review of the many groups targeted in self-injury outreach work goes beyond the scope of the present chapter, professionals working in educational settings will be used to illustrate these kinds of initiatives.

Over the past several years, numerous efforts to reach educational professionals (e.g. educators, mental health staff, or administrators) who can support students who self-injure in schools and on university campuses have been undertaken. Indeed, a large body of research indicates that self-injury is common among school-aged youth and that school professionals (teachers, administrators) often feel ill-equipped to respond to students who self-injure [6]. Similar reports have been made in university settings, with many campus stakeholders reporting more stigmatizing views towards self-injury [7]. As a result, groups such as the International Consortium on Self-injury in Educational Settings (ICSES: www.icsesgroup.org), an interdisciplinary and international research group composed of research and clinical leaders in the field, have used the Internet to disseminate helpful resources to augment responses to students who self-injure. This includes but is not limited to downloadable guides, infographics, and leaflets to assist schools in the support of students who self-injure. Relatedly, ICSES has created resources for university stakeholders to guide how they respond to and support students who self-injure; a position paper published by ICSES, intended to provide guidance for a campus-wide approach to support students with lived experience of self-injury, emphasizes the centrality of online outreach as a means to ensure resources are available to all university stakeholders – students, faculty, support staff, and administrators [8].

Although resources that include recommendations for use when interacting with students is important, in some contexts and for certain stakeholders, there is a need for more in-depth training. Efforts have therefore drawn on the Internet to provide more extensive training to school and other professionals (e.g. social workers). For example, Janis Whitlock at Cornell University has spearheaded 'Nonsuicidal Self-injury 101', a novel e-training series intended to improve how professionals respond to and work with people who engage in self-injury. The training can be done in one's own time and can be tailored in its level of comprehensiveness to meet varying training needs.

In sum, determining one's intended audience(s) represents a key first step in the development of online outreach work. At times, this may involve initiatives that carry broad appeal (not circumscribed to a specific group); however, this can also comprise more targeted approaches, to reach specific stakeholders. Irrespective of the group or groups targeted, and as discussed in the next section, once intended stakeholders have been identified, attention can be paid to the types of materials to develop and the associated platforms to use.

Determining the Content of Outreach Work

When making decisions about which kinds of material to utilize in outreach work, exploring existing outreach initiatives can assist in identifying: a) which content types (e.g. video, infographics, or social media campaigns) may be most relevant and helpful to identified stakeholders; b) where there may be duplicate efforts (and perhaps a lesser need for outreach); and c) potential gaps or needs, such as lack of treatment information, that should be incorporated in outreach efforts. Shedding light on these domains can also work to ensure key stakeholders are meaningfully targeted in any future outreach initiatives. For instance, if existing efforts seem focused on reaching youth but do not draw on the most relevant platforms to this age group, their relative impact will likely be limited.

Beyond accounting for existing outreach efforts, a broader focus on online content and communication pertinent to a health topic is recommended. This can help establish what types of platforms and materials may be most useful in one's outreach work – selecting the most salient social media platforms for a stakeholder, such as identifying concerns about a new treatment as discussed in an e-community. As noted later, insight into the scope and nature of online activity about a health topic can also illuminate motives for the use of the Internet for that topic, what impact certain kinds of online activity may have in areas like health behaviours or help seeking, and the overall quality of available health information that people may be exposed to when online.

Returning to self-injury as an example, and as is likely the case for many health and mental health concerns, there are many manifestations of online content (such as images and videos) and platforms used. This includes but is certainly not limited to social media sites such as Instagram, discussion fora, and blogs depicting people's experiences with self-injury. This has been documented since the inception of research examining online self-injury content (in the mid-late 2000s and early 2010s) and continues to be the case based on several reviews of the literature [1, 9, 10]. Consequently, outreach activities for self-injury have not relied on a singular online format. Rather, efforts have been wide-ranging, relying on imagery, videos, and text across numerous website types.

As self-injury content – including that used in outreach efforts – is multi-faceted and present on various platforms, a strategic approach is needed when engaging in outreach via the Internet. Indeed, effective efforts for self-injury have been tailored to specific stakeholders, accounting for platforms stakeholders most often use and incorporating the kinds of communication that resonate with them. For example, efforts such as SiOS and SIRR (described earlier) have content for people with lived experience as well as various others including families and health and school professionals. As a result, their content has been designed to appeal to these audiences. Sometimes, however, the use of social media is used as a primary means of outreach. For instance, 'Self-Harmer Problems' is an online initiative created by an advocate with lived experience to ensure that people who self-injure have good quality research-informed information as well as needed peer support. To increase its reach, the initiative makes use of social media sites such as Instagram that have appeal to age groups reporting the highest self-injury rates – namely, youth and emerging adults [5].

Before continuing, a final point merits discussion. Much like online activity is non-static, so too should outreach work be. Indeed, the nature of online material is fluid and bound to change with time. As a result, what may be a popular and relevant social media platform at one point may not be as salient an outreach tool at a later date. Individuals engaged in online outreach will therefore need to account for these changes to ensure the ongoing relevance, reach, and impact of their work.

Factoring in Motives for Online Communication

Knowledge about what motivates broader online activity (beyond outreach work specifically) as it pertains to a health concern can help shape the nature of intended outreach activities. Of note, this can elucidate key stakeholder needs (e.g. a need for acceptance due to stigma, or information about how to broach a topic with professionals or loved ones), thereby pinpointing what may be relevant in subsequent outreach endeavours. In what follows, examples of how motives for online self-injury communication have been identified will be summarized.

A scan of the literature points to numerous studies conducted to understand the motivations contributing to online self-injury activity. For instance, researchers have drawn on qualitative methods of analysis to investigate the motivations underlying the posting of online material across discussion forums, personally developed websites by people with lived experience, and major social media channels [11–17]. Collectively, these efforts have indicated a range of motives for online self-injury activity germane to outreach work. For example, and, in part, due to the aforementioned stigmatization of self-injury, many people with lived experience of self-injury go online in an effort to find a safe (and often anonymous) space to share their lived experience and obtain needed validation (typically of their emotional pain and the difficulties inherent in self-injury), acceptance, and understanding that they are not alone in their experience. As such, several websites (including SiOS) and social media efforts ('Self-Harmer Problems') centre these experiences and permit reciprocal support by virtue of people sharing their experiences.

Although motives for online activity can be gleaned through examination of what is already posted across different e-platforms, more traditional research methods are also useful. This includes but is not constrained to recruiting members of online communities and people with lived experience more broadly to directly ask about the nature and reasons for their online activity – using, for example, survey-based research or interviews. In terms of work conducted in the field of self-injury, there have been several studies in which people with lived experience of self-injury take part in online surveys employing both quantitative and open-ended, text-based questions [18, 19]. These efforts have permitted more focused (and at times in-depth) insight into specific domains of interest (what initiated online self-injury activity or why people continue visiting self-injury websites [18]). More comprehensive viewpoints can be identified via interview-based studies and those examining people's online activities and preferences over time. Taken together, researchers interested in their own online outreach work may wish to consider these approaches to understand motives more fully and to account for different types of online behaviour.

Accounting for the Impact of Online Material

How (and the extent to which) online material impacts people who interact with it will depend on many factors – like the topic of interest itself, or the nature of a particular message or video posted online. Nevertheless, to maximize the positive impact of outreach activities, an understanding of how online content and e-activity can affect key stakeholders is crucial. Typically, this can be achieved by reviewing the extant empirical literature. When a paucity of research exists, however, further investigation may be necessary. Should this be the case, some of the earlier mentioned approaches may be useful – such as examining the nature of content and communication on specific websites, or engaging with members of online communities. Indeed, this has been done for self-injury. For example, some of the initial studies in this area relied on content analysis to not only describe what is uploaded to websites such as YouTube (e.g. a hopeless versus hopeful video about recovery) but to also illuminate how this content may differentially affect people who access it – increasing or decreasing recovery motivation [12].

Overall, insight into the effect of online material is essential as even projects with the best of intentions may still be composed of messaging or material that inadvertently contributes to harm or that is otherwise unhelpful. For instance, attempts have been made to promote awareness and understanding about self-injury (via blogs or YouTube videos); however, sometimes the content uploaded is accompanied by terminology (such as self-injurer) or imagery (including pictures of self-injury) which can have adverse effects. Indeed, researchers have cautioned that specific terms used in reference to self-injury and people who self-injure can be stigmatizing [20]; and graphic representations of self-injury can be triggering (by provoking self-injury urges or behaviour) to people with lived experience [21]. An empirically informed approach that accounts for this kind of content can work towards avoiding unintentional consequences in outreach work.

Also relevant when accounting for impact is the degree of communication permitted between people on any platforms used. When interaction occurs between individuals (e.g. via a comment feature or messaging system on popular social media sites), there is potential for reciprocal sharing and support. At the same time, interaction can also lead to the sharing of misinformation and involve negative interactions. For example, although researchers have found people with lived experience of self-injury use the Internet to share their experiences to get support [18], this can sometimes elicit problematic responses such as vitriolic and trolling comments, mocking people who self-injure, and encouraging people to attempt suicide [1, 4, 5]. Therefore, moderation of posted content alongside efforts to ensure the accessibility of helpful resources has often been recommended for online outreach and social media use regarding self-injury [1, 4, 22]. To bolster these efforts, dissemination of community guidelines that articulate what is and is not appropriate can also be helpful. Furthermore, ensuring that helpful resources are readily available (clearly posted, shared regularly shared via social media) can also mitigate the potential of risks stemming from online interactions. In some cases, it may also be useful to have moderated discussion sessions or other ways that people can contact and obtain support from trained support staff.

Inasmuch as it is important to mitigate the potential risks tied to specific forms of online content, it is equally (if not more) important to optimize any associated benefits.

Accordingly, if there are specific kinds of content known to be helpful to specific stakeholders, efforts to promote and ensure easy access to such material are paramount. In the case of self-injury, some online platforms (including personal self-injury websites and YouTube videos) contain messages about self-injury that are melancholic, or even hopeless in nature, for example indicating that recovery is not possible [12, 16, 23]. Concern has thus been raised that accessing such material may thwart people's recovery efforts (for a review see [1]). Despite this, there is evidence that hopeful content (material emphasizing that recovery is possible) is readily posted online and may be beneficial when accessed [1, 5, 24]. Indeed, researchers have found that exposure to messaging from people with lived experience that acknowledges the difficulties inherent in self-injury, while portraying that recovery is a viable outcome, can evoke more positive views about one's own recovery [19]. It should therefore come as little surprise that many outreach efforts emphasize hope and that recovery is possible (see SiOS, or the UK-based website, LifeSIGNS: https://www.lifesigns.org.uk).

In sum, those engaged in online outreach may need to take into account the various ways that people can be affected by the material used. This is especially critical when there are potential risks associated with certain kinds of content. A dual approach that draws on the scientific literature to minimize harms, while maximizing benefits can go a long way in ensuring the impact of one's intended outreach efforts.

Understanding the Quality of Health Information Online

The quality of online health information should also be on the radar of people involved in online outreach work. Indeed, if poor quality information, such as myth spreading or sharing of deleterious treatment recommendations, is common and easily accessible, efforts would be needed to curtail the potential consequences of this content being accessed, while ensuring access to helpful, research-informed material. In part, the extent to which poor (or high) quality content is available may be gleaned through prior research or by one's own investigation into what is currently posted across online platforms. Important, however, is attention to health information websites which may not always be considered when examining online material such as that on social media sites.

Building on this, researchers have examined the nature of Google searches for self-injury content and the quality of health information available on websites in the associated search results [25]. Google was chosen in this study as, at the time, it was the most commonly used search engine worldwide. Specifically, the program Google AdWords Keywords was used as it permitted users to enter a set of keywords (such as 'self-injury' and 'self-harm help') in order to identify search terms (such as 'treatments for self-injury' and 'why do people self-harm') entered by Google users when searching for information. Also available in the program's output were relevant search data, including the frequency of each search term as well as the country of origin for that search term.

Results indicated that self-injury terms were commonly entered into Google, with well over 42 million searches in the year prior to the study being published (for terms with at least 1,000 searches per month) and widespread (not limited to one country). As a next step, the health information websites in the search results, which were the predominant website type, were subject to content analysis to evaluate the quality of information they offered. Unfortunately, these sites often perpetuated self-injury myths (including presenting it as attention-seeking, implying that only female youth self-injure) and carried poor quality health information. Taken together, these findings suggested that despite a clear need for self-injury information, people's informational needs may not be met. And, in turn, this may have consequences such as increased stigmatization through myth propagation or the provision of poor treatment information, which could impede help seeking. While it is not presumed that this will be the case for all health topics on the Internet, it does point to the value in systematically exploring what people may be exposed to when looking for health information and why this may need to be targeted in outreach work. Indeed, in line with the findings from this study, self-injury websites and related outreach activities work to dispel myths and ensure people's access to quality, research-informed content (see the earlier mentioned SiOS and SIRR websites and the Australian-based Shedding Light on Self-Injury).

Evaluation of Outreach Work

Once efforts for online support and resource provision have been realized, their evaluation is key. An ongoing and multifaceted approach to evaluating online support and outreach work can therefore go a long way in ensuring one's associated goals, such as reaching a certain number of people, likes, or downloads, are met. How this transpires will vary in part on the platforms utilized. For initiatives relying solely on the use of major social media platforms, relevant site analytics (such as number of likes, retweets, followers) can be used to gauge appeal and reach. Doing this over time can also help determine trends with respect to certain kinds of posts having more relevance and impact. Beyond these basic metrics, most social media platforms provide users with data to point to how people interact with the content posted. Depending on the platform used, this information may also include geographic regions reached, the number of times content is repeatedly accessed by users, and how long people interact with posted content.

When outreach websites are created as part of one's efforts, ensuring a means to measure relevant website analytics is recommended. This is important as it can help to determine what aspects of a website may be most appealing and which components may not be as relevant; this may also help to highlight areas that need revision. Finally, for outreach involving social media and/or use of stand-alone websites, qualitative data may also be fruitful in the context of evaluation. For example, this may come from examination of what people post in response to developed content, for example as a comment or a written response to a tweet. In this way, when relevant, both quantitative and qualitative approaches to evaluation can be useful.

Outside of data organically collected through social media and website usage, individuals involved in the provision of online outreach and resources may also wish to consider engaging directly with key stakeholders in the context of evaluation. This can be accomplished by drawing on an array of methodologies, including but not limited to focus groups, surveys, interviews, and studies asking people to engage with developed online content to elicit views on their experience with outreach content as they access it.

Enhancing Outreach Work: Additional Considerations

The considerations discussed thus far have potential to increase the relevance, reach, and impact of online outreach endeavours for a variety of health and mental health concerns. Another set of approaches that may also function to enhance outreach work are those in which people with lived experience can play a direct role in all stages of the outreach process. In particular, the application of participatory-based methods – namely, collection of research approaches in which people with lived experience play a direct and active role in planning, application, and dissemination [26, 27] – may have salience.

In line with the World Health Organization's long-standing advocacy for the direct involvement of people with lived experience in various aspects of research and service provision, their involvement in outreach work arguably carries much potential. This can grant unique opportunities to ensure that any developed content has relevance to intended stakeholders given their role in this process. They can thus provide valuable insight on intended outreach goals early in the process – providing for example suggestions about the relative import of goal or the kinds of messages to use. Likewise, individuals with lived experience can play a role in the dissemination of outreach outputs and in its later evaluation. This may be an especially potent means of presenting information as it affords a chance to centre people's experiences which may be more effective given that contact-based approaches tend to be more potent in addressing stigma and fostering awareness [28, 29]. A participatory approach to online outreach can also be a positive experience for people involved in that it can offer a sense of community and empowerment. This may be especially important if this involves people who have been historically marginalized (including Black, Indigenous, and People of Colour) and/or stigmatized due to health-related difficulties such as people living with mental illness or AIDS. In the case of self-injury, direct involvement of people who have self-injured has been advocated for in the field as an effective way to combat stigma, promote greater understanding, and enhance the lives of people with lived experience [24, 27].

Finally, effective outreach approaches should look to how their impact can be maximized through the cultivation of networks with existing professional organizations and social media initiatives relevant to their goals and intended audiences. For example, several self-injury outreach projects are featured on websites of prominent organizations in the field such as the International Society for the Study of Self-Injury. By building relationships with organizations or even working with other outreach initiatives, a larger audience can be reached. Attention to broader-based organizations is also warranted. For example, self-injury outreach efforts have been featured on many major websites that are broader in scope (not only focused on self-injury but also other mental health concerns), such as To Write Love On Her Arms (https://twloha.com/) and The Mighty. To further increase the reach of one's outreach work developing media releases, such as through a university media and communications office, or writing opinion pieces for media outlets may also be useful. Finally, there may be merit in launching online campaigns or capitalizing on those that already exist. For instance, 1 March is Self-Injury Awareness Day and it is common to see support messages, trending hashtags, and online resources featured with higher degrees of frequency across social media at this time of the year. By way of harnessing these various avenues of dissemination, outreach efforts will be better situated to achieve their goals.

Conclusion

There is clearly much potential in the use of the Internet and social media to disseminate resources and provide support to individuals for a wide range of health and mental health concerns. At the same time, even with the best of intentions, outreach efforts are not guaranteed to yield their intended benefits. Hence, reflection on the various considerations articulated throughout this chapter may help to inform the relevance, impact, and overall effectiveness of one's planned outreach work. Although the significance of each consideration discussed will undoubtedly vary across the focus of any intended outreach initiatives, it is hoped they can both guide and enhance the online outreach work in *all* arenas of physical health and mental health.

Afterword

If there is a single message to emerge from the work presented here, it is this: there is no support for the idea that social media should be seen as an invariably harmful influence on the mental health of those who use it. For many people this new technology is a valued part of life that can be a positive resource in times of trouble. And in relation to understanding harms, much depends upon who is using which social media, how, why, and when. This is not to say, however, that social media have no harmful effects and we do have some idea about what those are and to whom they apply.

Probably the clearest evidence is in two areas, in the harmful effects of online gambling, and in social media representations (and promotion) of unrealistic body types and presentations of self. In each case the social media influence can be seen as supported by and reflecting wider offline social pressures – commercial in the first example, cultural as well as commercial in the second. By contrast, social media influence on mood disorders and self-harm is less clearcut and appears harmful mainly for vulnerable people using their online time in unhealthy ways.

What does this mean for how we should respond to social media, as individuals and as a society? As individuals we need to develop thoughtful ways of using a technology that seems at times to encourage rapid-response thoughtlessness. Much as with other socially influenced behaviours (for example, consumption of food or alcohol, sexual activity) we need to find ways to manage our behaviour so that our experiences are beneficial, and to educate and support young people and others to do the same.

As a society we need to make important decisions about the use of legal powers to limit the reach and content of social media. Although the main emphasis in discussions about regulation has been on harmful content, that is only one of three aspects of the problem to be considered.

A central issue is algorithmic pushing which increases duration and intensity of exposure. We know that people with existing mental health problems are more likely to spend long periods online and more likely to use sites with content related to their mental health problems, and there is some evidence that such extended exposure makes matters worse. So, what limits should be set on these quantitative aspects of social media viewing?

The question of what to do about algorithmic 'recommendations' is confounded with one about content. It is generally accepted that it would be no bad thing if searches for key terms (self-harm, suicide and so on) were to trigger responses offering links to helpful resources, which raises the question of how to identify resources as helpful (suitable to recommend) or harmful (not to be recommended). In relation to moderation of content, harmfulness is usually defined by terms like glamourizing, normalizing, and encouraging. These words are used without definition and yet proposed as the main criteria upon which any duty of care will be judged. How are they to be defined and identified in ways that don't just rely on individual opinion?

Monitoring and responding to problematic patterns of use is a key issue in debates about online gambling – how to achieve it without driving away those who resent the idea of surveillance and loss of privacy?

It is not our role to make specific suggestions beyond noting that any legislation should be proportionate, as clearly specified as it can be, and enforceable.

And as a society we need to invest more in developing and using positive interventions in social media – aimed at achieving benefit rather than simply restricting access to harm. Links to the pages or helplines of support organizations are unlikely to be sufficient. We know that users of social media value the fact that content is user-generated and thereby seen as most relevant to their needs – we therefore need more developments along the lines described in the later chapters of this volume.

One undoubted limitation of the research in this area is how dominated it is by English language publication and, by the same token, by findings from countries in which English is the primary language. As a result we have only limited understanding of, for example, cultural influences on social media use and its relation to mental health compared with what we know about the picture in those countries in the developed world from which most research comes. The other obvious limitation in research terms is that we have very limited evidence on the best ways to intervene to modify social media usage and experience for the benefit of all who use it.

The essays in this volume reflect, and we hope will encourage, a more nuanced approach to the discussion of social media in relation to mental health and what we might need to do – through legislation, education, or other means – to ensure they are a force for good and not for harm.

References

1 Introducing Social Media

1. Wells, G., J. Horwitz, and D. Seetharaman, *Facebook knows Instagram is toxic for teen girls, company documents show.* 2021; Available from: www.wsj.com/articles/facebook-knows-instagram-is-toxic-for-teen-girls-company-documents-show-11631620739 (last accessed 7 May 2023).
2. Baym, N.K., Social media and the struggle for society. *Social Media and Society*, 2015. **1**(1): p. 1–2.
3. Bercovici, J. *Who coined social media? Web pioneers compete for credit.* 9 December 2010; Available from: www.forbes.com/sites/jeffbercovici/2010/12/09/who-coined-social-media-web-pioneers-compete-for-credit/#1fada0c151d5 (last accessed 7 May 2023).
4. Jamieson, J., Many (to platform) to many: Web 2.0 application infrastructures. *First Monday*, 2016. **21**(6).
5. Grossman, L., *You – yes, you – are Time's Person of the Year.* 25 December 2006; Available from: http://content.time.com/time/magazine/article/0,9171,1570810,00.html (last accessed 7 May 2023).
6. Bruns, A., *Blogs, Wikipedia, Second Life, and Beyond: From Production to Produsage.* 2008, New York; Oxford: Peter Lang.
7. McLelland, M., H. Yu, and G. Goggin, Alternative histories of social media in Japan and China, in *The SAGE Handbook of Social Media*, J. Burgess, A. Marwick, and T. Poell, Editors. 2017, London; New York: SAGE. p. 53–68.
8. Boyd, D.M. and N.B. Ellison, Social network sites: Definition, history, and scholarship. *Journal of Computer-Mediated Communication*, 2007. **13**(1): p. 210–230.
9. Miltner, K.M. and Y. Gerrard, "Tom had us all doing front-end web development": A nostalgic (re)imagining of Myspace. *Internet Histories*, 2021. **21**(6): p. 1–20.
10. Burgess, J., A. Marwick, and T. Poell, *The SAGE Handbook of Social Media*. 2017, London; New York: Sage.
11. Maris, E., T. Libert, and J.R. Henrichsen, Tracking sex: The implications of widespread sexual data leakage and tracking on porn websites. *New Media and Society*, 2020. **22**(11): p. 2018–2038.
12. Bell, K. *How Sarahah became one of the most popular iPhone apps in the world.* 23 July 2017; Available from: https://mashable.com/article/the-story-of-sarahah-app (last accessed 7 May 2023).
13. Gerrard, Y., 'Too good to be true': The challenges of regulating social media startups. In: T. Gillespie, et al. Expanding the debate about content moderation: Scholarly research agendas for the coming policy debates. *Internet Policy Review*, 2020. **9**(4). DOI: 10.147. Available at SSRN: https://ssrn.com/abstract=4459448
14. Matamoros-Fernández, A., Inciting anger through Facebook reactions in Belgium: The use of emoji and related vernacular expressions in racist discourse. *First Monday*, 2018. **23**(9).
15. Roberts, S.T., *Behind the Screen: Content Moderation in the Shadows of Social Media.* 2019, New Haven, CT: Yale University Press.
16. Gillespie, T., The politics of 'platforms'. *New Media and Society*, 2010. **12**(3): p. 347–364.
17. McChesney, R.W., *Digital Disconnect: How Capitalism Is Turning the Internet against Democracy.* 2013, New York: New Press.
18. Gibbs, M., et al., #Funeral and Instagram: Death, social media, and platform vernacular. *Information, Communication & Society*, 2015. **18**(3): p. 255–268.
19. Patelis, K., Political economy and monopoly abstractions: What social media demand, in *Unlike Us Reader:*

Social Media Monopolies and Their Alternatives, G. Lovink and M. Rasch, Editors. 2013, Amsterdam: Institute of Network Cultures. p. 117–126.
20. Hogan, B., Pseudonyms and the rise of the real-name Web, in *A Companion to New Media Dynamics*, J. Hartley, J. Burgess, and A. Bruns, Editors. 2013, Chichester: Wiley. p. 390–407.
21. Hine, C., *Ethnography for the Internet: Embedded, Embodied and Everyday*. 2015, London: Bloomsbury.
22. McCosker, A. and Y. Gerrard, Hashtagging depression on Instagram: Towards a more inclusive mental health research methodology. *New Media and Society*, 2020. **23**(7): p. 1899–1919.
23. Goffman, E., *The Presentation of Self in Everyday Life*. 1959, New York: Anchor Books.
24. Marwick, A.E. and D. Boyd, I tweet honestly, I tweet passionately: Twitter users, context collapse, and the imagined audience. *New Media and Society*, 2011. **13**(1): p. 114–133.
25. Hogan, B., The presentation of self in the age of social media: Distinguishing performances and exhibitions online. *Bulletin of Science, Technology and Society*, 2010. **30**(6): p. 377–386.
26. Van der Nagel, E., Alts and automediality: Compartmentalising the self through multiple social media platforms. *M/C Journal*, 2018. **21**(2). Available at: https://doi.org/10.5204/mcj.1379
27. Ditchfield, H., Behind the screen of Facebook: Identity construction in the rehearsal stage of online interaction. *New Media and Society*, 2019. **22**(6): p. 927–943.

2 The Legal and Ethical Status of Social Media

1. The Committee Office and House of Lords, *Communications Committee – First Report Social Media and Criminal Offences*. 2014, London: The Stationery Office Ltd.
2. *Suicide Act 1961* (9 & 10 Eliz 2 c 60). Available from: www.legislation.gov.uk/ukpga/Eliz2/9-10/60 (accessed 21 December 2022).
3. *Law Commission, Reform of the Communications Offences*. Available from: www.lawcom.gov.uk/project/reform-of-the-communications-offences/ (accessed 18 June 2022).
4. *Law Commission, Modernising Communications Offences* (Law Com No. 399, 2021). Available from: www.lawcom.gov.uk/ (last accessed 6 May 2023).
5. *Draft UK Online Safety Bill*. Available from: https://bills.parliament.uk/bills/3137 (accessed 18 June 2022).
6. Career Teachers, *Social media guide for UK teachers*. Available from: www.careerteachers.co.uk/-/media/careerteachers/images/social-media-guide-for-teachers.pdf (accessed 18 June 2022).
7. General Medical Council, *Doctors' use of social media*. Available from: www.gmc-uk.org/ethical-guidance/ethical-guidance-for-doctors/doctors-use-of-social-media (accessed 18 June 2022).
8. Wu, J.T. and J.B. McCormick, Why health professionals should speak out against false beliefs on the Internet. *AMA Journal of Ethics*, 2018. **20**(11): p. E1052–1058.
9. General Medical Council, *Good medical practice*. Available from: www.gmc-uk.org/ethical-guidance/ethical-guidance-for-doctors/good-medical-practice (accessed 18 June 2022).
10. British Medical Association, *Social media, ethics and professionalism*. 2018. Available at: www.bma.org.uk/media/1851/bma-ethics-guidance-on-social-media-2018.pdf (accessed 18 June 2022).
11. General Medical Council, *Confidentiality: Good practice in handling patient information*. Available at: www.gmc-uk.org/ethical-guidance/ethical-guidance-for-doctors/confidentiality (accessed 18 June 2022).

12. *Human Rights Act 1998 (c.42), Article 8.* Available at: www.legislation.gov.uk/ukpga/1998/42 (accessed 21 December 2022).
13. Medical Research Council Regulatory Support Centre, *Identifiability, anonymisation and pseudonymisation.* Available at: www.ukri.org/wp-content/uploads/2021/11/MRC-291121-GDPR-Identifiability-Anonymisation-Pseudonymisation.pdf (accessed 18 June 2022).

3 Social Media: An Everyday Reality

1. Parry, D., et al., A systematic review and meta-analysis of discrepancies between logged and self-reported digital media use. *Nature Human Behaviour*, 2021. **5**(11): p. 1535–1547.
2. Orben, A. and A.K. Przybylski, The association between adolescent well-being and digital technology use. *Nature Human Behaviour*, 2019. **3**(2): p. 173–182.
3. Vanden Abeele, M.M.P., A. Halfmann, and E.W.J. Lee, Drug, demon, or donut? Theorizing the relationship between social media use, digital well-being and digital disconnection. *Current Opinion in Psychology*, 2022. **45**: p. 101295.
4. Ellis, D.A., Are smartphones really that bad? Improving the psychological measurement of technology-related behaviors. *Computers in Human Behavior*, 2019. **97**: p. 60–66.
5. Bandura, A., Growing primacy of human agency in adaptation and change in the electronic era. *European Psychologist*, 2002. **7**(1): p. 2–16.
6. Nadkarni, A. and S.G. Hofmann, Why do people use Facebook? *Personality and Individual Differences*, 2012. **52**(3): p. 243–249.
7. Rosenfeld, M.J., R.J. Thomas, and S. Hausen, Disintermediating your friends: How online dating in the United States displaces other ways of meeting. *Proceedings of the National Academy of Sciences*, 2019. **116**(36): p. 17753–17758.
8. Joinson, A.N., Looking at, looking up or keeping up with people? Motives and use of Facebook, in *Proceedings of the SIGCHI Conference on Human Factors in Computing Systems*. 2008, Florence, Italy: Association for Computing Machinery. p. 1027–1036.
9. Orchard, L.J., et al., Individual differences as predictors of social networking. *Journal of Computer-Mediated Communication*, 2014. **19**(3): p. 388–402.
10. Seidman, G., Self-presentation and belonging on Facebook: How personality influences social media use and motivations. *Personality and Individual Differences*, 2013. **54**(3): p. 402–407.
11. Davidson, B.I. and A.N. Joinson, Shape shifting across social media. *Social Media and Society*, 2021. **7**(1): p. 2056305121990632.
12. Hoffman, B.L., et al., "Their page is still up": Social media and coping with loss. *Journal of Loss and Trauma*, 2021. **26**(5): p. 451–468.
13. Treré, E., Intensification, discovery and abandonment: Unearthing global ecologies of dis/connection in pandemic times. *Convergence*, 2021. **27**(6): p. 1663–1677.
14. Büchi, M. and E. Hargittai, A need for considering digital inequality when studying social media use and well-being. *Social Media and Society*, 2022. **8**(1): p. 20563051211069125.
15. Blank, G. and C. Lutz, Representativeness of social media in Great Britain: Investigating Facebook, LinkedIn, Twitter, Pinterest, Google+, and Instagram. *American Behavioural Scientist*, 2017. **61**(7): p. 741–756.
16. Lazer, D.M.J., et al., The science of fake news. *Science*, 2018. **359**(6380): p. 1094–1096.
17. Scharkow, M., et al., How social network sites and other online intermediaries increase exposure to news. *Proceedings of the National Academy of Sciences*, 2020. **117**(6): p. 2761–2763.

18. Vasalou, A. and A.N. Joinson, Me, myself and I: The role of interactional context on self-presentation through avatars. *Computers in Human Behavior*, 2009. **25**(2): p. 510–520.
19. McEwan, B. and C.J. Carpenter, Networked maintenance: The effect of Facebook relational maintenance on network centrality. *Communication Studies*, 2020. **71**(2): p. 187–202.
20. Taylor, S.H. and N.N. Bazarova, Always available, always attached: A relational perspective on the effects of mobile phones and social media on subjective well-being. *Journal of Computer-Mediated Communication*, 2021. **26**(4): p. 187–206.
21. Halfmann, A. and D. Rieger, Permanently on call: The effects of social pressure on smartphone users' self-control, need satisfaction, and well-being. *Journal of Computer-Mediated Communication*, 2019. **24**(4): p. 165–181.
22. Matassi, M., P.J. Boczkowski, and E. Mitchelstein, Domesticating WhatsApp: Family, friends, work, and study in everyday communication. *New Media & Society*, 2019. **21**(10): p. 2183–2200.
23. Horvát, E.-Á. and E. Hargittai, Birds of a feather flock together online: Digital inequality in social media repertoires. *Social Media and Society*, 2021. **7**(4): p. 20563051211052897.
24. Barros, P.B., et al., Circumspect users: Older adults as critical adopters and resistors of technology, in *Proceedings of the 2021 CHI Conference on Human Factors in Computing Systems*. 2021, Yokohama, Japan: Association for Computing Machinery. p. 1–14.
25. Bayer, J.B., I.A. Anderson, and R.S. Tokunaga, Building and breaking social media habits. *Current Opinion in Psychology*, 2022. **45**: p. 101303.
26. Hinds, J., et al., Integrating insights about human movement patterns from digital data into psychological science. *Current Directions in Psychological Science*, 2021. **31**(1): p. 88–95.
27. Taylor, S.H., P. Zhao, and N.N. Bazarova, Social media and close relationships: A puzzle of connection and disconnection. *Current Opinion in Psychology*, 2022. **45**: p. 101292.
28. Haythornthwaite, C., Exploring multiplexity: Social network structures in a computer-supported distance learning class. *The Information Society*, 2001. **17**(3): p. 211–226.
29. Kubovy, M., Lives as collections of strands: An essay in descriptive psychology. *Perspectives on Psychological Science*, 2020. **15**(2): p. 497–515.
30. Karhulahti, V.-M., Registered reports for qualitative research. *Nature Human Behaviour*, 2022. **6**(1): p. 4–5.

4 How Social Media Can Influence Group and Individual Behaviour

1. Vuorre, M., A. Orben, and A.K. Przybylski, There is no evidence that associations between adolescents' digital technology engagement and mental health problems have increased. *Clinical Psychological Science*, 2021. **9**(5): p. 823–835.
2. Dahl, S., *Social Media Marketing, Theories and Applications*. 2015, London: Sage Publishing.
3. Habermas, J., *Theory of Communicative Action, Volume One: Reason and the Rationalization of Society*. Translated by Thomas A. McCarthy. 1981, Boston, MA: Beacon Press.
4. Horton, D. and R.R. Wohl, Mass communication and para-social interaction; Observations on intimacy at a distance. *Psychiatry*, 1956. **19**(3): p. 215–229.
5. Lueck, J.A., Friend-zone with benefits: The parasocial advertising of Kim Kardashian. *Journal of Marketing Communications*, 2012. **21**(2): p. 91–109.
6. Ad Council. *Popular TikTok creators join #AloneTogether campaign to address*

mental health challenges during COVID-19 crisis. 12 May 2020; Available from: www.adcouncil.org/learn-with-us/press-releases/popular-tiktok-creators-join-alonetogether-campaign-to-address-mental-health-challenges-during-covid-19-crisis (last accessed 8 May 2023).
7. Fogg, B.J., Persuasive technologies. *Communications of the ACM*, 1999. **42**(5): p. 26–29.
8. Torning, K. and H. Oinas-Kukkonen, Persuasive system design: State of the art and future directions, in *Proceedings of the 4th International Conference on Persuasive Technology, Association for Computing Machinery*. 2009, Claremont, CA.
9. Sharma, M.K., N. John, and M. Sahu, Influence of social media on mental health: A systematic review. *Current Opinion in Psychiatry*, 2020. **33**(5): p. 467–475.
10. Bekalu, M.A., R.F. McCloud, and K. Viswanath, Association of social media use with social well-being, positive mental health, and self-rated health: Disentangling routine use from emotional connection to use. *Health Education & Behavior*, 2019. **46**(2_suppl): p. 69S–80S.
11. Andreassen, C.S., S. Pallesen, and M.D. Griffiths, The relationship between addictive use of social media, narcissism, and self-esteem: Findings from a large national survey. *Addictive Behaviors*, 2017. **64**: p. 287–293.
12. Andreassen, C.S., Online social network site addiction: A comprehensive review. *Current Addiction Reports*, 2015. **2**(2): p. 175–184.
13. Pantic, I., Social networking and depression: An emerging issue in behavioral physiology and psychiatric research. *The Journal of Adolescent Health*, 2014. **54**(6): p. 745–746.
14. Churchman, C.W., Wicked problems. *Management Science*, 1967. **14**(4): p. 141–142.
15. Hagi, S. *Cancel culture is not real – at least not in the way people think*. 21 November 2019; Available from: https://time.com/5735403/cancel-culture-is-not-real/ (last accessed 7 May 2023).
16. The International Society for Mental Health Online (ISMHO). *About ISMHO*. 2021; Available from: https://ismho.org/ismho/about-ismho/ (last accessed 7 May 2023).
17. Grönroos, C. and P. Voima, Critical service logic: Making sense of value creation and co-creation. *Journal of the Academy of Marketing Science*, 2013. **41**(2): p. 133–150.
18. Vivaldi Partners Group. *What is social currency?* [cited 15 October 2021]; Available from: www.vivaldipartners.com/vpsocialcurrency/abo.
19. Freeman, B., et al., Social media campaigns that make a difference: What can public health learn from the corporate sector and other social change marketers? *Public Health Research and Practice*, 2015. **25**(2): p. e2521517.
20. Obar, J.A., P. Zube, and C. Lampe, Advocacy 2.0: An analysis of how advocacy groups in the United States perceive and use social media as tools for facilitating civic engagement and collective action. *Journal of Information Policy*, 2012. **2**: p. 1–25.
21. French, J. and R. Gordon, *Strategic Social Marketing*. 2020, Los Angeles: Sage.

5 Researching Social Media: Qualitative and Mixed-Methods Research Approaches

1. Biddle, L., et al., Using the Internet for suicide-related purposes: Contrasting findings from young people in the community and self-harm patients admitted to hospital. *PLoS ONE*, 2018. **13**(5): p. e0197712.
2. Räisänen, U. and K. Hunt, The role of gendered constructions of eating disorders in delayed help-seeking in men: A qualitative interview study. *BMJ Open*, 2014. **4**(4): p. e004342.

3. O'Reilly, M., et al., Is social media bad for mental health and wellbeing? Exploring the perspectives of adolescents. *Clinical Child Psychology and Psychiatry*, 2018. **23**(4): p. 601–613.
4. Lavis, A. and R. Winter, #Online harms or benefits? An ethnographic analysis of the positives and negatives of peer-support around self-harm on social media. *Journal of Child Psychology and Psychiatry*, 2020. **61**(8): p. 842–854.
5. Braun, V. and V. Clarke, One size fits all? What counts as quality practice in (reflexive) thematic analysis? *Qualitative Research in Psychology*, 2021. **18**(3): p. 328–352.
6. Jacob, N., R. Evans, and J. Scourfield, The influence of online images on self-harm: A qualitative study of young people aged 16–24. *Journal of Adolescence*, 2017. **60**: p. 140–147.
7. Heyes, K., Socialization or social isolation?: Mental health community support in the digital age, in *Research Anthology on Mental Health Stigma, Education, and Treatment*, I.R. Management Association, Editor. 2021, Hershey, PA: IGI Global. p. 360–380.
8. Brennan, C., et al., Self-harm and suicidal content online, harmful or helpful? A systematic review of the recent evidence. *Journal of Public Mental Health*, 2022. **21**(1): p. 57–69.
9. Arendt, F., Suicide on Instagram – Content analysis of a German suicide-related hashtag. *Crisis: Journal of Crisis Intervention & Suicide*, 2019. **40**(1): p. 36–41.
10. Kędra, J., To see more: A model for press photograph story analysis. *Journal of Visual Literacy*, 2013. **32**(1): p. 27–50.
11. Rose, G., *Visual Methodologies: An Introduction to Researching with Visual Materials*. 4th ed. 2016, Oxford, UK: SAGE Publishing.
12. Shanahan, N., C. Brennan, and A. House, Self-harm and social media: Thematic analysis of images posted on three social media sites. *BMJ Open*, 2019. **9**(2): p. e027006.
13. Ellis, D.A., Are smartphones really that bad? Improving the psychological measurement of technology-related behaviors. *Computers in Human Behavior*, 2019. **97**: p. 60–66.
14. Eccles, D.W. and G. Arsal, The think aloud method: What is it and how do I use it? *Qualitative Research in Sport, Exercise and Health*, 2017. **9**(4): p. 514–531.

6 Researching Social Media: Quantitative Approaches

1. Bowers, D., et al., *Understanding Clinical Papers*. 4th ed. 2020, Chichester: John Wiley & Sons.
2. Marshall, J.M., D.A. Dunstan, and W. Bartik, Effectiveness of using mental health mobile apps as digital antidepressants for reducing anxiety and depression: Protocol for a multiple baseline across-individuals design. *JMIR Research Protocols*, 2020. **9**(7): p. e17159.
3. Hawton, K., et al., Clustering of suicides in children and adolescents. *The Lancet Child and Adolescent Health*, 2020. **4**(1): p. 58–67.
4. Jones, P., et al., Identifying probable suicide clusters in Wales using national mortality data. *PLoS One*, 2013. **8**(8): p. e71713.
5. Mars, B., et al., Exposure to, and searching for, information about suicide and self-harm on the Internet: Prevalence and predictors in a population based cohort of young adults. *Journal of Affective Disorders*, 2015. **185**: p. 239–245.
6. Ma, X. and H. Sayama, Mental disorder recovery correlated with centralities and interactions on an online social network. *PeerJ*, 2015. **3**: p. e1163–e1163.
7. Doll, R. and A.B. Hill, Smoking and carcinoma of the lung. *British Medical Journal*, 1950. **2**(4682): p. 739–748.
8. Yao, B., et al., Freshman year mental health symptoms and level of adaptation as predictors of internet addiction: A retrospective nested case-control study

of male Chinese college students. *Psychiatry Research*, 2013. **210**(2): p. 541–547.

9. Thom, R.P., D.S. Bickham, and M. Rich, Internet use, depression, and anxiety in a healthy adolescent population: Prospective cohort study. *JMIR Mental Health*, 2018. **5**(2): p. e44.

10. Bridge, J.A., et al., Association between the release of Netflix's *13 Reasons Why* and suicide rates in the United States: An interrupted time series analysis. *Journal of the American Academy of Child & Adolescent Psychiatry*, 2020. **59**(2): p. 236–243.

11. Till, B., et al., Beneficial and harmful effects of educative suicide prevention websites: Randomised controlled trial exploring Papageno v. Werther effects. *British Journal of Psychiatry*, 2017. **211**(2): p. 109–115.

12. Arendt, F., S. Scherr, and D. Romer, Effects of exposure to self-harm on social media: Evidence from a two-wave panel study among young adults. *New Media and Society*, 2019. **21**(11–12): p. 2422–2442.

13. Escobar-Viera, C.G., et al., Association between LGB sexual orientation and depression mediated by negative social media experiences: National Survey Study of US young adults. *JMIR Mental Health*, 2020. **7**(12): p. e23520.

14. Stapelberg, N.J.C., et al., Efficacy of the Zero Suicide framework in reducing recurrent suicide attempts: Cross-sectional and time-to-recurrent-event analyses. *The British Journal of Psychiatry*, 2020. **219**(2): p. 427–436.

7 The Harms and Benefits of Social Media

1. Rheingold, H., Attention, and other 21st-century social media literacies. *Educational Review*, 2010. **45**: p. 14.

2. Ofcom, *Online Nation 2020 Report*. 2020. p. 176.

3. Willard, N., *Cyberbullying and Cyberthreats: Responding to the Challenge of Online Social Aggression, Threats, and Distress*. 2007. Champaign, IL: Research Press.

4. Jenaro, C., N. Flores, and C. Frias Butrón, Systematic review of empirical studies on cyberbullying in adults: What we know and what we should investigate. *Aggression and Violent Behavior*, 2018. **38**: p. 113–122.

5. Betts, L.R., T. Baguley, and S.E. Gardner, Examining adults' participant roles in cyberbullying. *Journal of Social and Personal Relationships*, 2019. **36**(11–12): p. 3362–3370.

6. Pacheco, E., N. Melhuish, and J. Fiske, Digital self-harm: prevalence, motivations and outcomes for teens who cyberbully themselves. 1 May 2019, Netsafe: https://apo.org.au/node/252376 (last accessed 7 May 2023).

7. Mori, C., et al., The prevalence of sexting behaviors among emerging adults: A meta-analysis. *Archives of Sexual Behaviour*, 2020. **49**(4): p. 1103–1119.

8. Livingstone, S., et al., In their own words: What bothers children online? *European Journal of Communication*, 2014. **29**(3): p. 271–288.

9. Madigan, S., et al., Prevalence of multiple forms of sexting behavior among youth: A systematic review and meta-analysis. *JAMA Pediatrics*, 2018. **172**(4): p. 327–335.

10. Gámez-Guadix, M. and E. Mateos-Pérez, Longitudinal and reciprocal relationships between sexting, online sexual solicitations, and cyberbullying among minors. *Computers in Human Behavior*, 2019. **94**: p. 70–76.

11. Klettke, B., D.J. Hallford, and D.J. Mellor, Sexting prevalence and correlates: A systematic literature review. *Clinical Psychology Review*, 2014. **34**(1): p. 44–53.

12. Pennycook, G. and D.G. Rand, The psychology of fake news. *Trends in Cognitive Sciences*, 2021. **25**(5): p. 388–402.

13. Apuke, O.D. and B. Omar, Fake news and COVID-19: Modelling the predictors of fake news sharing among social media users. *Telematics and Informatics*, 2021. **56**: p. 101475–101475.
14. Berryman, C., C.J. Ferguson, and C. Negy, Social media use and mental health among young adults. *Psychiatric Quarterly*, 2018. **89**(2): p. 307–314.
15. Gao, J., et al., Mental health problems and social media exposure during COVID-19 outbreak. *PLoS One*, 2020. **15**(4): p. e0231924.
16. Piazza, J.A., Fake news: The effects of social media disinformation on domestic terrorism. *Dynamics of Asymmetric Conflict*, 2021. **15**(1): p. 55–77.
17. Singer, P., et al. Why we read Wikipedia, in *Proceedings of the 26th International Conference on World Wide Web*. 2017. p. 1591–1600.
18. Zhao, Y. and J. Zhang, Consumer health information seeking in social media: A literature review. *Health Information and Libraries Journal*, 2017. **34**(4): p. 268–283.
19. Liu, D., S.E. Ainsworth, and R.F. Baumeister, A meta-analysis of social networking online and social capital. *Review of General Psychology*, 2016. **20**(4): p. 369–391.
20. Alencar, A., Refugee integration and social media: A local and experiential perspective. *Information, Communication & Society*, 2018. **21**(11): p. 1588–1603.
21. Higgins, E.T., Self-discrepancy: A theory relating self and affect. *Psychological Review*, 1987. **94**(3): p. 319–340.
22. Twomey, C. and G. O'Reilly, Associations of self-presentation on Facebook with mental health and personality variables: A systematic review. *Cyberpsychology, Behavior and Social Networking*, 2017. **20**(10): p. 587–595.
23. Reinecke, L. and S. Trepte, Authenticity and well-being on social network sites: A two-wave longitudinal study on the effects of online authenticity and the positivity bias in SNS communication. *Computers in Human Behavior*, 2014. **30**: p. 95–102.
24. Lucero, L., Safe spaces in online places: Social media and LGBTQ youth. *Multicultural Education Review*, 2017. **9**(2): p. 117–128.
25. Furr, J.B., A. Carreiro, and J.A. McArthur, Strategic approaches to disability disclosure on social media. *Disability & Society*, 2016. **31**(10): p. 1353–1368.
26. Caton, S. and M. Chapman, The use of social media and people with intellectual disability: A systematic review and thematic analysis. *Journal of Intellectual & Developmental Disability*, 2016. **41**(2): p. 125–139.

8 Social Media and Disorders of Mood

1. Heffer, T., et al., The longitudinal association between social-media use and depressive symptoms among adolescents and young adults: An empirical reply to Twenge et al. (2018). *Clinical Psychological Science*, 2019. **7**(3): p. 462–470.
2. Radloff, L.S., The CES-D scale: A self-report depression scale for research in the general population. *Applied Psychological Measurement*, 1977. **1**(3): p. 385–401.
3. Cunningham, S., C.C. Hudson, and K. Harkness, Social media and depression symptoms: A meta-analysis. *Research on Child and Adolescent Psychopathology*, 2021. **49**(2): p. 241–253.
4. Vidal, C., et al., Social media use and depression in adolescents: A scoping review. *International Review of Psychiatry*, 2020. **32**(3): p. 235–253.
5. Valkenburg, P.M., A. Meier, and I. Beyens, Social media use and its impact on adolescent mental health: An umbrella review of the evidence. *Current Opinion in Psychology*, 2021. **44**: p. 58–68.
6. Jelenchick, L., J.C. Eickhoff, and M.A. Moreno, "Facebook depression?" Social

networking site use and depression in older adolescents. *Journal of Adolescent Health*, 2013. **52**(1): p. 128–130.

7. Berryman, C., C.J. Ferguson, and C. Negy, Social media use and mental health among young adults. *Psychiatric Quarterly*, 2018. **89**(2): p. 307–314.

8. Orben, A., T. Dienlin, and A.K. Przybylski, Social media's enduring effect on adolescent life satisfaction. *Proceedings of the National Academy of Sciences*, 2019. **116**(21): p. 10226–10228.

9. Vernon, L., K. Modecki, and B. Barber, Tracking effects of problematic social networking on adolescent psychopathology: The mediating role of sleep disruptions. *Journal of Clinical Child & Adolescent Psychology*, 2017. **46**(2): p. 269–283.

10. Perlis, R.H., et al., Association between social media use and self-reported symptoms of depression in US adults. *JAMA Network Open*, 2021. **4**(11): p. e2136113.

11. Primack, B.A., et al., Temporal associations between social media use and depression. *American Journal of Preventive Medicine*, 2021. **60**(2): p. 179–188.

12. Primack, B.A., et al., Use of multiple social media platforms and symptoms of depression and anxiety: A nationally-representative study among U.S. young adults. *Computers in Human Behavior*, 2017. **69**: p. 1–9.

13. Escobar-Viera, C.G., et al., Passive and active social media use and depressive symptoms among United States adults. *Cyberpsychology, Behavior, and Social Networking*, 2018. **21**(7): p. 437–443.

14. Livingstone, S., et al., In their own words: What bothers children online? *European Journal of Communication*, 2014. **29**(3): p. 271–288.

15. Alonzo, R., et al., Interplay between social media use, sleep quality, and mental health in youth: A systematic review. *Sleep Medicine Reviews*, 2021. **56**: p. 101414.

16. Lovato, N. and M. Gradisar, A meta-analysis and model of the relationship between sleep and depression in adolescents: Recommendations for future research and clinical practice. *Sleep Medicine Reviews*, 2014. **18**(6): p. 521–529.

17. Shensa, A., et al., Emotional support from social media and face-to-face relationships: Associations with depression risk among young adults. *Journal of Affective Disorders*, 2020. **260**: p. 38–44.

18. Valkenburg, P., J. Peter, and J. Walther, Media effects: Theory and research. *Annual Review of Psychology*, 2016. **67**: p. 315–338.

19. Göritz, A.S. and K. Moser, Web-based mood induction. *Cognition and Emotion*, 2006. **20**(6): p. 887–896.

20. Bell, A.C. and T.J. D'Zurilla, Problem-solving therapy for depression: A meta-analysis. *Clinical Psychology Review*, 2009. **29**(4): p. 348–353.

9 Social Media Use, Body Image, and Eating Disorders

1. Thompson, J.K., et al., *Exacting Beauty: Theory, Assessment, and Treatment of Body Image Disturbance*. 1999, Washington, DC: American Psychological Association.

2. Bourdieu, P., The forms of capital, in *Handbook of Theory and Research for the Sociology of Education*, J.G. Richardson, Editor. 1986, New York: Greenwood Press. p. 241–258.

3. Rubin, A.M., Media uses and effects: A uses-and-gratifications perspective, in *Media Effects: Advances in Theory and Research*, J. Bryant and D. Zillmann, Editors. 1994, New Jersey: Lawrence Erlbaum Associates, Inc. p. 525–548.

4. Paxton, S., S.A. McLean, and R. Rodgers, "My critical filter buffers your app filter": Social media literacy as a protective factor for body image. *Body Image*, 2022. **40**: p. 158–164.

5. Saiphoo, A.N. and Z. Vahedi, A meta-analytic review of the relationship between social media use and body image disturbance. *Computers in Human Behavior*, 2019. **101**: p. 259–275.
6. de Valle, M.K., et al., Social media, body image, and the question of causation: Meta-analyses of experimental and longitudinal evidence. *Body Image*, 2021. **39**: p. 276–292.
7. Burnette, C.B., M.A. Kwitowski, and S.E. Mazzeo, "I don't need people to tell me I'm pretty on social media": A qualitative study of social media and body image in early adolescent girls. *Body Image*, 2017. **23**: p. 114–125.
8. Feltman, C.E. and D.M. Szymanski, Instagram use and self-objectification: The roles of internalization, comparison, appearance commentary, and feminism. *Sex Roles*, 2018. **78**(5): p. 311–324.
9. Rodgers, R.F. and A. Rousseau, Social media and body image: Modulating effects of social identities and user characteristics. *Body Image*, 2022. **41**: p. 284–291.
10. Rodgers, R.F., S.J. Paxton, and E.H. Wertheim, #Take idealized bodies out of the picture: A scoping review of social media content aiming to protect and promote positive body image. *Body Image*, 2021. **38**: p. 10–36.
11. Norris, M.L., et al., Ana and the Internet: A review of pro-anorexia websites. *International Journal of Eating Disorders*, 2006. **39**(6): p. 443–447.
12. Mento, C., et al., Psychological impact of pro-anorexia and pro-eating disorder websites on adolescent females: A systematic review. *International Journal of Environmental Research and Public Health*, 2021. **18**(4): p. 2186.
13. Linardon, J., et al., E-mental health interventions for the treatment and prevention of eating disorders: An updated systematic review and meta-analysis. *Journal of Consulting and Clinical Psychology*, 2020. **88**(11): p. 994–1007.
14. National Eating Disorder Association. *Help & support*. 2018; Available from: www.nationaleatingdisorders.org/help-support (last accessed 7 May 2023).

10 Social Media and Gambling

1. Potenza, M.N., et al., Gambling disorder. *Nature Reviews Disease Primers*, 2019. **5**(1): p. 51.
2. Gainsbury, S.M., Online gambling addiction: The relationship between internet gambling and disordered gambling. *Current Addiction Reports*, 2015. **2**(2): p. 185–193.
3. Calado, F. and M.D. Griffiths, Problem gambling worldwide: An update and systematic review of empirical research (2000–2015). *Journal of Behavioral Addictions*, 2016. **5**(4): p. 592–613.
4. Goodwin, B., et al., A typical problem gambler affects six others. *International Gambling Studies*, 2017. **17**(2): p. 276–289.
5. Hodgins, D.C., J.N. Stea, and J.E. Grant, Gambling disorders. *The Lancet*, 2011. **378**(9806): p. 1874–1884.
6. Lorains, F.K., S. Cowlishaw, and S.A. Thomas, Prevalence of comorbid disorders in problem and pathological gambling: Systematic review and meta-analysis of population surveys. *Addiction*, 2011. **106**(3): p. 490–498.
7. Gainsbury, S.M., J. Tobias-Webb, and R. Slonim, Behavioral economics and gambling: A new paradigm for approaching harm-minimization. *Gaming Law Review*, 2018. **22**(10): p. 608–617.
8. Wardle, H., et al., Gambling and public health: We need policy action to prevent harm. *British Medical Journal*, 2019. **365**: p. l1807.
9. Rossi, R., et al., "Get a £10 free bet every week!" – gambling advertising on Twitter: Volume, content, followers, engagement, and regulatory compliance. *Journal of Public Policy & Marketing*, 2021. **40**(4): p. 487–504.

10. Bouguettaya, A., et al., The relationship between gambling advertising and gambling attitudes, intentions and behaviours: A critical and meta-analytic review. *Current Opinion in Behavioral Sciences*, 2020. **31**: p. 89–101.
11. Ipsos MORI. *The effect of gambling marketing and advertising on children, young people and vulnerable adults.* 2020; Available from: www.begambleaware.org/media/2160/the-effect-of-gambling-marketing-and-advertising-synthesis-report_final.pdf (last accessed 7 May 2023).
12. James, R.J.E. and A. Bradley, The use of social media in research on gambling: A systematic review. *Current Addiction Reports*, 2021. **8**(2): p. 235–245.
13. Torrance, J., et al., Emergent gambling advertising: A rapid review of marketing content, delivery and structural features. *BMC Public Health*, 2021. **21**(1): p. 718.
14. Hörnle, J., et al., Regulating online advertising for gambling – once the genie is out of the bottle… *Information & Communications Technology Law*, 2019. **28**(3): p. 311–334.
15. Houghton, S., et al., Comparing the Twitter posting of British gambling operators and gambling affiliates: A summative content analysis. *International Gambling Studies*, 2019. **19**(2): p. 312–326.
16. Hollingshead, S., et al., Motives for playing social casino games and the transition from gaming to gambling (or vice versa): Social casino game play as harm reduction? *Journal of Gambling Issues*, 2021. **46**: p. 43–61.
17. King, D.L. and P.H. Delfabbro, Early exposure to digital simulated gambling: A review and conceptual model. *Computers in Human Behavior*, 2016. **55**: p. 198–206.
18. King, D. and P. Delfabbro, The convergence of gambling and monetised gaming activities. *Current Opinion in Behavioral Sciences*, 2020. **31**: p. 32–36.
19. Abarbanel, B. and M.R. Johnson, Gambling engagement mechanisms in Twitch live streaming. *International Gambling Studies*, 2020. **20**(3): p. 393–413.
20. Sirola, A., et al., The role of virtual communities in gambling and gaming behaviors: A systematic review. *Journal of Gambling Studies*, 2021. **37**(1): p. 165–187.
21. Blank, L., et al., Interventions to reduce the public health burden of gambling-related harms: A mapping review. *Lancet Public Health*, 2021. **6**(1): p. e50–e63.
22. Swanton, T.B., et al., Problematic risk-taking involving emerging technologies: A stakeholder framework to minimize harms. *Journal of Behavioral Addictions*, 2020. **9**(4): p. 869–875.

11 Social Media, Self-Harm, and Suicide

1. Muehlenkamp, J.J., et al., International prevalence of adolescent non-suicidal self-injury and deliberate self-harm. *Child and Adolescent Psychiatry and Mental Health*, 2012. **6**(1): p. 10.
2. Carr, M.J., et al., The epidemiology of self-harm in a UK-wide primary care patient cohort, 2001–2013. *BMC Psychiatry*, 2016. **16**(1): p. 53.
3. Morgan, C., et al., Incidence, clinical management, and mortality risk following self harm among children and adolescents: Cohort study in primary care. *BMJ*, 2017. **359**: p. j4351.
4. Arensman, E., et al., Factors associated with self-cutting as a method of self-harm: Findings from the Irish National Registry of Deliberate Self-Harm. *European Journal of Public Health*, 2014. **24**(2): p. 292–297.
5. Owens, D., et al., Switching methods of self-harm at repeat episodes: Findings from a multicentre cohort study. *Journal of Affective Disorders*, 2015. **180**: p. 44–51.
6. World Health Organization (WHO), *Suicide worldwide in 2019: Global health estimates.* 16 June 2021; Available from: www.who.int/publications/i/item/9789240026643 (last accessed 7 May 2023).
7. Hawton, K., et al., Suicide following self-harm: Findings from the Multicentre

Study of self-harm in England, 2000–2012. *Journal of Affective Disorders*, 2015. **175**: p. 147–151.

8. Shanahan, N., C. Brennan, and A. House, Self-harm and social media: Thematic analysis of images posted on three social media sites. *BMJ Open*, 2019. **9**(2): p. e027006.

9. Geulayov, G., et al., Incidence of suicide, hospital-presenting non-fatal self-harm, and community-occurring non-fatal self-harm in adolescents in England (the iceberg model of self-harm): A retrospective study. *Lancet Psychiatry*, 2018. **5**(2): p. 167–174.

10. Brennan, C., et al., Self-harm and suicidal content online, harmful or helpful? A systematic review of the recent evidence. *Journal of Public Mental Health*, 2022. **21**(1): p. 57–69.

11. Lavis, A. and R. Winter, #Online harms or benefits? An ethnographic analysis of the positives and negatives of peer-support around self-harm on social media. *Journal of Child Psychology and Psychiatry*, 2020. **61**(8): p. 842–854.

12. Berman, R. and Z. Katona, Curation algorithms and filter bubbles in social networks. *Marketing Science*, 2020. **39**(2): p. 296–316.

13. Arendt, F., S. Scherr, and D. Romer, Effects of exposure to self-harm on social media: Evidence from a two-wave panel study among young adults. *New Media & Society*, 2019. **21**(11–12): p. 2422–2442.

14. Biddle, L., et al., Online help for people with suicidal thoughts provided by charities and healthcare organisations: A qualitative study of users' perceptions. *Social Psychiatry and Psychiatric Epidemiology*, 2020. **55**(9): p. 1157–1166.

12 Safely Navigating the Terrain

1. Adams, R., Social media urged to take 'moment to reflect' after girl's death, in *The Guardian*. 30 January 2019; Available from: www.theguardian.com/media/2019/jan/30/social-media-urged-to-take-moment-to-reflect-after-girls-death (last accessed 7 May 2023).

2. eSafety Commissioner. *Best Practice Framework for Online Safety Education*. n.d. [cited 14 April 2022]; Available from: www.esafety.gov.au/educators/best-practice-framework (last accessed 7 May 2023).

3. esafety Commissioner. *Safety by Design*. n.d. [cited 14 April 2022]; Available from: www.esafety.gov.au/industry/safety-by-design (last accessed 7 May 2023).

4. Facebook. *Safety@Facebook*. 2022 [cited 14 April 2022]; Available from: www.facebook.com/safety (last accessed 7 May 2023).

5. Instagram. *Safety*. 2022 [cited 14 April 2022]; Available from: https://about.instagram.com/safety (last accessed 7 May 2023).

6. Snapchat. *Snapchat Safety Centre*. 2022 [cited 14 April 2022]; Available from: https://snap.com/en-US/safety/safety-center (last accessed 7 May 2023).

7. TikTok. *Safety Centre*. 2022 [cited 14 April 2022]; Available from: www.tiktok.com/safety/en/ (last accessed 7 May 2023).

8. Robinson, J., et al., Social media and suicide prevention: A systematic review. *Early Intervention in Psychiatry*, 2016. **10**(2): p. 103–121.

9. Thorn, P., et al., Developing a suicide prevention social media campaign with young people (the #Chatsafe project): Co-design approach. *JMIR Mental Health*, 2020. **7**(5): p. e17520.

10. Bailey, E., et al., An enhanced social networking intervention for young people with active suicidal ideation: Safety, feasibility and acceptability outcomes. *International Journal of Environmental Research and Public Health*, 2020. **17**(7): p. 2435.

11. La Sala, L., et al., Can a social media intervention improve online communication about suicide? A feasibility study examining the acceptability and potential impact of the

#chatsafe campaign. *PLoS ONE*, 2021. **16**(6): p. e0253278.

12. Robinson, J., et al., The #chatsafe project. Developing guidelines to help young people communicate safely about suicide on social media: A Delphi study. *PLoS One*, 2018. **13**(11): p. e0206584.

13. Orygen. *#chatsafe resources*. 2022; Available from: www.orygen.org.au/chatsafe/Resources (last accessed 7 May 2023).

14. Johansson, L., P. Lindqvist, and A. Eriksson, Teenage suicide cluster formation and contagion: Implications for primary care. *BMC Family Practice*, 2006. **7**(1): p. 32.

15. Pirkis, J.E., et al., The relationship between media reporting of suicide and actual suicide in Australia. *Social Science & Medicine*, 2006. **62**(11): p. 2874–2886.

16. Robinson, J., et al., Developing social media-based suicide prevention messages in partnership with young people: Exploratory study. *JMIR Mental Health*, 2017. **4**(4): p. e40.

13 Technological Interventions for Adolescent Mental Health

1. Polanczyk, G.V., et al., Annual research review: A meta-analysis of the worldwide prevalence of mental disorders in children and adolescents. *Journal of Child Psychology and Psychiatry*, 2015. **56**(3): p. 345–365.

2. Collishaw, S. and R. Sellers, Trends in child and adolescent mental health prevalence, outcomes, and inequalities, in *Mental Health and Illness of Children and Adolescents*, E. Taylor, et al., Editors. 2020, Singapore: Springer Singapore. p. 1–11.

3. Whitehorne-Smith, P. and M. Irons-Morgan, *Final Report: Risk Factors Associated with Youth Suicidality in Jamaica*. 2014, UNICEF: www.unicef.org/jamaica/reports/final-report-risk-factors-associated-youth-suicidality-jamaica (last accessed 7 May 2023).

4. Rideout, V., Measuring time spent with media: The Common Sense census of media use by US 8- to 18-year-olds. *Journal of Children and Media*, 2016. **10**(1): p. 138–144.

5. Lee, J., Mental health effects of school closures during COVID-19. *The Lancet Child and Adolescent Health*, 2020. **4**(6): p. 421.

6. The American College of Obstetricians and Gynecologists (ACOG). *Mental Health Disorders in Adolescents*. 2021 [cited 16 November 2021]; Available from: www.acog.org/en/clinical/clinical-guidance/committee-opinion/articles/2017/07/mental-health-disorders-in-adolescents (last accessed 7 May 2023).

7. World Health Organization (WHO). *Adolescent mental health*. 2020 [cited 16 November 2021]; Available from: www.who.int/news-room/fact-sheets/detail/adolescent-mental-health (last accessed 7 May 2023).

8. Whittaker, R., et al., MEMO: An mHealth intervention to prevent the onset of depression in adolescents: A double-blind, randomised, placebo-controlled trial. *Journal of Child Psychology and Psychiatry*, 2017. **58**(9): p. 1014–1022.

9. O'Dea, B., et al., A randomised controlled trial of a relationship-focussed mobile phone application for improving adolescents' mental health. *Journal of Child Psychology and Psychiatry*, 2020. **61**(8): p. 899–913.

10. McManama O'Brien, K.H., et al., A pilot study of the acceptability and usability of a smartphone application intervention for suicidal adolescents and their parents. *Archives of Suicide Research*, 2017. **21**(2): p. 254–264.

11. Kenny, R., B. Dooley, and A. Fitzgerald, Ecological momentary assessment of adolescent problems, coping efficacy, and mood states using a mobile phone app: An exploratory study. *JMIR Mental Health*, 2016. **3**(4): p. e51.

12. Ranney, M.L., et al., A depression prevention intervention for adolescents in the emergency department. *The Journal of Adolescent Health*, 2016. **59**(4): p. 401–410.
13. Dawson, A.E., et al., Exploring how adolescents with ADHD use and interact with technology. *Journal of Adolescence*, 2019. **71**: p. 119–137.
14. David, O.A., R.A.I. Cardoș, and S. Matu, Is REThink therapeutic game effective in preventing emotional disorders in children and adolescents? Outcomes of a randomized clinical trial. *European Child & Adolescent Psychiatry*, 2019. **28**(1): p. 111–122.
15. UNICEF. *UNICEF U-Report poll on COVID-19: One third of Jamaican youth believe they are not at risk*. 2020 [cited 2 December 2021]; Available from: www.unicef.org/jamaica/press-releases/unicef-u-report-poll-covid-19-one-third-jamaican-youth-believe-they-are-not-risk (last accessed 7 May 2023).
16. UNICEF. *Community-based mental health care in Peru*. 2021 [cited 2 December 2021]; Available from: www.unicef.org/stories/community-based-mental-health-care-peru (last accessed 7 May 2023).
17. Ssewamala, F.M., et al., Suubi4Her: A study protocol to examine the impact and cost associated with a combination intervention to prevent HIV risk behavior and improve mental health functioning among adolescent girls in Uganda. *BMC Public Health*, 2018. **18**(1): p. 693.
18. Scalzi, L.V., et al., Improvement of medication adherence in adolescents and young adults with SLE using web-based education with and without a social media intervention, a pilot study. *Pediatric Rheumatology*, 2018. **16**(1): p. 18.
19. Hetrick, S.E., et al., Youth codesign of a mobile phone app to facilitate self-monitoring and management of mood symptoms in young people with major depression, suicidal ideation, and self-harm. *JMIR Mental Health*, 2018. **5**(1): p. e9.
20. McCarty, C.A., et al., Screening and brief intervention with adolescents with risky alcohol use in school-based health centers: A randomized clinical trial of the Check Yourself tool. *Substance Abuse*, 2019. **40**(4): p. 510–518.
21. Punukollu, M., et al., SafeSpot: An innovative app and mental health support package for Scottish schools – a qualitative analysis as part of a mixed methods study. *Child and Adolescent Mental Health*, 2020. **25**(2): p. 110–116.
22. Newbold, A., et al., Promotion of mental health in young adults via mobile phone app: Study protocol of the ECoWeB (emotional competence for well-being in young adults) cohort multiple randomised trials. *BMC Psychiatry*, 2020. **20**(1): p. 458.
23. UNICEF. *How many children and young people have internet access at home?* 2020 [cited 12 January 2022]; Available from: https://data.unicef.org/resources/children-and-young-people-internet-access-at-home-during-covid19/ (last accessed 7 May 2023).
24. Gleaner, J. *Teen Hub to provide counselling, Internet, HIV testing in HWT*. 2017 [cited 12 January 2022]; Available from: www.pressreader.com/jamaica/jamaica-gleaner/20171130/281638190525478 (last accessed 7 May 2023).

14 Online Outreach and Support Provision

1. Lewis, S.P. and Y. Seko, A double-edged sword: A review of benefits and risks of online nonsuicidal self-injury activities. *Journal of Clinical Psychology*, 2016. **72**(3): p. 249–262.
2. Staniland, L., et al., Stigma and nonsuicidal self-injury: Application of a conceptual framework. *Stigma and Health*, 2021. **6**(3): p. 312–323.
3. Rosenrot, S.A. and S.P. Lewis, Barriers and responses to the disclosure of non-suicidal self-injury: A thematic analysis.

Counselling Psychology Quarterly, 2018. **33**(2): p. 121–141.

4. Lewis, S.P., Kenny, T. E., and Pritchard, T. R., Toward an understanding of online self-injury activity: Review and recommendations for researchers and clinicians, in *Nonsuicidal Self-Injury: Advances in Research and Practice*, J.J. Washburn, Editor. 2019, New York: Routledge.

5. Pritchard, T.R. and S.P. Lewis, Understanding online self-injury activity: Implications for research, practice and outreach, in *Oxford Handbook on Self-Injury*, J.L. Whitlock, E. Lloyd-Richardson, and I. Baettens, Editors. in press, New York: Routledge.

6. Hasking, P.A., et al., Position paper for guiding response to non-suicidal self-injury in schools. *School Psychology International*, 2016. **37**(6): p. 644–663.

7. Hamza, C.A., et al., Educational stakeholders' attitudes and knowledge about nonsuicidal self-injury among university students: A cross-national study. *Journal of American College Health*, 2021: p. 1–11. DOI: 10.1080/07448481.2021.1961782.

8. Lewis, S.P., et al., Addressing self-injury on college campuses: Institutional recommendations. *Journal of College Counseling*, 2019. **22**(1): p. 70–82.

9. Dyson, M.P., et al., A systematic review of social media use to discuss and view deliberate self-harm acts. *PLoS One*, 2016. **11**(5): p. e0155813.

10. Marchant, A., et al., A systematic review of the relationship between internet use, self-harm and suicidal behaviour in young people: The good, the bad and the unknown. *PLoS One*, 2017. **12**(8): p. e0181722.

11. Lewis, S.P., et al., Non-suicidal self-injury, youth, and the Internet: What mental health professionals need to know. *Child and Adolescent Psychiatry and Mental Health*, 2012. **6**(1): p. 13.

12. Lewis, S.P., et al., Helpful or harmful? An examination of viewers' responses to nonsuicidal self-injury videos on YouTube. *Journal of Adolescent Health*, 2012. **51**(4): p. 380–385.

13. Lewis, S.P., S.A. Rosenrot, and M.A. Messner, Seeking validation in unlikely places: The nature of online questions about non-suicidal self-injury. *Archives of Suicide Research*, 2012. **16**(3): p. 263–272.

14. Niwa, K.D. and M.N. Mandrusiak, Self-injury groups on Facebook. *Canadian Journal of Counselling and Psychotherapy*, 2012. **46**(1): p. 1–20.

15. Seko, Y. and S.P. Lewis, The self – harmed, visualized, and reblogged: Remaking of self-injury narratives on Tumblr. *New Media & Society*, 2018. **20**(1): p. 180–198.

16. Lewis, S.P., et al., The scope of nonsuicidal self-injury on YouTube. *Pediatrics*, 2011. **127**(3): p. e552–e557.

17. Rodham, K., et al., An investigation of the motivations driving the online representation of self-injury: A thematic analysis. *Archives of Suicide Research*, 2013. **17**(2): p. 173–183.

18. Lewis, S.P. and N.J. Michal, Start, stop, and continue: Preliminary insight into the appeal of self-injury e-communities. *Journal of Health Psychology*, 2016. **21**(2): p. 250–260.

19. Lewis, S.P., Y. Seko, and P. Joshi, The impact of YouTube peer feedback on attitudes toward recovery from non-suicidal self-injury: An experimental pilot study. *Digital Health*, 2018. **4**: p. 2055207618780499.

20. Hasking, P. and M. Boyes, Cutting words: A commentary on language and stigma in the context of nonsuicidal self-injury. *Journal of Nervous and Mental Disease*, 2018. **206**(11): p. 829–833.

21. Baker, T.G. and S.P. Lewis, Responses to online photographs of non-suicidal self-injury: A thematic analysis. *Archives of Suicide Research*, 2013. **17**(3): p. 223–235.

22. Westers, N.J., et al., Media guidelines for the responsible reporting and depicting of non-suicidal self-injury. *The British Journal of Psychiatry*, 2021. **219**(2): p. 415–418.

23. Lewis, S.P. and T.G. Baker, The possible risks of self-injury web sites: A content analysis. *Archives of Suicide Research*, 2011. **15**(4): p. 390–396.

24. Lewis, S.P. and P.A. Hasking, Putting the 'self' in self-injury research: Inclusion of people with lived experience in the research process. *Psychiatric Services*, 2019. **70**(11): p. 1058–1060.

25. Lewis, S.P., et al., Googling self-injury: The state of health information obtained through online searches for self-injury. *JAMA Pediatrics*, 2014. **168**(5): p. 443–449.

26. Gubrium, A. and K. Harper, *Participatory Visual and Digital Methods*. 1st ed. Vol. 10. 2016, New York: Routledge.

27. Lewis, S.P., N.L. Heath, and R. Whitley, Addressing self-injury stigma: The promise of innovative digital and video action-research methods. *Canadian Journal of Community Mental Health*, 2022. **40**(3): p. 45–54.

28. Corrigan, P.W., et al., Key ingredients to contact-based stigma change: A cross-validation. *Psychiatric Rehabilitation Journal*, 2014. **37**(1): p. 62–64.

29. Thornicroft, G., et al., Evidence for effective interventions to reduce mental-health-related stigma and discrimination. *The Lancet*, 2016. **387**(10023): p. 1123–1132.

Index

activism-for-bad, 36
addiction, 51, 85
Adly Influence Index, 34
adolescents, 47, 68, 70, 95, 136
   digital exclusion, 137
   mental health, 84, 131, 132, 136, 138
   social media, 132–134
   treatment, 131, 135, 138
   use of technology, 135, 137
Adults Psychiatric Morbidity Survey (APMS), 63
AIDS/HIV, 135, 148
algorithms, 16, 28, 91
   curation, 113
   modification of, 116
   use of, 116
analytic studies, 53, 57
anhedonia, 81
anthropology, 47, 50
anxiety, 70, 73, 82, 92, 131, 134
   disorders, 101
   physical appearance, 36
   symptoms, 36, 54, 57, 59
appearance, 91, 92, 93
   activism, 93
   comparisons, 91, 92, 94, 96
   concerns, 97
   ideals, 91, 92, 93, 95, 96
   preoccupation with, 90, 93
   unrealistic ideals, 91, 94
appearance-related content, 93
apps, 7, 133, 135–136
   applied, 23
   detox, 27
   development of, 35
   mental health, 54, 129
   mobile, 103, 131, 132, 137
   notifications, 30
   online counseling, 42
   persuasive technology-based, 35
   screen monitoring, 27
   social media, 35
   social networking, 36
aspiration, 42

assessment, 46, 48, 58
   formative, 75
   standardized, 57
   summative, 75
attention, 28, 54, 68, 73, 77, 80
authentic self, 78, 79

Bandura, Albert, 31
Bebo, 9
before-and-after study, 59, 60
behaviour change, 36, 37, 42
behavioural theory, 33
belonging, 25, 44, 51, 76, 79, 136
belongingness, 36, 77, 115
   sense of, 67, 68
   sense of group, 75
   thwarted, 115
benefits of social media, 74
   online information-seeking, 68
   opportunities for identity exploration, 68
   self-expression, 68
   social capital, 68
Best Practice Framework for Online Safety Education, 123
BetterHelp, 40, 41
bias, 53, 56, 61, 62, 64, 73
binary model of distress, 134
biopsychosocial model, 87
Blackboard, 75
BlackPlanet, 9, 11
blocking, 80
   of access, 116
   of content, 116
body dissatisfaction, 36, 91, 93
body image, 3, 19, 65, 87, 90, 91, 93
   concerns, 90, 91, 92, 93, 95
   disturbance, 94
   effects of social media, 92, 94, 95, 97
   negative, 90, 92
   positive, 90, 93, 96, 97
body liberation, 93, 95
body neutrality, 93, 95
body positive content, 93, 96

body positive movement, 96
brand owners, 37
British Medical Association, 20, 22
browsing, 50, 52, 86
   disorganised, 46
   history, 103
   mindless, ix, 36
   social media and news portal, 28
bulletin board systems, 4
bullying, 68, 87, 88, 115, see also cyberbullying
   traditional, 68, 69
burdensomeness, 115
business models, 3, 6, 11

cancel culture, 36
caregivers, 141, 142
case-control studies, 58
casino games, 103–105, 107
CBT-based interventions, 132
Center for Epidemiologic Studies Depression Scale (CES-D), 83
characteristics, 3
chatsafe, 126–130
   campaign, 127, 129
   guidelines, 127
   initiative, 126, 127, 128
Children's Online Privacy Protection (COPPA), 122
chronic illnesses, 4, 28
co-designing with end-users, 129
coercion, 67, 68, 70, 71, 74
cognitive behavioural therapy, see CBT
cognitive symptoms, 82
cohort studies, 58, 59
collective group action, 29
Commercial Content Moderators (CCMs), 9
Common Sense Census, 131
communicating about suicide, 121, 126, 127, 130
Communications Act 2003, 17
compulsive use of social media, 43

Index

computer programs, 132
computer-driven searching, 62
  mental health, 143
confidentiality, 20, 122
confirmation bias, 28, 73
conflict resolution, 80, 132
confounding factors, 59
congenital abnormalities, 54
connectedness, 36, 76, 78, 115, 136
conspiracy theories, 73, 80
content analysis, 49, 50, 51, 145, 147
content of outreach work, 140, 143
content providers, 9, 39
content warnings, 125
context collapse, 10
context-based behavioural change, 28
controlled trial, 61
coping mechanisms, 132, 135, 136, 137
COVID-19 pandemic, 26, 29, 65, 72, 75, 131, 137
critical awareness, 92
critical consumption, 73, 74, 80
cultural context, 95
cultural influences on social media use, 151
cyberaggression, 67, 68, 69, 74, 79
cyberbullying, 67, 68–70, 71, 72, 74, 79, 80, 122
  behaviours, 69
  externalizing effects, 70
  internalizing effects, 70
  risk factors, 70
  roles, 69
cybergrooming, 71, 80

data analytics, 102, 106
data collection, 9, 45, 63, 136
Data for Children Collaborative, 132
data mining, 7
dating
  platform, 25, 27, 29
  profile, 28
  services, 25
Delphi expert consensus methodology, 127
depression, 10, 36, 47, 70, 82, 84, 87, 115, 136
  causes of, 87
  history of, 57

prone to, 59, 87
psychotic, 82
self-reported, 86
symptoms, 54, 57, 59, 82, 83, 136
Depression Anxiety Distress Scale (DASS-21), 136
descriptive studies, 53
digital environment, 52, 107
digital exclusion, 23, 28, 137
digital literacy, 67, 74, 75, 79, 80, 125
digital science, 56, 62
digital self-harm, 70
discourse analysis, 48
disinformation, 72, 74
disinhibition, 71, 77
disordered eating behaviours, 91, 92, 94
disorders of mood, 81, 83
distress, 16, 81, 83, 93, 110
  emotional, 82
  expressions of, 114
  psychological, 71, 72, 101
  serious, 15, 19
dual-system models, 73

Early AI-supported Response with Social Listening (EARS), 40
eating disorder, 12, 19, 47, 65, 73, 90, 96, 126, 135
  behaviours, 139
  recovery, 96
  related to body image, 90
  treatment of, 90
ecological momentary assessment designs, 52
e-counselling, 37, 40
e-learning, 36, 40
electronic health records, 59, 64
e-mental health
  interventions, 97
  resources, 97
emoji, 4, 8, 9
emotional support, 67, 115
end-users, 129, 130
e-newsletter, 38
eSafety Commission, 123
escapism, 25
ethnography, 45, 46, 47
everyday reality, 23, 31
evidence-based information, 72
evolution of social media, 3
extraversion, 25

Facebook, 6, 11, 25, 35, 124, 129
  activities, 24
  adverts, 49
  breaks, 43
  content warnings, 125
  founders of, 9
  friends, 28
  likes, 42
  profiles, 25
  recruitment, 49
  use, 26, 133
  users, 26
Facebook Help Centre, 124
Facebook Messenger, 8, 10
Facebook Safety Advisory Board, 124
fake news, 72, 80
fake reviews, 74
false communications, 17
Family Centre and Parental Supervision tools, 125
fear of missing out (FOMO), 36, 85
feelings of isolation, 78, 112, 113, 114
focus group discussions, 45, 46, 47
freedom of expression, 13, 14, 16, 17
functional triad model, 35
functional triad of computer persuasion, 34

gambling
  activities, 100, 101, 103, 105
  advertisements, 98, 103, 107
  disorder, 65, 99, 100
  excessive, 98, 105
  legal definitions, 104, 107
  marketing practices, 102, 103
  operators, 102–103, 106–107
  problems, 99, 100, 102, 104, 105, 106
  products, 99, 101
  websites, 98, 99, 101, 107
gambling harm, 99, 105, 106, 108
  reduction, 106
gambling on social media, 102, 106, 107
gambling-related
  accounts, 102
  communities, 105

gambling-related (cont.)
  content, 99, 102, 105, 107, 108
  engagement mechanisms, 104, 105, 107
  harms, 100, 101, 102, 105
  monetization strategies, 105
gamification, 133, 134
gender, 89
  differences, 26, 95, 136
  presentation of, 51
General Medical Council, 12, 19, see also GMC
GMC, 12, 19, 20, 21
Google AdWords Keywords, 146
governance, 8, 9
  models, 3
  structures, 11
graphic imagery, 50, 112
grieving process, 27
Grindr, 25
grounded theory, 48
group
  behaviour, 33, 44
  discussion, 47
  dynamics, 47
  forum, 47
  members, 47

Habermas, Jurgen, 33, 34
harassment, 13, 16, 23, 87, 88
harmful content, 24, 112, 114, 116, 122, 123, 150
  management of, 116
harmful information, 14, 16, 19, 73, 116
harms-based law, 19
harms-based offence, 17, 18
hashtag search, 50
health information, 12, 28, 75, 139, 143
health information websites, 146
health-related decisions, 75
help-seeking, 113, 136, 143, 147
high-value social media content, 42
holistic approach to online safety, 80
Holistic Psychologist, 38
hopeful content, 146
How Couples Meet and Stay Together (HCMST), 25
hypodermic needle model, 3

identifying intended audiences, 141
identity, 9, 10, 38, 51, 78
  characteristics, 77
  concealment, 10
  development, 77, 95
  exploration, 67, 68, 77, 78, 79
  formation, 78
iDove texting intervention, 133
image-based data, 50
image-based sexual abuse, 71
images
  nature of, 50, 51, 111, 112
  pornographic, 7
  of self-harm, xi, 49, 50, 51, 59, 111, 112
  of self-injury, 51, 112, 113
  of suicide, 59
  on social media, 51, 91, 92, 94
impact of online material, 140, 145
individual behaviour, 33, 44
individual characteristics, 70, 93, 94, 95, 97, 100
influencers, 34, 37, 40, 103
infodemic, 72
information-seeking, 67, 68, 74
informed consent, 45, 48
Instagram, 3, 11, 35, 36, 42, 48, 50, 51, 113, 124, 125, 129
  help centre, 125
  Safety Centers, 125, 129
instant messaging, 5
interaction with harmful online groups, 67, 68
interactive
  educational resources, 75
  online tutoring, 75
International Association for Suicide Prevention, 124
International Consortium on Self-Injury in Educational Settings (ICSES), 142
International Society for Mental Health Online, 37
International Society for the Study of Self-injury, 148
internet addiction, 57
interpersonal media ecosystem, 29

interpersonal relationships, 24, 31
Interpersonal Skills Group, 133
interpretation, 47, 48, 49, 51
interpretative analysis, 48, 51
interrupted time series, 60
intervention strategies, 79
intervention studies, 54, 59
interviews, 30, 43, 45, 46, 51
  conversation with a purpose, 46
  individual, 46
  narrative, 46
  one-off, 52
  semi-structured, 46
  structured, 46
  walking, 52
intrusiveness, 85, 89

jigsaw identification, 21
Joiner, Thomas, 115

key benefits of social media, 67, 68
Kids Online Safety Act, 122
knowledge and consent, 45, 46

Law Commission, 12–17, 18, 22
law reform, 12, 13, 21
legal standards, 19, 20
lesbian, gay and bisexual (LGB), 63, 79
LGBTQ (Lesbian, Gay, Bisexual, Transgendered and Questioning) identity, 10, 79
Lifeline Program, 137
lifespan, 26, 30, 69, 70
LinkedIn, 25, 29
low self-esteem, 47, 78, 87, 88
lurking, 10

Malicious Communications Act 1988, 15
management of harmful content, 116
marketers, 37, 106
massive open online courses (MOOCs), 75
measurement error, 53, 64
mechanisms
  of benefit, 115
  of harm, 114
  of social influence, 33
  of support provision, 139

Index

media attention, 79
media literacy skills, 95
MEMO intervention, 132, 136
mental health, 143
  awareness, 34, 37, 40
  concerns, 40, 96, 134, 148
  interventions, 44, 134, 137
  management, 38, 43
  problems, 56, 61, 62, 64, 65, 86, 134, 136, 150
  promotion, 33, 37, 39
  services, 40, 83, 131
mental illness, 58, 82, 88, 134, 148
mental well-being, 47, 116, 126, 137
Meta, 3, 26, 125
MeToo movement, 36
Millennium Cohort Study (MCS), 63
misinformation, 12, 19, 20, 21, 22, 28, 68, 72–74, 79
misleading information, 20, 21, 67, 72
mixed-methods research, 51, 63
models
  7s framework, 35
  conceptual, 35
  dual-system, 73
  functional triad, 35
  hypodermic needle, 3
  integrative, 31
  press photograph story analysis, 51
  social affiliation, 30
  traditional, 13
mood disorders, 63, 65, 81, 83, 84, 87, 88, 101, 114
  common causes of, 81, 87
  as illness, 82
mood-induction effect, 88
Moodle, 75
multi-faceted approach, 147
myside bias, 73
Myspace, 5, 9
myths, 73, 139, 146, 147

National Eating Disorders Association (NEDA), 97
National Institute for Health and Care Excellence (NICE), 109
national policy approaches, 126

natural language processing, 63
Neopets, 9
Netflix, 60
netiquette, 68, 80
network awareness, 71, 80
neural markers, 32
neuroticism, 25
non-aggressive interactions, 70
non-consensual sexual images, 122, 123
non-consensual sharing of sexting material, 71
non-judgemental environment, 113, 115
non-suicidal self-injury (NSSI), 18, 110

objectification theory, 91, 92, 94
offensive material, 28
Office of Communications (OFCOM), 122
offline
  behaviours, 31
  communication, 27
  outreach tactics, 37
online
  aggression, 67, 68
  authenticity, 78
  ethnography, 48
  identity, 25, 26, 85
  self-disclosure, 77
  self-injury activity, 144
  sexual solicitation, 71
  support, 75, 141, 147
online gambling, 99
  debates about, 150
  regulations, 99
online outreach, 139, 144, 145, 147, 148, 149
  efforts, 141
  initiatives, 139
  work, 140, 142, 144, 146, 149
Online Safety Act, 122
Online Safety Bill, 17, 122
ought self, 78
outreach activities, 140, 144, 145, 147
  for self-injury, 143

parasocial interaction theory, 34
participation, 3, 4, 8, 33, 38, 42, 47, 56, 62, 80, 86

participatory culture, 4
participatory web, 4
participatory-based methods, 148
passive use, 88
peer support, 48, 51, 105, 106, 121, 143
personal distress, 81, 82, *see also* distress
personal information, 69, 71, 77, 87, 122
persuasion modes, 35
physical appearance, 36, 77
physical disabilities, 79
Pinterest, 26
Poole, Chris, 10
poor truth discernment, 72, 73
population surveys, 56, 112
pornography, 87
potential harms, 16, 121
precautionary approach, 106, 107
predisposition to critical thinking, 73
pre-existing mental health condition, 32, 101
press photograph story analysis model, 51
prevention and intervention, 79, 96
principles of social media applications, 35
privacy, 10, 12, 20, 27, 30, 48, 68, 121
  and confidentiality, 22
  settings, 68, 80
problem gambling, 99–101, *see also* gambling
professional
  conduct, 19, 20
  development, 40, 75
  obligations, 22
  regulators, 19
prosumer, 4
pseudonymity, 10

qualitative
  analysis, 48
  approaches, 45, 147
  health research, 46
  research, 45, 48, 52
  study, 46, 48, 49, 51
qualitative data, 48, 50, 147
  analysis, 48
  collection, 45

quality of health information, 140, 146
quality of life, 70, 83
quality of online health information, 146
quantitative
  approaches, 147
  methods, 45
  research, 51, 53, 54
  study, 46, 49, 51, 52, 63
quantitative research designs, 53
  analytical studies, 53
  intervention studies, 54, 59
questionnaires, 59, 63, 82, 83, 84

real-world approach, 129
real-world social support, 115
reasonable excuse, 15, 17, 18, 19
recognized medical conditions, 15
Reddit, 9, 25, 26, 28, 48, 49
rehearsal stage, 10
relational assurances, 29
relational maintenance behaviours, 29
relationship dissatisfaction, 29
relationship status, 25
research, 24, 53, 84
  interviews, 63, 83
  methods, 49, 50
  participants, 61
  question, 46, 48, 61
  study, 54, 64
response seeking, 29
REThink, 135
REThink therapeutic game, 133
retrospective studies, 57
revenge porn, 71
risk factors for sexting, 71
risks associated with social media, 74
risks of social media, 67
  behaviour, 87, 101, 135, 137
  gambling behaviours, 105
  health behaviours, 73
  online experiences, 67
  online interactions, 67, 68
risks for suicide, 115
Russell, Molly, 116, 122

safety, 17, 49
safety advisory boards, 124

Safety by Design, 123
safety policies and functions, 124, 126
Safety Snapshot, 125
safety tools, 123, 124
samples, 30, 46, 50, 56, 62
  convenience, 62
  random, 62
  systematic, 62
sampling, 50, 53, 57, 62, 63
  quota, 62
  snowball, 46
search
  data, 146
  engine, 62, 146
  results, 146
  terms, 62, 146
selbstmord, 50
the self, 9, 10, 78, 87
  explorations of, 11
  on social media, 9
self-censorship, 29
self-disclosure, 77, 78, 79, 114
self-discrepancy theory, 78
the self-domains, 78
self-expression, 67, 68, 77
self-harm
  act of, 51, 109, 110, 111, 112, 114
  definition, 109
  encouragement or assisting, 18
  method of, 46, 63, 110, 111
  non-fatal, 110, 111
  rates, 59, 63, 110
  and suicidal ideation, 70, 115, 132
  and suicide, 50, 53, 62, 109
self-harm content on social media, 48, 111, 113, 115
  experiences with, 18
  impact of, 113
Self-Harm Recovery Guide, 141
Self-Harmer Problems, 143, 144
selfhealers movement, 38
self-help interventions, 137
self-injury, 18, 51, 109, 110, 111, 139, 142, 143
  content, 143, 146
  engage in, 141, 142
  myths, 147
  outreach, 142, 148
  stigma, 141, 142
  terms, 146
  websites, 144, 146, 147

Self-Injury & Recovery Resources, see SIRR
Self-Injury Awareness Day, 148
Self-Injury Outreach & Support, see SiOS
self-monitoring, 135, 137
self-objectification, 92, 94
self-presentation, 24, 25, 77, 78, 92
  online, 78, 92
self-relevance, 35
self-supervision, 35
sensitivity analysis, 57
sentiment analysis, 62, 63
sexting, 67, 68, 70, 71, 74, 79, 87
sexual
  harassment, 7, 36
  identity exploration, 71
  objects, 92
  orientation, 63, 77
  solicitation, 71, 72, 79
sign-posting, 35
sign-up fees, 6
Silicon Valley, 4
simulated gambling games, 103, 104, 108
single case design, 54
single case study, 54
SiOS, 141, 142, 143, 144, 146, 147
SIRR, 141, 142, 143, 147
situational characteristics, 101
SixDegrees, 5, 6
sleep disturbance, 1, 82, 87
Snapchat, 6, 7, 25, 26, 35, 124, 125, 133
  Safety Centre, 125
social capital, 67, 68, 76, 77, 79, 92
  bonding, 76
  bridging, 76
social characteristics, 88, 131
social connection, 5, 25, 75, 79
social contact, 29, 82
social dialogue, 34
social identity, 77, 79, 105
social isolation, 59, 141
social media
  excessive use of, 36, 43
  interventions, 35, 37
social media and the relationship with
  body image, 91, 92, 93, 95
  disordered eating, 92, 93, 94

gambling, 98, 104
mental health, 45
social media engagement, 34, 42, 68, 133
social media literacy, 67, 71, 74, 92
social media platforms, 35, 36, 42, 44
  advertising, 107
  gambling, 104, 105
social media as a resource, 119
social media use, 24, 27, 29, 45, 122
  active use, 52, 86
  negative aspects of, 36, 67, 79
  passive use, 52, 86
social media-based research study, 133
social network analysis, 56
social network sites (SNSs), 4, 6, 76
social sciences, 24
social support, 67, 68, 76, 87, 135
socialization, 35
sociocultural and objectification theories, 92, 95
sociocultural theories, 91, 94
socio-economic status, 71
socio-technical systems, 23
stigmatization, 147
  of self-harm, 116
  of self-injury, 142, 144
stress, 19, 29, 43, 47
subjectivity, 48, 51
substantial effect, 15
suicidal ideation, 47, 73, 131, 135
suicidal intent, 109, 110, 111
suicidal thinking, 61, 110, 111
suicide, 13, 54, 82, 100, 109, 110, 126
  attempted, 64, 109, 111, 127
  encouragement or assisting, 18
  pacts, 111, 114

prevention, 61, 64, 121, 124, 127, 128–130
  rates, 59, 60
  reference to, 50
  risk, 110, 111, 129
Suicide Act 1961, 18
Suicide Prevention Help Centre, 125
Suicide and Self-injury Advisory Group, 124

target audience, 37, 141
target group, 37, 44, 141
technological infrastructure, 71
technological innovation, 23, 31
technological interventions, 131, 132, 134, 135, 138
terrorism
  acts of, 31, 123
  domestic, 74
texting intervention, 131, 133
texting programs, 133
The Mighty, 141, 148
thematic analysis, 48, 49, 51
theory of critical body awareness, 95
theory of development of critical body awareness, 92
theory of social spheres, 33
thin-ideal internalization, 91
TikTok, 6, 11, 34, 40, 124, 126
  Content Advisory Council, 124
  Safety Centre, 126
  Safety Partners, 124
TIME magazine, 4, 36
Tinder, 25
traditional media, 13, 14, 19, 34, 90, 98, 102, 103, 106, 107
treatment programs, 133
Trusted Flagger Programme, 124
Tumbler, 51
Twitch, 105
Twitter, 25, 28, 30, 34, 35, 36, 48, 51, 102, 103

UNICEF, 131, 132, 134, 137
usage scales, 24
user-generated content, 4, 14, 91, 103, 107, 111, 113
uses and gratification theory, 25, 91, 92

vaccine hesitant, 19
vexatious complaint, 16
victimization, 70
violence against women and girls, 122
violent content, 87
virtual communities, 23, 29
virtual ethnography, 47
virtual learning management systems, 75
virtual private networks (VPNs), 28
Virtual Reality (VR), 125
visual analysis, 50
visual content, 50, 51, 112, 125
visual data, 50
VR technologies, 125

Wall Street Journal, 3
Web 1.0, 4
Web 2.0, 3, 4, 9, 23
WeClick, 132
well-being, 24, 27, 30, 31, 36, 67, 74, 76, 79, 126
  emotional, 24, 81, 136
  financial, 98
  subjective, 78
WhatsApp, 26
Wikipedia, 68, 74
withdrawal, 27, 82, 83, 88
World Health Organization (WHO), 30, 40, 81, 100, 109, 148

YouTube, 11, 26, 37, 38, 42, 75, 107, 145

Zika virus, 54
Zuckerberg, Mark, 6, 10

Printed in the United States
by Baker & Taylor Publisher Services